Automotive CAN Bus and In-Vehicle Networks

I0346768

Welcome to Automotive CAN Bus and In-Vehicle Networks

As electronics and software continue to take centre stage in modern vehicle design, technicians need to embrace the knowledge and tools necessary to understand how these systems communicate in order to develop effective diagnostic and repair strategies.

The power of the CAN Bus to connect and coordinate the dozens of control units and sensors in a vehicle is significant; it's like the nervous system of the car, constantly transmitting information that allows each part to function in harmony. Understanding this system allows you to diagnose faults more intelligently and repair them more efficiently.

An effective diagnostic routine should always begin with a clear understanding of automotive electrics and how information flows around the vehicle, followed by logical reasoning to narrow down the possible causes before taking precise measurements and readings to identify the fault.

A sound knowledge of CAN Bus helps you see this information flow more clearly.

An important thing to remember about CAN and in-vehicle networks is that although they may appear complicated or intimidating, you can often use familiar test methods to diagnose issues and faults quickly and accurately.

Once you get used to interpreting the data and using the right equipment, it will soon become an indispensable part of your diagnostic routine.

This book has been written to help you get the most from your understanding of CAN Bus and in-vehicle networks, and it has been designed to give both straightforward and practical methods that can be used effectively for diagnosis, as well as more advanced techniques to help reinforce and expand on the concepts explained.

The chapters will introduce you to electrical and network principles, health and safety, CAN Bus structure and terminology, including key points of interest, diagnostic strategies and tips to support the information provided within the text.

Chapters

How to use this book………….………..Page 3
Chapter 1 Electrical Essentials …………...Page 7
Chapter 2 Introduction to CAN Bus Systems …………………………………………………...Page 25
Chapter 3 Circuit Theory …….…………...Page 55
Chapter 4 Electromagnetic Principles ……Page 79
Chapter 5 Communication Protocol & Voltage Regulation……………………………………....Page 93
Chapter 6 Diagnostics & Testing Principles ………………………………………………....Page 123

This book offers:

Information to help Automotive Technicians systematically diagnose in-vehicle network faults.

Ideal support for learners and tutors undertaking automotive qualifications.

A large number of illustrations to support knowledge and understanding, with an analysis of automotive in-vehicle networks.

Text © Graham Stoakes 2025

Original illustrations © Graham Stoakes 2025

The rights of Graham Stoakes to be identified as author of this work have been asserted by them in accordance with the Copyright, Designs and Patents Act 1988.

Preface

Copyright notice ©

All rights reserved. No part of this publication may be reproduced in any form or by any means (including photocopying or storing it in any medium by electronic means and whether or not transiently or incidentally to some other use of this publication) without the written permission of the copyright owner, except in accordance with the provisions of the Copyright, Designs and Patents Act 1988 or under the terms of a licence issued by the Copyright Licensing Agency, Saffron House, 6 - 10 Kirby Street, London EC1N 8TS (www.cla.co.uk). Applications for the copyright owners' written permission should be addressed to the author.

Acknowledgements

Graham Stoakes would like to thank Anita and Holly Stoakes for their support during this project.

Thank you to alerrandre for the cover design.

Author

Graham Stoakes AAE MIMI MSET QTLS is a trainer/lecturer and author of college textbooks in automotive engineering for light vehicles and motorcycles.

With his background as a qualified Master Technician, senior automotive manager, and specialist diagnostic trainer, he brings over 40 years of technical industry experience to this title.

www.grahamstoakes.com

Cover design - fiverr.com/alerrandre

Published by Graham Stoakes

First published 2025

First edition

ISBN 978-1-9192995-0-1

Introduction

How to use this book

Are you new to CAN Bus, or do you want to enhance your current knowledge?

If so, then you are ready to use CAN Bus and in-vehicle network diagnostics to better understand modern automotive systems.

This book is specifically crafted to assist mechanics and technicians in the aftermarket with diagnosing and resolving in-vehicle network issues, rather than serving as a resource for CAN Bus designers or software programmers.

The CAN Bus allows you to access the normally hidden world of communication between electronic control units (ECUs), sensors, actuators, and more. Once you become familiar with the function and operation of in-vehicle networks, you'll be able to interpret data traffic, pinpoint faults, and diagnose issues that would otherwise remain invisible.

This book is fully illustrated to provide detailed information about the structure, operation, and diagnostic procedures used when working with CAN Bus and other in-vehicle networks. Although it is impractical to cover every manufacturer, protocol, or test routine in detail, this book aims to offer a solid overview of principles, methods, and examples. This approach is intended to help you build the confidence necessary to explore more advanced diagnostic strategies.

Throughout this book, you will find features that aim to support and enhance your understanding and use, such as:

The information in these boxes highlights safety features to consider when working on vehicles and electrical circuits, especially any high-voltage systems associated with EVs. These features aim to minimise the risk of injury or damage to vehicles or equipment. Even if specific safety advice is not provided, always evaluate potential risks before starting any activity or diagnostic routine.

The guidance in these boxes is intended to support the information about the construction and operation of in-vehicle network systems. It provides material that enhances understanding and strengthens knowledge of system components and testing methods.

This feature explains the key terms related to in-vehicle network operation, components, and diagnostic testing. Understanding and correctly using technical vocabulary is the foundation for effective repairs. Words highlighted in **bold** within the text are defined here.

Introduction

These tips offer useful diagnostic advice for specific systems and components. Although not all of them may be relevant to your current task or vehicle, they may inspire ideas that you can modify and incorporate into your diagnostic routines. Always take care when implementing any diagnostic process to avoid the possibility of damage or injury to yourself, others, vehicles, or equipment.

The guidance in these boxes uses analogies to compare complex operational systems or component designs to simple concepts. The purpose of these explanations is to clarify and improve understanding, even though they are not scientifically accurate. However, they are only a tool to aid comprehension, not a replacement for correct information.

Preparing for assessment

The information in this book can help you with theory or practical assessments that measure your skills or competence in vehicle repairs or a recognised qualification. You may be able to use some of the evidence you produce for more than one qualification. You should make the best use of all your evidence to maximise the opportunities for cross-referencing between units or qualifications.

You should choose the type of evidence that suits the type of assessment you are undertaking (either theory or practical).

The types of evidence you could use are listed below:

- Direct observation by a qualified assessor
- Witness testimony
- Computer-based
- Audio recording
- Video recording
- Photographic recording
- Professional discussion
- Oral questioning
- Personal statement
- Competence/Skills tests
- Written tests
- Multiple-choice tests
- Assignments/Projects

Before taking a written or multiple-choice test, review the key terms related to the subject. Read all questions and answers thoroughly to understand what is being asked as multiple-choice tests often have similar options that can be confusing.

For practical assessments, make sure you have had ample practice and feel confident in your ability to pass. Having a plan of action and a work method can be helpful.

Ensure you have the correct technical information, such as vehicle data, wiring diagrams, and the necessary tools and equipment. Check your work regularly to ensure accuracy and prevent issues from developing as you go along.

Always prioritise safety when performing any practical task.

Introduction

Information sources

The complex nature of light vehicle electric and electronic systems and in-vehicle networks requires a good source of technical information and data. In order to conduct diagnostic and repair procedures, you need to gather as much information as possible before you start.

Sources of information may include:

Table 0.1 Possible information sources

Verbal information from the driver	Vehicle identification numbers
Service and repair history	Warranty information
Vehicle handbook	Technical data manuals
Workshop manuals/Wiring diagrams/Topology maps	Safety recall sheets
Manufacturer specific information	Information bulletins
Technical helplines	Advice from other technicians/colleagues
Internet	Parts suppliers/catalogues
Jobcards	Diagnostic trouble codes
Oscilloscope waveforms	On-vehicle warning labels/stickers
On-vehicle displays	Reference/Textbooks

Always compare the results of any inspection, testing or diagnosis to suitable sources of data. Remember that no matter which information or data source you use, it is important to evaluate how useful and reliable it will be to your safety, diagnostic, maintenance and repair routine.

Electronic and electrical safety procedures

Working with any electrical system has its hazards, and you must take safety seriously. When working with light vehicle electrical and electronic systems, the main hazard is the risk of electric shock. Although most systems operate with low voltages of around 12V, an accidental electrical discharge caused by incorrect circuit connection can be enough to cause severe burns. Where possible, isolate electrical systems before repairing or replacing components.

If working on hybrid or fully electric vehicles, take care not to disturb the high-voltage system. The high-voltage system can normally be identified by its reinforced insulation and shielding, often coloured bright orange. These systems carry voltages that can cause severe injury or death.

Always use the correct tools and equipment. Damage to components, tools or personal injury could occur if the wrong tool is used or misused. Check tools and equipment before each use.

If you are using electrical measuring equipment, check that it is correctly rated, accurate, and calibrated before you take any readings.

If you need to replace any electrical or electronic components, always check that the quality meets the original equipment manufacturer (OEM) specifications. (If the vehicle is under warranty, inferior parts or deliberate modification might make the warranty invalid. Also, if parts of an inferior quality are fitted, it might affect vehicle performance and safety). You should only carry out the replacement of electrical components if the parts comply with the legal requirements for road use and environmental protection.

Introduction

Personal Protective Equipment (PPE)

To reduce the possibility of personal injury, always use the appropriate personal protection equipment (PPE):

   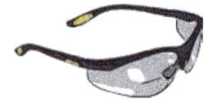 

When selecting PPE, make sure that the equipment:

- Is the right PPE for the job – ask for advice if you are not sure.
- Fits correctly – it needs to be adjustable, so it fits you properly.
- Is properly looked after.
- Prevents or controls the risk for the job you are doing.
- Does not create a new risk, e.g. Overheating.
- Is comfortable enough to wear for the length of time you need it.
- Does not impair your sight, communication or movement.
- Is compatible with other PPE worn.
- Does not interfere with the job you are doing.

Vehicle Protective Equipment (VPE)

To reduce the possibility of damage to the car, always use the appropriate vehicle protection equipment (VPE):

 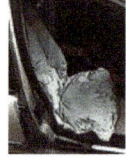  

Wing covers   Seat covers   Steering wheel covers   Floor mats

Electrical Essentials

Chapter 1 Electrical Essentials

In order to develop a clear understanding of CAN Bus and in-vehicle networks, it is important to first have a solid grasp of electrical fundamentals. This chapter will help you build on your knowledge of basic electrical principles as they apply to vehicle communication systems. It also introduces the key operating theories that link electrical behaviour to data transmission and network performance, providing a strong foundation for effective diagnosis and repair. Remember to work safely at all times and observe the relevant health and safety regulations, while developing diagnostic routines that are systematic and effective.

Contents

What is Electricity	8
Electrical Units & Terminology	11
Circuit Properties & Voltage Types	15
Electromagnetism & EMI	17
High & Low Voltage	19
Ohms & Watts (Power) Law	20
Analog vs Digital	22
Pulse Width Modulation & Duty Cycle	22
Pull-up & Pull-down Circuits	23

The automotive industry is a high-risk environment, especially when dealing with electrical systems. The hazards of electricity are well-known but can be easily ignored due to its invisible nature. This can lead to complacency if the fundamentals of electricity are not well understood. Even with this understanding, caution is necessary. Assume that any safety systems designed for protection have failed and take precautions to minimise the risk of vehicle damage, injury or even death. Always evaluate the risks associated with any activity and implement measures to eliminate or reduce the hazards involved in any task, diagnosis, or repair.

Additional risks associated with working on, or around electrical systems may include:

- Electrocution
- Strong magnetic fields
- Falling from heights
- Short circuits
- Electrical discharge/arcing
- Fire and explosion
- Chemicals

Electrical Essentials

What is Electricity

The discovery of electricity

Approximately 2,500 years ago, a Greek scientist named Thales discovered that rubbing amber (fossilised tree sap) with a cloth attracted small dust and fluff particles. This was his discovery of static electricity. While Thales did not fully understand the phenomenon, he did document his findings.

Around 1550, William Gilbert, who was Queen Elizabeth I's doctor, discovered that rubbing a silk cloth on a glass rod could attract even heavier objects, like feathers. He called this phenomenon 'electricus', taking the name from the Greek word for amber, 'elektron', leading to the word electricity.

While static electricity is interesting, it's hard to convert into a practical energy source because electricity needs to move to be useful. In the late 18th century, two Italian scientists, Luigi Galvani, and Alessandro Volta, were competing with each other and ended up creating the first moving electricity, known as electric **current**. This electric current was produced through a chemical reaction and eventually led to the invention of the battery.

 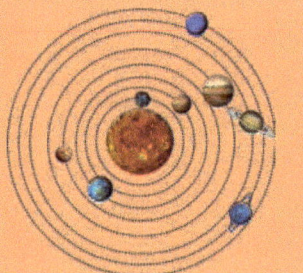

Understanding electricity can be challenging because it exists within tiny atoms. You can picture an atom as a miniature solar system, where the **nucleus** is like the sun and the electrons orbit it like planets. The nucleus contains positively charged protons and neutral neutrons, while the electrons that orbit it have a negative charge. When electrons move from one atom to another, they create electric current.

Atoms and molecules

Every substance is composed of **molecules**, which are made up of **atoms**. For instance, water is a molecule denoted as H_2O, comprising two hydrogen (H) atoms and one oxygen (O) atom.

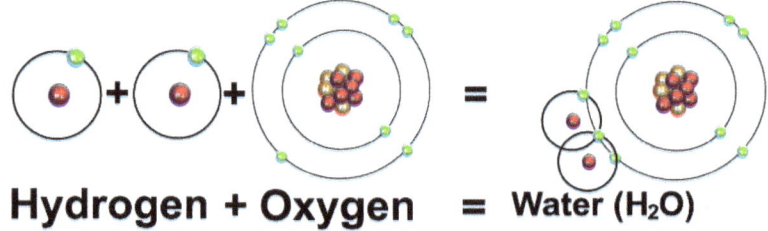

Hydrogen + Oxygen = Water (H_2O)

Figure 1.1 Hydrogen and oxygen making up a water molecule

Current - the flow of electric charge though a conductor.

Nucleus - the central part of an atom.

Atom - the smallest unit of matter that has the characteristic properties of a chemical element.

Molecule - a group of two or more atoms that are held together by chemical bonds.

Electrical Essentials

The number of **protons** and **electrons** varies among atoms, as depicted in the periodic table. This chart organises elements by atomic number, which mainly corresponds to the number of protons in their nucleus.

1 H																	2 He
3 Li	4 Be											5 B	6 C	7 N	8 O	9 F	10 Ne
11 Na	12 Mg											13 Al	14 Si	15 P	16 S	17 Cl	18 Ar
19 K	20 Ca	21 Sc	22 Ti	23 V	24 Cr	25 Mn	26 Fe	27 Co	28 Ni	29 Cu	30 Zn	31 Ga	132 Ge	33 As	34 Se	35 Br	36 Kr
37 Rb	38 Sr	39 Y	40 Zr	41 Nb	42 Mo	43 Tc	44 Ru	45 Rh	46 Pd	47 Ag	48 Cd	49 In	50 Sn	51 Sb	52 Te	53 I	54 Xe
55 Cs	56 Ba	57-71	72 Hf	73 Ta	74 W	75 Re	76 Os	77 Ir	78 Pt	79 Au	80 Hg	81 Tl	82 Pb	83 Bi	84 Po	85 At	86 Rn
87 Fr	88 Ra	89-103	104 Rf	105 Db	106 Sg	107 Bh	108 Hs	109 Mt	110 Ds	111 Rg	112 Cn	113 Nh	114 Fl	115 Mc	116 Lv	117 Ts	118 Og

57 La	58 Ce	59 Pr	60 Nd	61 Pm	62 Sm	63 Eu	64 Gd	65 Tb	66 Dy	67 Ho	68 Er	69 Tm	70 Yb	71 Lu
89 Ac	90 Th	91 Pa	92 U	93 Np	94 Pu	95 Am	96 Cm	97 Bk	98 Cf	99 Es	100 Fm	101 Md	102 No	103 Lr

Figure 1.2 The periodic table of elements

Movement of electrons

To generate an electric current, electrons need to move from one atom to another. Electron movement requires an external force or pressure, which can be created by magnetic fields or a chemical reaction.

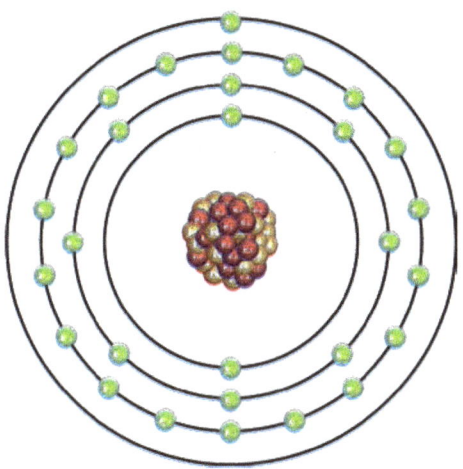

Electrons orbit the nucleus of an atom, much like planets orbit the sun due to gravity. In atoms with simple structures, the attraction between the nucleus and electrons is very strong, making it difficult for electrons to move. Elements where electrons do not move easily are known as **insulators**.

However, in other atoms, the attraction force between the nucleus and electrons is weaker. For example, a copper atom, which has 29 electrons and 29 protons. The electrons orbit in increasingly larger circles. The outermost electrons, known as 'free electrons', have a weaker bond to the nucleus than those in simpler atoms. If external pressure is applied, these free electrons can be made to move from one atom to another, creating an electric current. When electrons move easily, the element is known as a **conductor**.

Figure 1.3 A copper atom

In vehicles, conductors are used where we want electricity to flow easily, such as in wiring. Insulators are used to restrict the movement of electricity, such as the coating on the outside of a wire or cable.

Electrical Essentials

 Certain elements, such as silicon and germanium, can be engineered into components that function as either conductors or insulators. They can even be switched between these two states, acting as controls in electronic systems. These versatile elements are known as **semiconductors**.

For electrons to move from one atom to another, they need a continuous path, known as a **circuit**. This allows an electron to be replaced by another one from behind as it moves. Without a complete circuit, electrons can't flow because the last electron in the conductor has nowhere to go. If the circuit is interrupted, it loses **continuity** and current stops flowing.

 Imagine a relay race where runners pass a baton to one another in a continuous loop around the track. If at any point a runner drops the baton or doesn't show up at the next handoff, the race comes to an abrupt stop. In the same way, electrical continuity ensures that electrons can 'pass the baton' seamlessly in a complete, unbroken circuit. Without this unbroken path, the 'race' of electric current halts entirely.

Proton - a subatomic particle that has a positive electric charge and is found in the nucleus of every atom.

Electron - a subatomic particle that has a negative electric charge and is one of the main components of matter.

Insulator - an electrical component that restricts or prevents the flow of electric current.

Conductor - an electrical component which allows the flow of electric current.

Semiconductor - a material that can have the properties of both a conductor and an insulator when used in an electric circuit.

Circuit - a continuous, unbroken loop that allows the steady flow of electricity.

Continuity - refers to a complete, unbroken conductor that enables the uninterrupted flow of electricity.

Electrical Essentials

Electrical Units & Terminology

To better understand how electricity works in a circuit, we use specific units of measurement. Correct use of electrical terminology is crucial to avoid misinterpretation, which could lead to incorrect testing and diagnosis.

Table 1.1 outlines the primary units associated with electricity and the function of electrical systems.

Table 1.1 Units of measurement

Unit	Description
Volts 	Voltage, named after Alessandro Volta, is the electrical pressure or potential force in any part of an electrical circuit. There are two main types of voltage in electrical circuits: • **Electromotive Force (EMF)**: This is the potential pressure when all electrical devices are turned off and no current is flowing, often considered as the **open circuit voltage (OCV)**. • **Potential Difference (Pd)**: This is the voltage drop caused by electricity flow when the circuit is active or switched on. When the circuit is active, this is known as the **closed-circuit voltage (CCV)**. Voltage is often represented in technical information or documentation as: V - Volts named after Alessandro Volta. E - EMF to describe electromotive force.
Amps	Amps, named after André-Marie Ampère, are the units used to quantify the amount of electricity in any part of an electrical circuit. It's measured when electricity is allowed to flow in a circuit, a phenomenon known as current. There are two main types of electrical current: • Direct Current (DC): This is electricity that flows in one direction only. • Alternating Current (AC): This is electricity that **oscillates** back and forth in a circuit. Regardless of where you measure it in the circuit (at the beginning, middle, or end), the amperage remains the same. Current (amps) is often represented in technical information or documentation as: I - which originates from the French phrase intensité du courant, (current intensity). A - amps, named after André-Marie Ampère.

Electrical Essentials

Table 1.1 Units of measurement

Unit	Description
Ohms 	Ohms, named after Georg Ohm, are the units used to measure **resistance** to electrical flow. Resistance directly impacts the functioning of any electrical circuit as it slows down the flow of electricity. As resistance increases in a circuit, both current and voltage decrease. This can limit the operation of electrical components. While resistance can be used to control electrical components in some circuits, high resistance is generally undesirable. Resistance in electrical circuits is often closely associated with heat. Therefore, heat can be seen as an indication of resistance, and vice versa. Resistance (ohms) is often represented in technical information or documentation as: Ω - the Greek letter Omega (meaning 'great'), which sounds similar to ohms and ensures that the letter 'O' is not confused with a zero.
Watts 	Watts, named after James Watt, are the units used to measure electrical power produced or consumed. **Power** is essentially the speed at which work is done. In the context of electrical components, a higher wattage indicates a more powerful component that uses more electrical energy. Power is often represented in technical information or documentation as: W - Watts, named after James Watt. P - to represent the word power. The word horsepower is often attributed to James Watt but considered to be an imperial measurement. The International System of Units (Si) unit of power is the Watt. 1 horsepower (hp) is equivalent to approximately 746 Watts. 1.34 horsepower (hp) equals 1 kilowatt (kW).
Hertz 	Hertz, named after Heinrich Hertz, are the units used to measure **frequency**. Frequency relates to how often something happens in one second of time. In automotive terms, it can be used to describe things like the frequency of electrical signals, vibrations, or oscillations. For example, if a sensor operates at 1,000 Hz, it means it cycles or measures 1,000 times per second. Frequency is often represented in technical information, documentation or on oscilloscope displays as: Hz - Hertz, named after Heinrich Hertz.

Electrical Essentials

Electromotive Force (EMF) - the voltage generated by a power source, such as a battery or alternator, to drive electric current through a vehicle's electrical system.

Open circuit voltage (OCV) - the voltage measured across a power source when no load is connected, and no current is flowing.

Potential Difference (Pd) - the voltage difference between two points in a vehicle's electrical circuit, driving current flow.

Closed-circuit voltage (CCV) - the voltage measured across a power source when it is connected to a circuit and supplying current.

Oscillate - the repetitive variation of a signal, voltage, or mechanical movement in a vehicle system.

Resistance - the opposition to electrical current flow in a vehicle's circuit, measured in ohms (Ω).

Power - the rate/speed at which work is done.

Frequency - the rate at which an electrical or mechanical signal oscillates in a vehicle system, measured in Hertz (Hz).

How electrical voltage drives signals across vehicle networks

At the heart of any in-vehicle **network**, including **CAN Bus**, are simple electrical signals. These networks operate by sending information in the form of voltage changes along wires. To understand how the network communicates, it helps to think of voltage as the 'push' that moves the signal through the circuit.
When you're diagnosing or testing a CAN Bus, you're really looking at these small voltage changes. Understanding that voltage is what 'drives' the signal through the network and that the **ECU** creates and senses these voltage differences is key to making sense of how the system works and what can go wrong.

Recognising the flow of electrical signals in communication circuits

When working with in-vehicle networks like CAN Bus, it's important to remember that behind every data signal is a flow of electrical **current**. Current is the movement of electrons through a conductor, in this case, through the network wires. Without current, no signal can be sent, because no **charge** would move to create the voltage differences that carry the data.

In a communication circuit, the control units (ECUs) on the network send messages by creating small, rapid changes in voltage. These changes cause a corresponding flow of current in the network wires. Although the current is very small compared to what you'd see in traditional automotive circuits and systems, it is still a real flow of electrons that makes the network work.

Figure 1.4 An ECU creating a network message

Electrical Essentials

Think of voltage as the force or pressure pushing the electrons, and current as the movement of those electrons through the circuit. Both are necessary; voltage alone without a path to flow through won't move electrons, and current can't exist without voltage to push it.

When diagnosing a network fault, keep in mind that current is the physical movement of charge carrying the signal. Checking connections, continuity, and resistance is just as important on a CAN Bus circuit as it is on any other electrical system, because these factors directly affect the current flow that the network depends on.

How impedance can affect signal integrity and network performance

Every electrical circuit resists the flow of current to some degree. This property is called **resistance**, and it plays an important role in how well in-vehicle networks like CAN Bus function. On a CAN Bus, the concept of resistance extends to something called **impedance**, which describes how the circuit resists the flow of a fast-changing signal such as the data messages sent on the network.

In simple terms, resistance and impedance are what the electrical signals have to 'work against' as they travel through the wires and connections. If the resistance or impedance is too high or too low, the signals can become weak, distorted, or even fail completely, leading to communication errors between control units (ECUs).

Corrosion, poor connections, or damaged wires can add unwanted resistance into the circuit. Even a few ohms of extra resistance in the wrong place can weaken the current flow and degrade the voltage signals, causing intermittent or total network failure.

Network - systems of connected electronic control units (ECUs) in a vehicle that communicate with each other by sending electrical signals over shared wiring, instead of using separate wires for each signal.

CAN Bus - a type of automotive communication network that allows electronic control units (ECUs) in a vehicle to exchange information with each other using just two wires.

ECU (Electronic Control Unit) - a small computer in a vehicle that controls or monitors a specific system or function.

Current - the flow of electric charge in a vehicle's electrical system, typically measured in amperes (amps).

Charge - the property of particles, like electrons, that makes electricity possible. In a vehicle, electrical charge is what flows through wires and circuits to power components and carry signals.

Resistance - the opposition to the flow of electrical current in a vehicle's electrical system, usually caused by components like wires, switches, and electrical devices.

Impedance - the total opposition to the flow of alternating current (AC) or changing signals in a circuit.

Electrical Essentials

Circuit Properties & Voltage Types

Electric circuits

For electrons to move from one atom to another, they need a continuous path, known as a **circuit**. This allows an electron to move forward as it is replaced by another one from behind. Without a circuit, the electrons cannot flow because the last electron in the conductor has nowhere to go. If the circuit is broken, we refer to it as losing **continuity**.

In other words, electrons need a complete loop to move. If the loop is broken, the electrons can't move because they have nowhere to go.

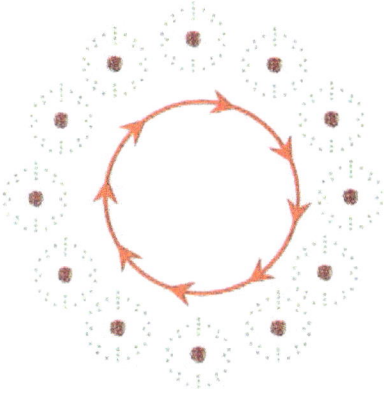

Figure 1.5 Copper atoms forming a loop

Series and parallel circuits

Two main types of electrical circuit are used in the construction of motor vehicles:

- **Series**
- **Parallel**

Series circuit

In a series circuit, devices are connected one after another in a single line. They all share the same circuit, so they divide the electricity based on how much power each device uses. If you add more devices to the circuit, each one gets only a portion of the available voltage. The more power a device needs, the more electricity it uses.

In simpler terms, in a series circuit, all devices are lined up in a row. They share the electricity, and each device only gets a part of it. The stronger the device, the more electricity it takes.

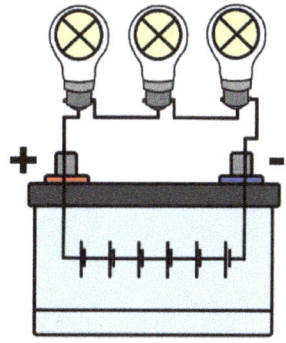

Figure 1.6 Bulbs connected in series

In a series circuit, if any one device stops working, it breaks the circuit and stops the flow of electricity. This means all the other devices in the circuit will also stop working.

Parallel circuit

In a parallel circuit, devices are connected side by side. Each device has its own power supply and return path to the supply. Because of this, all devices receive the full voltage and can operate at full **power**.

When you add a device to a parallel circuit, it creates a new branch or pathway. This allows more current to flow, which is **inversely proportional** to the resistance in that branch. This is known as a **current divider**.

If one device in a parallel circuit stops working, the others will continue to work. This is because each device has its own separate pathway for electricity.

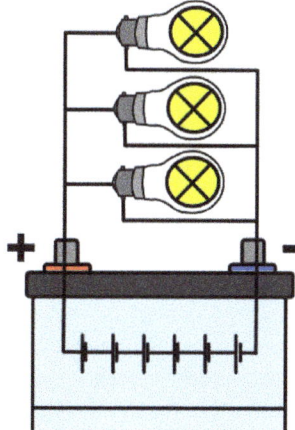

Figure 1.7 Bulbs connected in parallel

Electrical Essentials

In a series circuit, the components are connected one after the other, and the current flows through each component in turn. The voltage across each component can be different and is determined by its resistance according to Ohm's law. The total resistance of a series circuit is equal to the sum of the individual resistances. (They add up).

In a parallel circuit, the components are connected on different branches of the circuit and the voltage across each component is the same. The current flowing through each branch is determined by its resistance according to Ohm's law. The total resistance of a parallel circuit is less than any of the individual resistances.

Circuit - a continuous and unbroken loop.

Continuity - the unbroken electrical path in a vehicle's circuit, ensuring current flows properly.

Series - connected one after another.

Parallel - connected side-by-side.

Power - the amount of electrical energy used or produced by a vehicle's electrical system, typically measured in watts. It represents the rate at which electrical energy is transferred or converted to do work in the vehicle.

Inversely proportional - a relationship between two variables (in this case current and resistance), where an increase in one variable leads to a decrease in the other and vice versa.

Current divider - a circuit configuration that splits the total current among different branches, allowing different components to receive varying amounts of electrical current.

The difference between EMF, Pd, OCV, CCV

Voltage, or electrical potential (pressure or force), behaves differently depending on whether an electrical circuit is switched on or off. The acronyms OCV (Open Circuit Voltage) and CCV (Closed Circuit Voltage) are often used to differentiate between these two states.

- OCV – Open Circuit Voltage (switched off).
- CCV – Closed Circuit Voltage (switched on).

An electromotive force (EMF) often represents the highest electrical pressure waiting to do some work and is mostly associated with the voltage when the circuit is switched off. Conversely, a potential difference (Pd) is the voltage measured when a circuit is switched on and current is flowing. A potential difference can be higher than an electromotive force if a circuit is under the influence of electric charge, or lower than the electromotive force if components are consuming electrical energy or the circuit is discharging.

Electrical Essentials

Ground and earth

Two automotive electrical terms that are often confused or misused are 'Ground' and 'Earth.' The confusion might arise from the common association with 'planet Earth' and 'the ground'. However, in automotive electrical circuits, it is crucial to understand the distinct meanings of these terms:

- Ground represents the lowest common voltage potential on an electrical circuit. This is often accepted to be 0 volts but will depend on the circuit being tested.
- Earth describes a low-resistance electrical connection returning back to the power source in a direct current (DC) circuit or a low-resistance path away from the main circuit in alternating current (AC), often used to protect the system and operator, normally via some form of circuit breaker.

Think of 'ground' in a DC electrical circuit as the floor of a building, where all the furniture rests at a common level—it's the reference point or base level.

In contrast, 'earth' can be compared to the way out or a safety exit that allows people to leave the same way they came in or directs unwanted guests (excess electrical energy) out of the building and away from harm.

While 'ground' gives stability within the circuit, 'earth' ensures electrical energy can return unhindered to its original supply source or provides protection by safely diverting energy away when needed.

Electromagnetism & EMI

Electricity and magnetism are closely related, like two sides of the same coin. Both have positive and negative poles, or north and south, and both can attract and repel.

When a magnet passes a copper conductor (wire), the magnetic attraction moves electrons through the conductor, creating an electric current. Conversely, when an electric current passes through a copper conductor, it generates an invisible magnetic field. The magnetic effect of an electric current can cause movement through attraction or repulsion. This movement can be harnessed to create a motor.

Similarly, the movement of magnets past a conductor can generate an electric current, which is the principle behind a generator.

- Motors convert electrical energy into mechanical energy.
- Generators convert mechanical energy into electrical energy.

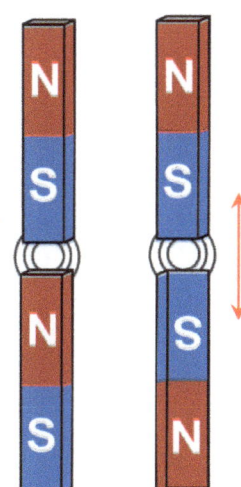

Figure 1.8 Magnets attracting and repelling

Electrical Essentials

Electromagnetic interference

When working with automotive electrical and network systems, you may hear the terms **EMI** (electromagnetic interference) and **RFI** (radio frequency interference). Both refer to unwanted **electrical noise** that can disrupt how circuits and communication networks work. Understanding what they are and how they affect systems like CAN Bus is important for diagnosing faults and keeping the vehicle reliable.

Electromagnetic interference (EMI) happens when one electrical circuit creates a magnetic field that disturbs another circuit nearby. Whenever current flows through a wire, it creates an invisible magnetic field around it. In normal operation, these fields don't cause problems, but if wires are routed poorly, damaged, or run too close to noisy components like high-voltage electric vehicle drive systems, ignition coils or alternators for example, they can pick up or radiate **interference**. This interference can cause false signals, data errors, or even communication loss in sensitive circuits like CAN Bus.

Radio frequency interference (RFI) is a type of EMI that happens at very high frequencies, the kind used by radio waves. RFI is essentially 'high-speed' electrical noise that can come from things like spark plugs firing, relays switching, or even external sources like nearby radio transmitters. In vehicles, RFI can interfere with AM/FM radio reception, Bluetooth, GPS, or even the proper operation of data networks if **shielding** is poor or components are faulty.

Modern vehicle networks such as CAN Bus are designed to resist EMI and RFI. For example:

- The CAN wires are twisted together to cancel out electromagnetic fields.
- Termination resistors prevent signals from reflecting and turning into noise.
- Shielding and proper grounding help keep stray signals out of sensitive circuits.

EMI (electromagnetic interference) - unwanted electrical noise caused by magnetic fields from other circuits or components.

RFI (radio frequency interference) - unwanted electrical noise made up of high-frequency signals, similar to radio waves.

Electrical noise - unwanted or stray electrical signal that gets into a circuit and can interfere with how it works.

Interference - any unwanted electrical signal or disturbance that disrupts how a vehicle's circuits, sensors, or communication networks work.

Shielding - the protective measures used to block electromagnetic interference (EMI) or physical damage. This can involve using materials like metal or special coatings around electrical wiring, components, or entire systems to prevent interference from external electromagnetic fields or to protect sensitive parts from environmental factors such as heat, moisture, or debris.

Electrical Essentials

High & Low Voltage

Electrical voltage creates a potential danger when it comes to the possibility of electric shock or electrocution. Once the electrical pressure (voltage) reaches a point where it can overcome the natural resistance of the human body and a circuit is created with two points of contact in parallel to a power source, electric current will start to flow. The touch threshold (resistance) for dry human skin is often considered to be 50 volts; however, this value can be lower if the skin is wet, there are wounds present or the electrodes penetrate the skin. Once current starts to flow, 80 milliamps (remember that a milliamp is just 1000th of an amp) has the potential to cause injury or even death.

Consider lightly placing your hand on a sharp, upturned nail. Your skin has resistance, so as long as the pressure is light, the nail won't cause damage. However, if you increase the pressure on your hand, the nail will eventually overcome the skin's resistance and pierce it. In this analogy, the pressure is like voltage. It's the cause of any injury. But the size of the nail, which is similar to the amount of current, determines the extent of the damage. If the pressure or voltage stays below the threshold where it can overcome skin resistance, then the size of the nail or current doesn't matter. That's why warning signs say, 'Danger High Voltage' and not 'Danger High Current'.

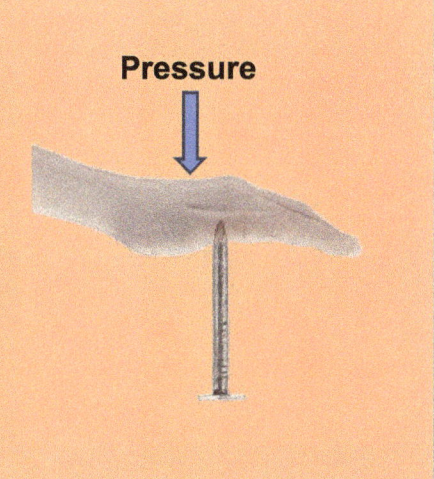

Regarding the hazards of voltage and current (amps), voltage is often considered the dangerous element, which is why warning signs typically state 'Danger High Voltage'. If a voltage exceeds the touch threshold of dry human skin, it can cause an electric current to flow, and it's this current that can cause harm. Keeping the voltage potential low reduces the risk of electric shock or electrocution. However, even with low voltage, there's still a risk of a short circuit that can lead to arcing, vehicle/circuit damage, fire, or explosion.
Make sure you are continually evaluating the risks of electricity when conducting any diagnosis or repair.

It is also important to consider the voltages being tested during a diagnostic procedure, in order to protect the operator, equipment and vehicle.

Ohms Law & Watts (Power) Law

Ohms law

Ohm's Law states that current flowing in a circuit is proportional to the voltage supplied and inversely proportional to the resistance.

Put simply, Ohm's Law explains how voltage, current (amps), and resistance (ohms) in a circuit are related. If you change one of these factors, it affects the others. Here's a simpler explanation using a water analogy:

1. Voltage (Pressure): If you increase the voltage in a circuit, it's like increasing the water pressure in a pipe. This makes more current flow, just like more water would flow through the pipe.

2. Resistance (Tap): If you increase the resistance in a circuit, it's like partially closing the tap on a pipe. This makes less current flow, just like less water would flow through the pipe.

Georg Ohm explained this with these formulas:

- Current (Amps) = Voltage ÷ Resistance
- Resistance (Ohms) = Voltage ÷ Current
- Voltage = Current × Resistance

Therefore, with Ohm's Law, if you know two of these measurements, you can calculate the third one. The Ohm's Law triangle is a handy tool for doing these calculations.

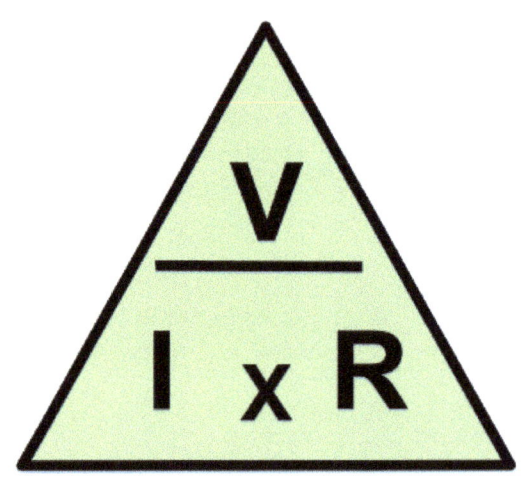

Figure 1.9 Ohms law triangle

In electrical equations, we often use the following symbols:

- **V** represents Volts.

  Sometimes, you might see the letter 'E' used instead to represent EMF (Electromotive Force), but it still means Volts.

- **I** stands for Amps.

  This letter is used to represent intensité du courant, (current intensity).

- **R** is used for Ohms.

  We use 'R' for resistance to avoid confusion with zero.

The Ohms Law triangle can help you calculate unknown units.

Here's how to use it:

Cover the unknown unit with your thumb, and the remaining letters form the calculation you need.
For example, if you don't know the amperage (I), cover the 'I' in the triangle. You'll be left with V ÷ R, which means Volts divided by resistance.

Electrical Essentials

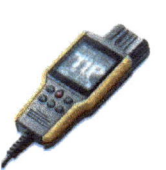

By taking measurements and comparing them using Ohms Law calculations, you can identify where the fault might be:

- Voltage (Pressure): If the voltage is lower than expected, the performance of the component might be reduced. If it's higher than expected, it could cause the component to be overworked and damaged.
- Current (Quantity/Amps): If the current is lower than expected, the component might not operate correctly. If it's higher than expected, it could mean that the component or system is being overworked.
- Resistance (Ohms): If the resistance is lower than expected, it could indicate a short circuit, where current is taking an alternative path to earth. If it's higher than expected, it could consume electrical energy and reduce system performance.

Therefore, if your voltage, current, or resistance measurements are different from what you expect, it could indicate a problem with your circuit.

Watt's (power) law

Power, measured in Watts, can be calculated similarly to Ohms Law:

- Current (Amps) = Power ÷ Voltage
- Voltage = Power ÷ Current
- Power (Watts) = Current × Voltage

You can use a power triangle, like the Ohms Law triangle, to help with these calculations.

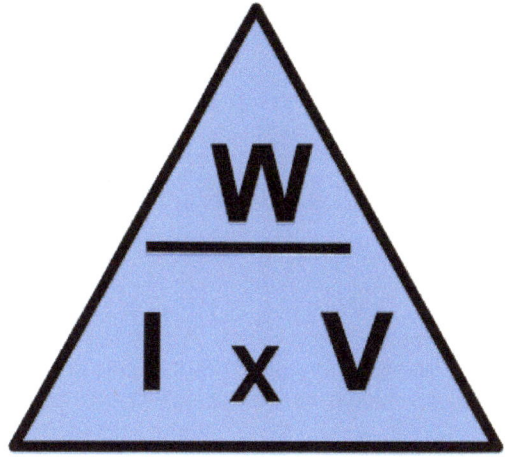

Figure 1.10 Power law triangle

- **W** represents power in Watts.

  Sometimes, you might see the letter 'P' used instead to represent power, but it still means Watts.

- **V** represents volts.

  Sometimes, you might see the letter 'E' used instead to represent EMF (electromotive Force), but it still means Volts.

- **I** stands for Amps.

  This letter is used to represent intensité du courant, (current intensity).

The Power Law triangle can help you calculate unknown units.

Here's how to use it:

Cover the unknown unit with your thumb, and the remaining letters form the calculation you need.
For example, if you don't know the amperage (I), cover the 'I' in the triangle. You'll be left with W ÷ V, which means Watts divided by Volts.

Analog vs Digital

Many vehicles use a mix of **analogue** and **digital** signals to operate and communicate and it's important to understand what these terms mean, because you'll come across both when diagnosing systems and networks like CAN Bus.

- An analogue signal is a smooth, continuous signal that can have any value within a range. Think of it like the needle on an old style fuel gauge moving up and down smoothly to show how much fuel is left. In electrical terms, an analogue voltage might change gradually from 0 volts up to 5 volts for example, depending on what the sensor is measuring. Many sensors, like temperature or throttle position sensors, produce analogue signals because the things they measure (like heat or movement) also change gradually.
- A digital signal, on the other hand, is made up of only two states: on or off, high or low, 1 or 0. It looks more like a square wave than a smooth line. In a digital circuit, the voltage switches quickly between two fixed levels, such as 0 volts (off) and 5 volts (on). This makes digital signals perfect for carrying information in **binary code**, which is how computers and control units process data. Vehicle networks like CAN Bus use digital signals to send messages between ECUs.

Analogue - electrical signals that change smoothly and continuously to represent a physical value, like temperature, pressure, or position.

Digital - electrical signals that switch quickly between just two values, on or off, high or low, 1 or 0.

Binary code - a way of representing information using only two numbers: 1 and 0.

Pulse Width Modulation & Duty Cycle

Pulse width modulation (PWM) and duty cycle, are two key terms that need to be understood, especially when using an automotive oscilloscope.

Many electrical devices and electronic actuators can be controlled by duty cycle or pulse width modulation (PWM). These methods work by rapidly switching components on and off so that they only receive a portion of the available current or voltage, thus regulating power. Depending on the reaction time of the component being switched and the duration of power supply, variable control is achieved. This method is more efficient than using resistors to control current or voltage in a circuit. Resistors waste electrical energy as heat, whereas duty cycle and PWM operate with minimal power loss.

Even though these terms are often interchanged, there is a subtle difference in their meaning:

- Pulse width modulation PWM often refers to how long something is switched on and is normally represented by a measurement of time.
- Although created by pulse width modulation, duty cycle, on the other hand, refers to the comparison between the amount of time something is switched on to the amount of time it is switched off (i.e., on-duty is when it's switched on; off-duty is when it's switched off). This is normally represented as a percentage.

Electrical Essentials

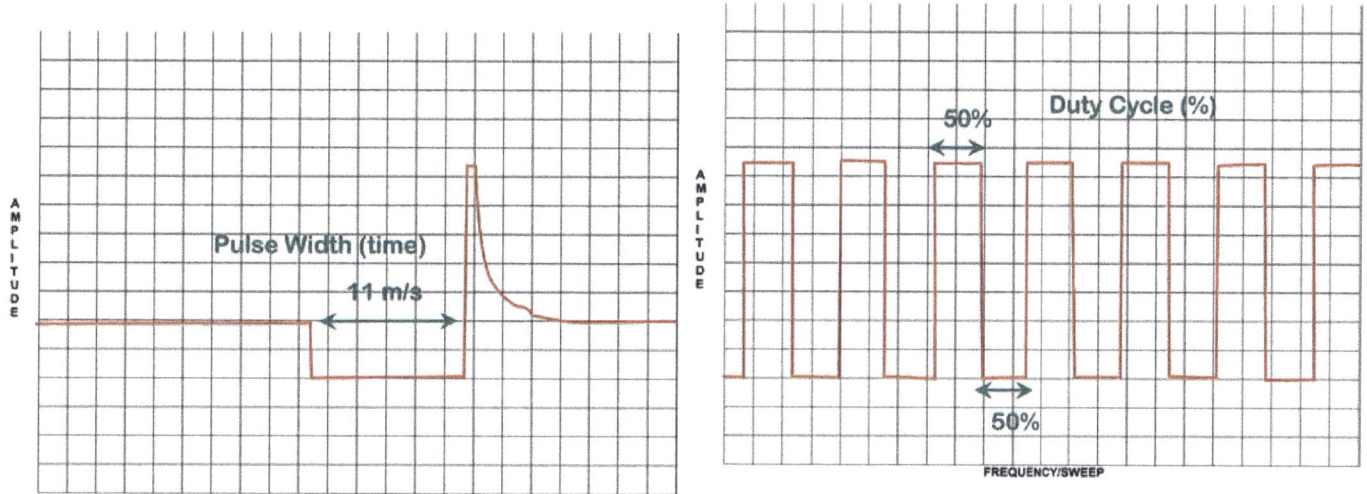

Figure 1.11 Pulse width and duty cycle

Pull-up & Pull-down Circuits

Pull-up or pull-down circuits refer to whether a circuit is switched on by connecting it to a power source or earth.

- Connecting to the positive side of the circuit will pull the voltage 'up'.
- Alternatively, switching on the circuit by earthing to a common ground will pull the voltage 'down'.

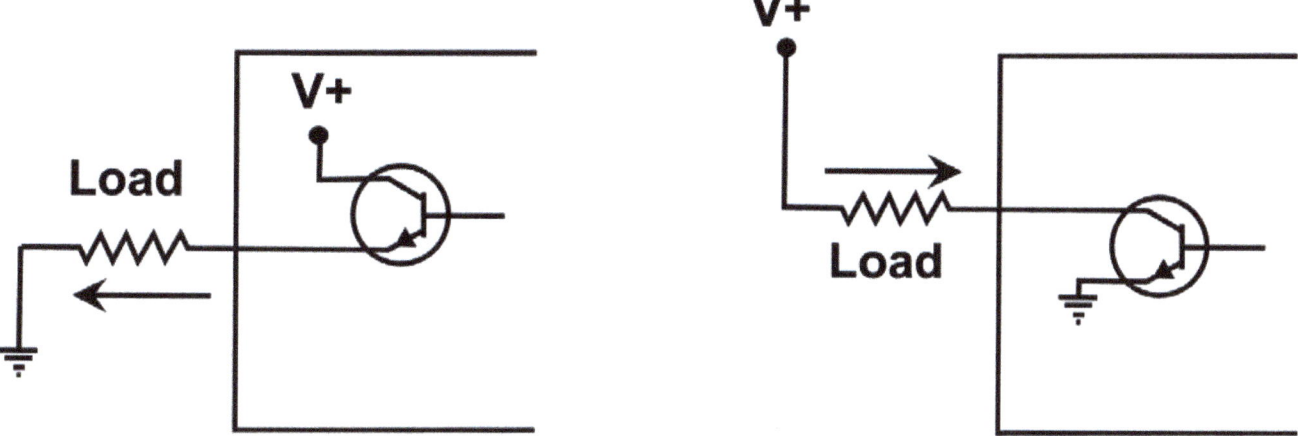

Figure 1.12 Pull-up and pull-down circuit switching

It is often commonplace for automotive electrical control circuits to be designed as pull down.
This is because it is easier for an electronic control unit (ECU) to 'earth-out' multiple circuits or components to a common ground than provide a power supply to separate components. This is especially important when the voltage of the power supply may vary between circuit requirements.
However, this does mean that to understand duty cycle for control operation, you will need to know whether the circuit uses pull-up or pull-down.

Conclusion

This chapter has explored the fundamental principles that underpin automotive electrical systems. Understanding how electricity works and how it interacts within circuits is essential for diagnosing, troubleshooting, and repairing modern vehicle electronics and in-vehicle network systems. These core concepts form the foundation for working safely and effectively with increasingly complex electrical and electronic components, helping you develop the skills needed to keep vehicles operating reliably and efficiently.

Chapter 2 Introduction to CAN Bus Systems

Chapter 2 Introduction to CAN Bus Systems

In order to work effectively with vehicle electrics, it is important to be familiar with the basics of CAN Bus systems and how they enable communication between control units. This chapter will help you develop an understanding of the key principles behind the Controller Area Network (CAN) used in automotive engineering by vehicle manufacturers. It also introduces the fundamental concepts of how digital data is transmitted across the network and how multiple electronic control units (ECUs) share information to operate the vehicle's systems.

Contents

What is a CAN Bus	26
Terminology	29
Principles of Parallel & Serial Communication	38
Multiplexing Network Architecture	40
Components of a CAN Network	44
CAN Protocol Basics	46
Common CAN Bus Architectures	49
Digital Signals	51
Timing & Synchronisation	52
Voltage Levels	53

When working on CAN Bus systems and vehicle networks, always remember that these circuits are part of the vehicle's critical control systems. Disconnecting, shorting, or applying the wrong voltage to CAN wiring can cause damage to electronic control units (ECUs), erase data, or even disable safety systems like airbags and ABS.
Before testing or repairing any CAN circuits:

- Always disconnect the battery if specified by the manufacturer's procedures.

- Use the correct diagnostic tools and avoid using standard test lights on CAN wires, as they can overload sensitive circuits.

- Never cut, splice, or tap into CAN wiring without proper guidance, as this can introduce faults and communication errors.

- Be aware that CAN systems operate even when the ignition is off; some ECUs stay awake for a short time after key-off.

Work methodically, follow the vehicle manufacturer's repair information, and always observe health and safety regulations. Taking care around CAN networks will help prevent costly damage and keep vehicle systems operating safely and reliably.

Chapter 2 Introduction to CAN Bus Systems

What is a CAN Bus

Over the last few decades, electrics and computing have completely transformed the modern world. From smartphones to factories, computers now control and automate almost everything we use in our daily lives. Transportation is no exception. The same advances in **electronics** and **digital technology** have driven huge changes in the way vehicles are designed, built, and maintained.

Modern vehicles no longer rely only on mechanical parts and simple wiring to operate. Today's cars, trucks, and buses use dozens of **microcomputers**, called **Electronic Control Units (ECUs),** to monitor and control nearly every system on the vehicle. These ECUs are constantly working in the background, making decisions thousands of times per second to keep the engine running efficiently, to control emissions, to manage braking and stability, and to keep passengers safe and comfortable.

In fact, modern vehicles depend on computers for almost every aspect of their operation. From starting the engine to deploying airbags in a crash, from regulating fuel injection to controlling the climate system, all of these functions are handled by ECUs working together. Even the steering, lighting, and driver assistance systems (like lane keeping and parking sensors) rely on networks of computers exchanging information. Hybrid, electric, and other alternative propulsion vehicles take this even further, they rely heavily on advanced electronics and powerful ECUs to manage battery systems, electric motors, regenerative braking, energy efficiency, and even communication with external charging equipment. These vehicles cannot operate without complex, high-speed communication networks connecting all of their systems.

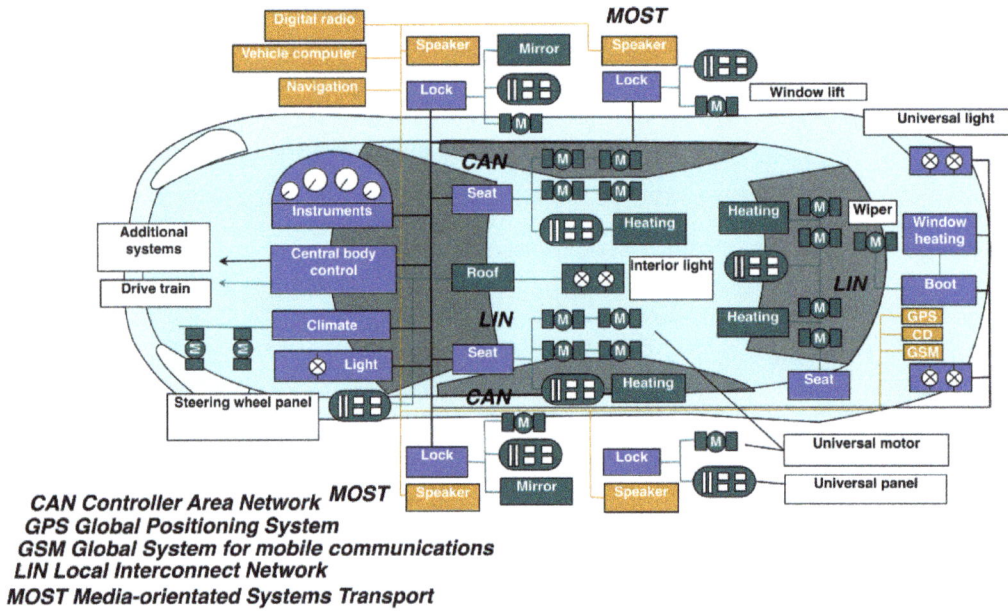

CAN Controller Area Network
GPS Global Positioning System
GSM Global System for mobile communications
LIN Local Interconnect Network
MOST Media-orientated Systems Transport

Figure 2.1 In-vehicle network systems

As electronics and ECUs became more widespread in vehicles during the 1980s, the amount of wiring and the number of signals needed grew rapidly. **Point-to-point wiring** (where every sensor and actuator is connected directly to its control unit) became bulky, heavy, and unreliable. A more efficient solution was needed. In 1986, engineers at Bosch developed the **Controller Area Network (CAN Bus),** a standardised in-vehicle **network** that allows all ECUs to communicate with each other over a single pair of wires. CAN Bus reduced wiring complexity, saved weight and cost, improved reliability, and provided a fast, robust way for systems to share information.

Chapter 2 Introduction to CAN Bus Systems

CAN Bus is probably one of the most widely used networks within vehicle design, and the name 'CAN Bus' has become synonymous with ECU communication to the point where it is often used to describe all in-vehicle networking, even if another type is actually being used.

Since its introduction, CAN Bus has become the backbone of in-vehicle communication. It is now used in nearly every modern vehicle to connect powertrain, chassis, body, and safety systems. As vehicles continue to evolve, especially with hybrid and electric propulsion, the demand for fast, reliable communication networks like CAN Bus (and newer networks that build on its principles) continues to grow.

As a technician, understanding how and why electronics and computing have become central to vehicle operation, and how CAN Bus networks make it all possible, is the first step toward diagnosing and repairing today's sophisticated systems.

The idea of a '**computer**', a machine that can process information, has been around for over a century. One of the earliest pioneers was *Charles Babbage*, who designed a mechanical 'difference engine' in the 1800s to perform calculations. His colleague *Ada Lovelace* is often credited as the world's first programmer, because she worked out how to write instructions for Babbage's machine.

Fast-forward to the 20th century, and during World War II, electronic computers began to appear. In 1936, *Alan Turing* described the idea of a universal machine that could perform any calculation given the right instructions and this became the foundation of modern computing theory. During the war, *Turing* and his team helped develop machines like Colossus to break enemy codes, proving how powerful computing could be.

In the decades that followed, inventors like *John von Neumann* helped define how computers store **programs** and process data, while engineers developed the first electronic circuits using **vacuum tubes**, then **transistors**, and finally **microchips**. The invention of the **microprocessor** in the 1970s was a turning point, suddenly, powerful computers could fit into small, affordable packages. This is what made it possible for carmakers to start putting computers (ECUs) into vehicles.

Electronics - electrical and electronic systems in a vehicle that control, monitor, and improve how it operates.

Digital technology - the use of computers, networks, and electronic systems in vehicles that process and communicate information in digital form, using binary (1s and 0s).

Microcomputers - small, specialised computers built into vehicles to control specific systems.

Chapter 2 Introduction to CAN Bus Systems

Electronic Control Units (ECUs) - small computers in a vehicle that control and monitor specific systems responsible for one or more functions, such as running the engine, controlling the brakes, managing airbags, or operating the climate control.

Point-to-point wiring - a type of wiring where each electrical component is connected directly to the control unit or switch it works with, using its own dedicated wires.

Controller Area Network (CAN Bus) - a communication system that allows all the electronic control units (ECUs) in a vehicle to share information with each other over just two wires.

Network - a system of connected electronic control units (ECUs) in a vehicle that communicate with each other to operate and monitor different functions.

Computer - an electronic device that processes information by following instructions (programs).

Programs - sets of instructions written into the software of electronic control units (ECUs) that tell the vehicle's computers how to operate different systems.

Vacuum tubes - early electronic components that control electric current by using a vacuum inside a glass tube. They were used in the first electronic computers and radios to amplify signals before transistors were invented.

Transistors - small electronic components used in vehicle circuits to amplify or switch electrical signals.

Microchips - tiny electronic circuits embedded in control units that process data and control vehicle systems.

Microprocessor - the central processing unit (CPU) inside an electronic control unit (ECU) that executes instructions and processes data to control vehicle systems. It acts like the vehicle's brain, managing functions such as engine timing, braking, and safety features.

The purpose and advantages of CAN Bus in automotive systems

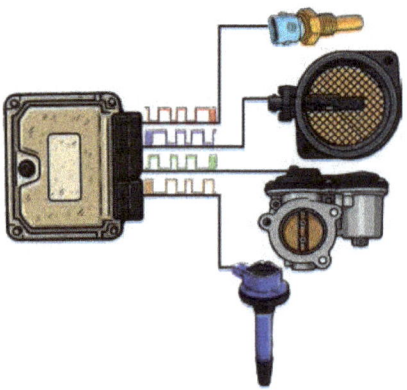

Vehicle systems are made up of many electronic control units (ECUs) that each manage different parts of the car. These ECUs need to share information with each other quickly and reliably so that they work seamlessly together.

Point-to-point wiring, used in older cars, was where each ECU or sensor was connected directly to the components it controlled. As vehicles became more advanced, this method created big problems. The wiring looms became heavy, bulky, complicated to install, and harder to repair. There was also more chance of wiring faults, and adding new features required even more wires.

Figure 2.2 Parallel communication – point-to-point

Chapter 2 Introduction to CAN Bus Systems

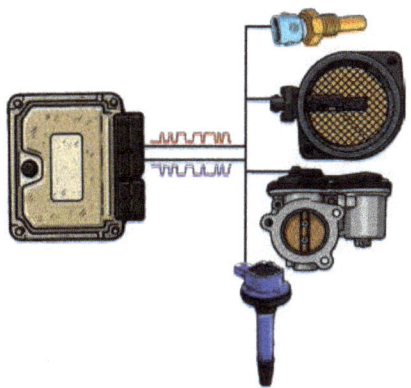

The Controller Area Network was developed to solve these problems. The purpose of CAN Bus is to provide a simple, reliable, and efficient way for all ECUs or nodes to communicate with each other over just two wires, instead of needing a separate wire for every signal. This is known as a networked communication system.

Figure 2.3 Serial communication - networked

Using CAN Bus brings several key advantages:

- Less wiring: Since all ECUs connect to the same two-wire Bus, the wiring harness is lighter, smaller, and easier to install. Fewer wires and connectors mean lower manufacturing and repair costs.

- Faster communication: CAN Bus can transmit data quickly enough for real-time control of critical systems like braking and stability.

- High reliability: CAN Bus is designed to resist electrical noise and keep working even in harsh automotive environments.

- Easier to add features: New ECUs, components and systems can be added to the network without running lots of extra wires; this also gives manufacturers a straightforward method of configuring vehicle options late in the manufacturing process.

- Better diagnostics: Since all ECUs are on the same network, you can access diagnostic codes and live data more easily using diagnostic tools.

- It provides the opportunity to update software to overcome running issues and fix bugs once the vehicle has been launched.

Terminology

In order to better understand in-vehicle network systems, it is necessary to describe some associated terminology and basic acronyms. **Table 2.1** explains some common vocabulary or **nomenclature** to help overcome confusing **jargon**. Understanding these terms will help you read wiring diagrams, use diagnostic tools, and communicate clearly with other technicians and engineers.

Table 2.1 Common terminology and vocabulary

Term	Description
Multiplex	In automotive electronics, **multiplexing**, derived from Latin roots 'multi-' meaning 'many' and 'plex' from 'plectere' meaning 'to weave,' refers to transmitting multiple signals over a single communication channel rather than using separate wires for each signal. This 'weaving together' of signals allows various devices to share the same communication Bus, often termed as a multiplexed network, improving efficiency in vehicle wiring systems.

Chapter 2 Introduction to CAN Bus Systems

Table 2.1 Common terminology and vocabulary

Term	Description
Network 	The word 'network' originates from two older English words: 'net,' meaning a woven mesh used for catching things, and 'work,' referring to something made or constructed. It initially described anything made of interconnecting threads or lines, like a fishing net, and has evolved in technical fields to mean systems of interconnected parts. In automotive electronics, a network describes the interconnected system of electronic control units (ECUs), sensors, actuators, and other devices exchanging information through communication links. Common automotive networks include the CAN network (Controller Area Network) for general in-vehicle communication, the LIN network (Local Interconnect Network) for simpler body electronics, and the Ethernet network for high-speed communication with cameras and advanced driver assistance systems (ADAS). These networks are also described by their **topology**, such as Bus, star, or ring patterns.
Local Area Network (LAN) 	The term 'Local Area Network' or LAN comes from Latin words: 'local,' meaning 'restricted to a specific place,' and 'area,' meaning a physical space, combined with 'network,' which originally described a woven net. So, LAN literally means 'a network operating within a specific place.' In computers, a LAN connects devices like computers in an office or home. In vehicles, a LAN refers to the network that connects many electronic control units (ECUs), sensors, and actuators inside the car, allowing quick and reliable communication. Although specific protocols like CAN or LIN are often mentioned, all these systems are examples of a LAN inside the vehicle.
Wide Area Network (WAN) 	The term 'Wide Area Network,' or WAN, comes from Latin words: 'wide,' meaning 'covering a large distance,' and 'area,' meaning a region, combined with 'network,' which originally meant a woven net. A WAN is a network that covers large geographical areas, such as between cities or countries. The internet is the biggest example of a WAN. In vehicles, WANs are used to connect the car to the outside world through technologies like cellular networks (4G, 5G), Wi-Fi, satellite, or dedicated short-range communication (DSRC). This allows cars to communicate with servers, share information with other vehicles, access the internet, and perform remote updates. While the term WAN is not often seen in wiring diagrams, it's helpful to know that when a vehicle sends or receives data beyond itself, like reporting its location or downloading maps, it is using some form of a Wide Area Network.
Controller Area Network (CAN)	The term 'Controller Area Network,' or CAN, comes from Latin roots: 'controller' meaning a device that manages or directs (from contra and rotulus, meaning to keep things in order), 'area' referring to a specific space, and 'network' from Old English meaning a woven net. CAN is a communication system that allows multiple electronic control units (ECUs) in a vehicle to share and exchange data over a single shared Bus. Developed by Bosch in the 1980s, CAN was created to reduce the heavy and complex wiring used before, by replacing point-to-point connections with a single, reliable network. This system helps different vehicle systems, like powertrain, brakes, or body electronics, communicate efficiently, even in the noisy electrical environment of a vehicle. Variants of CAN include high-speed for critical systems, low-speed for body electronics, and CAN FD for faster and larger data transfer.

Chapter 2 Introduction to CAN Bus Systems

Table 2.1 Common terminology and vocabulary

Term	Description
Bus 	The word 'Bus,' in automotive and electronic systems, comes from the Latin word 'omnibus,' meaning 'for all' or 'carrying everything.' Originally, an omnibus bar was a conductor that carried power to multiple circuits, and the term was shortened to 'Bus.' In vehicles, a Bus is a shared communication pathway, usually a pair of wires, that allows various electronic control units (ECUs), sensors, and actuators to send and receive data. Instead of each ECU having a separate wire to every other, all devices connect to the same Bus, taking turns to communicate. Common types include the CAN Bus, Data Bus, and specific protocols like LIN, FlexRay, or Ethernet, each designed for different communication needs within the vehicle.
Parallel 	The word 'parallel' comes from the Greek 'parallēlos,' meaning 'alongside one another,' with 'para-' meaning 'beside' and 'allēlōn' meaning 'of one another.' In automotive systems, parallel describes wiring where multiple components are connected so each has its own direct path to the power source or data line, running side by side. In a parallel circuit, if one component fails, the others can still operate because they each have their own connection, unlike a series circuit, where devices are connected in a line. Older vehicle systems sometimes used parallel data transmission, sending multiple bits of data simultaneously over separate wires. Today, most systems like CAN Bus use serial communication, sending data bits one after the other on a single pair of wires, which simplifies wiring and improves efficiency.
Serial 	The word 'serial' comes from the Latin 'series,' meaning 'a row, sequence, or succession,' referring to things happening one after the other. In automotive systems, serial describes data transmission where bits are sent one at a time in a continuous stream over a single wire or channel. This is different from parallel transmission, which sends multiple bits at the same time on separate wires. Modern vehicle networks like CAN, LIN, and FlexRay use serial communication to reduce wiring complexity and weight, while still providing fast and reliable data exchange between ECUs and sensors. You may see terms like serial communication protocol, serial data line, or serial transmission speed, which refer to how data is sent and received in these systems.
Universal Serial Bus (USB) 	The term 'Universal Serial Bus,' or USB, comes from Latin roots: 'universal,' meaning it works with many different devices; 'serial,' referring to the way data is sent one bit at a time over a single wire; and 'bus,' meaning a shared pathway that multiple devices connect to. USB is a standard way for devices to communicate and transfer power through a common port. In vehicles, USB ports are familiar for charging phones, playing media, or connecting diagnostic tools. Originally created for computers in the 1990s, USB is now widely used in cars for charging, data transfer, and diagnostics. Different versions (like USB 2.0 and 3.0) and connector types (such as USB-A, USB-B, and USB-C) are common in vehicles today, with newer models often using the reversible USB-C.

Chapter 2 Introduction to CAN Bus Systems

Table 2.1 Common terminology and vocabulary

Term	Description
Node 	The word '**node**' comes from the Latin 'nodus,' meaning 'knot.' Originally, it referred to a knot or point where things are tied together. Today, in networking and electronics, a node is a connection point or device on a communication system. In vehicles, a node can be any electronic control unit (ECU), sensor, or actuator connected to the network that can send or receive data. For example, the engine control module or a temperature sensor are nodes. Each node has a specific function and communicates with others by exchanging messages over the network. In automotive contexts, you'll see the term used in wiring diagrams and technical documents, like '10 active nodes on the CAN Bus,' or notes about faults affecting communication. Terms like control unit, module, or device are often used interchangeably with node.
Master/Slave 	The term 'Master/Slave' originates from Old English and Latin, meaning 'one who has authority' and 'one under authority,' respectively. In networked systems, it describes a control relationship where one device (the master) manages and directs other devices (the slaves). In automotive networks, this arrangement is common in protocols like LIN (Local Interconnect Network), where one master node controls communication and up to 15 slave nodes respond. Unlike CAN Bus, which allows any node to start the communication, LIN relies on the master to send scheduling signals while slaves wait to reply. Despite newer terms like primary/secondary or controller/device being used for neutrality, master/slave is still widely recognised among technicians. It appears in documents, particularly when discussing LIN Bus structures or older protocols.
Point-to-Point 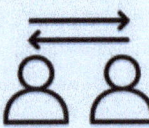	Point-to-Point derives from the words 'point,' meaning a specific location, and 'to,' indicating direction or connection. It describes a direct link between two devices, with no intermediaries. In automotive wiring, point-to-point refers to traditional systems where each switch, sensor, or device connects directly to its control unit with dedicated wires. This method was common for decades, but it led to bulky wiring harnesses and more complex troubleshooting as more devices were added. Today, while some circuits still use point-to-point wiring, especially for critical or simple components, many vehicles now rely on networked systems like CAN Bus, which share data across multiple devices using a common communication line, reducing wiring complexity.
Peer-to-Peer	Peer-to-Peer comes from Middle English, meaning 'equal' or 'someone of the same rank,' and literally means 'equal-to-equal.' It describes a communication system where all devices, or nodes, on a network have the same status and can talk to each other directly without a central controller. In vehicles, this is a key feature of CAN Bus, where any control unit (ECU) can initiate communication at any time if the Bus is free. Unlike systems with a master controlling the conversation, in a peer-to-peer setup, all nodes are equal, and message priority is managed through message identifiers (IDs). This design makes CAN Bus flexible, robust, and well-suited for modern vehicles, whereas other networks like LIN use a master-slave structure, where one device controls communication.

Chapter 2 Introduction to CAN Bus Systems

Table 2.1 Common terminology and vocabulary

Term	Description
Twisted Pair 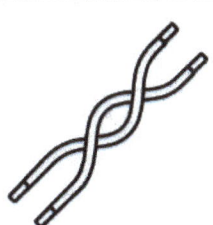	A Twisted Pair refers to a type of wiring used in automotive network systems like CAN Bus, where two insulated wires are wound around each other in a spiral. The name comes from 'twisted,' meaning the wires are wound together, and 'pair,' indicating two wires used as a set. This technique was first developed by telephone engineers in the late 19th century to reduce interference and improve signal clarity, and it is now used in vehicle networks to ensure reliable data transmission. In CAN systems, these wires are called CAN High (CAN H) and CAN Low (CAN L) and carry signals that are opposite in voltage (differential signalling). Twisting them cancels out electromagnetic interference (EMI) from electrical sources and minimises noise, helping maintain the integrity of network communication. It's essential for technicians to keep the twist intact during repairs to avoid data errors or network problems.
Local Interconnect Network (LIN) 	LIN, short for Local Interconnect Network, derives from Latin 'locus,' meaning 'place,' indicating its focus on local, limited-area communication within a vehicle. It links electronic components that don't need the high speed or complexity of CAN Bus. Developed in the 1990s by automakers, LIN is a simpler, slower protocol that uses a master/slave structure, where one device controls the communication with multiple controlled devices (slaves). It is ideal for low-cost, reliable control of components like power windows, mirrors, sunroofs, and climate fans. Unlike CAN's peer-to-peer communication, LIN is a single-wire network designed to reduce wiring complexity for non-critical systems.
Media Oriented Systems Transport (MOST) 	Media Oriented Systems Transport (MOST), from Latin 'media' meaning 'means of communication' and 'oriented' meaning 'focused on,' is a high-speed vehicle network designed to transport multimedia data like audio, video, and navigation information. Developed in the late 1990s, MOST is used for complex entertainment and infotainment systems, such as digital audio, video screens, cameras, and navigation. Unlike control networks like CAN or LIN, MOST is optimised for large data flows, often using optical fibres to prevent electromagnetic interference and ensure fast transmission. The system can operate at speeds like 50 or 150 Mbps, making it ideal for digital multimedia in vehicles.
Single Edge Nibble Transmission (SENT) 	Single Edge Nibble Transmission (SENT), from Latin 'singulus' meaning 'one, individual, or separate' and 'transmissio' meaning 'sending across' or 'sending through,' is a simple and cost-effective protocol used in vehicles to send high-resolution sensor data digitally. It is mainly used for engine sensors like throttle position or pressure sensors. SENT transmits data by timing voltage pulse edges, with each pulse representing four bits (a **nibble**). Being unidirectional, sending data from sensor to ECU, it replaces traditional analogue signals with more precise digital information less affected by electrical noise. SENT offers a straightforward, two-wire (SENT line and ground wire) communication method, making it ideal for high-resolution sensor data transmission in modern vehicles.

Chapter 2 Introduction to CAN Bus Systems

Table 2.1 Common terminology and vocabulary

Term	Description
FlexRay 	FlexRay is a high-speed, fault-tolerant communication protocol used in vehicles for critical systems such as electronic stability, steer-by-wire, and brake-by-wire. The name combines the Latin 'flectere,' meaning 'to bend,' reflecting flexibility, with 'ray,' symbolising fast, straight transmission, together suggesting an adaptable, rapid data highway. Developed in the early 2000s by major carmakers and suppliers like BMW, Daimler, and Bosch, FlexRay offers **deterministic communication**, ensuring that vital messages arrive precisely when needed, unlike CAN which prioritises speed but not timing accuracy. Operating at speeds up to 10 Mbps and using two channels for either higher bandwidth or **redundancy**, FlexRay is essential for advanced driver assistance systems and future automated driving.
Ethernet 	Ethernet is a widely used communication technology originally created for connecting computers in local networks. The name comes from 'ether,' a term from 19th-century physics that referred to an invisible medium thought to carry light waves, much like how Ethernet was imagined as an invisible medium for data signals. Developed in the 1970s by Robert Metcalfe and colleagues, Ethernet has since been adapted for vehicles, offering high-speed data transfer for advanced systems like cameras, sensors, and vehicle communication. Automotive Ethernet supports speeds from 100 Mbps up to 10 Gbps and uses a simpler, more robust cable design suitable for the tough conditions inside a car. It is essential for modern features like high-resolution infotainment, camera systems, and vehicle-to-vehicle communication. Terms like 100BASE-T1 and 1000BASE-T1 refer to specific Ethernet speeds used in automotive networks.
Differential Signalling 	Differential Signalling is a method of transmitting electrical signals over two wires, by sending the difference in voltage between them. The term 'differential' comes from Latin 'differentia,' meaning 'difference,' and 'signalling' refers to sending signals. Developed in telecommunications, this technique reduces noise and improves signal quality, especially in noisy environments like vehicles. In CAN Bus systems, the two wires, CAN High and CAN Low carry opposite voltages to represent the data. When interference affects both wires equally (common-mode noise), it cancels out because the system only reads the voltage difference. This makes differential signalling essential for reliable, high-speed data transfer in the electrically noisy environment of vehicles.
Dominant State and Recessive State 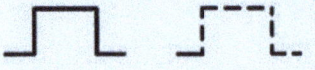	In CAN Bus systems, the two key signal levels are the Dominant and Recessive states, which represent data bits. 'Dominant' comes from Latin 'dominari,' meaning 'to rule,' and it describes the state that takes priority on the Bus. 'Recessive' comes from Latin 'recedere,' meaning 'to withdraw,' and it is the resulting, lower-priority state. The CAN Bus uses two wires, CAN High and CAN Low, with the voltage difference between them indicating the Bus state. The Dominant state (binary 0) actively pulls on CAN H and CAN L, overriding the Recessive (binary 1), where the lines float at similar voltages. This priority system allows multiple control units to share the network effectively, with the dominant state winning when messages occur at the same time, ensuring smooth and collision-free communication.

Chapter 2 Introduction to CAN Bus Systems

Table 2.1 Common terminology and vocabulary

Term	Description
Termination Resistor	A Termination Resistor is a special resistor placed at each end of a CAN Bus to ensure proper signal transmission. The word 'termination' comes from Latin 'terminare,' meaning 'to end,' and 'resistor; from Latin 'resistere,' meaning 'to resist.' In a CAN Bus, which uses two wires to carry data, the resistors (usually 120 ohms each) match the line's electrical impedance (about 120 ohms). This prevents signals from bouncing back and causing errors. Properly installed termination resistors ensure stable, clear communication; missing or faulty ones can lead to problems.
Baud Rate	Baud Rate describes the speed of data transmission over a vehicle's communication network, such as a CAN Bus. The term 'baud' comes from Émile Baudot, a French inventor, and originally meant the number of signal changes per second. In automotive systems, baud rate is measured in bits per second (bps), with common speeds like 125 kbps, 250 kbps, and 500 kbps. A higher baud rate allows faster communication between electronic control units (ECUs), but it can be more sensitive to interference. Conversely, a lower baud rate is slower but often more reliable in noisy environments. It's essential that all ECUs on the network use the same baud rate to ensure proper communication and avoid errors.
Bit	A **bit** is the smallest unit of digital information, representing a single 0 or 1. The word 'bit' is short for 'binary digit,' a term coined by John W Tukey in 1946, combining 'binary' (base-2 numbering) and 'digit' (a single number or symbol). In CAN Bus systems, data is transmitted as a series of bits, where each bit indicates a dominant or recessive state on the wires. Bits are grouped into bytes and messages to communicate information between electronic control units (ECUs). Because each bit is crucial for accurate communication, even small errors can cause network issues. Understanding bits helps you appreciate how digital signals **encode** and transfer data inside modern vehicle networks.
Topology	The word 'topology' comes from the Greek 'topos' meaning 'place' and 'logia' meaning 'study of.' In vehicle networks, topology describes how the electronic control units (ECUs) and wiring are arranged within the system. Common types include: • Bus topology, where all devices connect to a single line. • Star topology, where devices connect to a central hub. • Ring topology, where devices form a circle. • Hybrid topology, which combines methods.
Impedance	The word 'impedance' comes from the Latin 'impedire,' meaning 'to hinder' or 'obstruct.' In automotive electrical systems, impedance is the total opposition to the flow of electrical signals, involving both resistance (opposition to direct current) and reactance (opposition to changing signals caused by capacitors and inductors). Measured in ohms (Ω), impedance affects how well signals travel through wiring and components. If impedance is too high or mismatched, it can cause signal loss, distortion, or errors.

Chapter 2 Introduction to CAN Bus Systems

Table 2.1 Common terminology and vocabulary

Term	Description
Noise	The word 'noise' comes from the Latin 'nausea,' meaning sickness or discomfort, and in electronics, it refers to unwanted electrical signals that disrupt proper communication. In vehicle networks, noise includes any interference, such as electromagnetic interference (EMI), radio frequency interference (RFI), electrical spikes, or wiring issues that causes disturbances on data signals between ECUs and sensors. This interference appears as random or repetitive signals that can distort data, lead to errors, or cause system malfunctions. To ensure reliable operation, techniques like shielding, twisted cables, and good grounding are used to minimise noise and keep signals clear.
Bus Off	Bus Off is a term used in Controller Area Network communication systems, which originally comes from the Latin word 'bus' meaning 'a group of people traveling together,' or in this case, a shared communication pathway. 'Off' simply means turned off or disconnected. When a device like an Electronic Control Unit detects too many errors, such as corrupted messages or signal problems, it automatically turns itself off from the network to prevent disruption. This is a safety feature; the node stops sending messages, protecting the rest of the system from faulty signals. The device can often rejoin the network once the underlying issue is fixed and the error count resets.
Onboard Diagnostics (OBD)	Onboard Diagnostics, or OBD, is a system built into vehicles that monitors and reports the health of critical components like the engine and emissions controls. The word 'Onboard' means it is part of the vehicle itself, while 'Diagnostics' refers to identifying faults. The term comes from the Latin 'diagnosticare,' meaning to distinguish or recognise. OBD started in the 1980s with basic, manufacturer-specific systems, but in the 1990s, governments required standardisation to help reduce emissions. This led to OBDII, introduced in 1996 in the U.S., which uses a standard 16-pin connector and trouble codes to communicate issues. Today, all modern vehicles use OBDII or EOBD, which also allows technicians to read live data and diagnostic trouble codes via scan tools. The system supports various vehicle networks, like CAN Bus, but the OBD port remains the main access point for diagnostics.
Data Link Connector (DLC)	The Data Link Connector (DLC) is a standard diagnostic socket usually located under the dashboard of modern vehicles. It serves as the physical access point for technicians to connect scan tools to the vehicle's onboard computer systems, such as the CAN Bus. The term 'Data Link' refers to the communication path that carries data between the vehicle and diagnostic devices, while 'Connector' is the physical plug that joins these systems. The name means 'the plug that provides access to the vehicle's data communication link.' In vehicles with OBDII or EOBD, the DLC is a 16-pin standard connector, with each pin designated for functions like power, ground, and data transfer. This connector, also called the J1962 or OBD port, is key for reading trouble codes, live data, conducting tests, and reprogramming vehicle modules.

Chapter 2 Introduction to CAN Bus Systems

Table 2.1 Common terminology and vocabulary

Term	Description
Scan Tool 	A Scan Tool is a diagnostic device used by technicians to communicate with a vehicle's onboard computer systems, including the CAN Bus. The word 'scan' comes from Latin 'scandere,' meaning 'to examine carefully,' and 'tool' refers to an instrument for performing specific functions. Together, a scan tool is a device that carefully examines a vehicle's electronic systems. It connects to the Data Link Connector under the dashboard and retrieves information from the control units via the CAN Bus. Scan tools can read and clear trouble codes, monitor sensor data, reset warning lights, and even perform programming or calibration. They range from simple code readers to advanced analysers, helping technicians diagnose issues quickly and accurately in complex vehicle networks.
Diagnostic Trouble Code (DTC) 	A Diagnostic Trouble Code (DTC) is a code stored by a vehicle's electronic control units (ECUs) when a fault or abnormal condition is detected. The word 'diagnostic' comes from Greek 'diagnōstikos,' meaning 'able to distinguish,' and 'trouble' refers to a problem. 'Code' indicates a system of symbols or numbers used for identification. DTCs are generated when sensors or systems report data outside normal ranges and are often formatted with a letter and four digits (e.g., P0301). The letter shows the system area (like Powertrain, Body, Chassis or Network), and the numbers relate to the specific issue. Technicians use scan tools to retrieve DTCs through the Data Link Connector, helping them quickly identify and focus on problems, saving time and making troubleshooting more efficient.
Gateway 	A gateway in vehicle networking comes from the words 'gate' (an entry or exit point) and 'way' (a route), meaning a 'gateway' is a pathway between different areas. In cars, a gateway is a device that connects two or more communication networks, such as CAN Bus, LIN, or Ethernet, enabling them to exchange information. It acts like a bridge, translating protocols and managing data flow between different systems; like connecting the engine control system with the infotainment system, so all parts of the vehicle can work together smoothly. Gateways are critical in vehicles because they allow multiple ECUs on different networks to communicate with each other, ensuring the vehicle's many electronic systems operate as a coordinated whole.
Broadcast 	The term 'broadcast' comes from the early 20th century, originally meaning to spread seeds widely by hand, and later used in radio and TV to describe sending signals to a large audience. In automotive networks like CAN Bus, broadcast refers to sending data from one ECU to all other ECUs on the network at once. Instead of direct, one-to-one messages, a broadcast message is received by all connected devices simultaneously, like engine speed data shared with the transmission or ABS. This method simplifies communication, keeps systems synchronised, and ensures all relevant modules get real-time information, improving overall vehicle coordination.

Chapter 2 Introduction to CAN Bus Systems

Table 2.1 Common terminology and vocabulary

Term	Description
Identifier (ID) 	The word 'identifier' comes from the Latin 'identificare,' meaning 'to recognise as the same.' In vehicle networks like CAN Bus, an identifier (or ID) is a unique number assigned to each message. It serves two main purposes. First, it determines the message's priority; lower numerical IDs have higher priority and are sent first during simultaneous communication. Second, identifies the transmitting device, and filters messages for relevance among network nodes, so ECUs know how to process it. Identifiers can be 11 bits for simple systems or 29 bits for more complex ones. They are essential for organising and ensuring reliable communication between vehicle ECUs.
Protocol 	The word **'protocol'** comes from the Greek 'protokollon,' meaning 'first sheet' or 'first draft,' originally referring to the first version of a document. Today, in automotive systems, a protocol is a set of rules that govern how ECUs communicate with each other. It defines how messages are formatted, when devices send data, how errors are handled, and how devices respond. Different protocols like CAN, LIN, FlexRay, or Ethernet are used depending on the communication needs. These rules ensure that all parts of the vehicle's network understand each other, allowing for smooth operation, accurate diagnostics, and reliable control. Without protocols, devices wouldn't be able to communicate effectively.
Arbitration 	The word **arbitration** comes from the Latin 'arbitrari,' meaning 'to judge' or 'consider,' and in general refers to settling disputes through judgment. In vehicle networks like CAN Bus, arbitration is the process that determines which ECU gets to send its message when multiple ECUs try to communicate at the same time. Each message has an identifier that indicates its priority, with lower numbers representing higher priority. The CAN system quickly compares these identifiers bit by bit, and the highest-priority message wins and transmits while others wait. Arbitration ensures smooth, collision-free communication, giving priority to important messages like safety or engine control, making the network reliable and efficient.

These words and abbreviations are part of the everyday language of vehicle networking. Being familiar with them will make it much easier for you to diagnose network faults, understand service information, and communicate with colleagues. As you gain experience, these terms will become second nature.
A list of generic acronyms can be found in the appendix.

Nomenclature - a system of names and terms used to identify and describe the different parts, components, and features of a vehicle.

Jargon - words or phrases used in the automotive industry that are understood by people in that field but may be confusing to outsiders.

Chapter 2 Introduction to CAN Bus Systems

Multiplexing - a system in a vehicle that allows multiple electronic devices to share the same communication wiring by sending signals in turns (like a network).

Topology - the way the electronic control units (ECUs) and communication networks in a vehicle are arranged and connected to each other.

Node - an electronic device or control unit in a vehicle that sends, receives, or processes data on the vehicle's network.

Nibble - a group of four bits of data.

Deterministic communication - a way of sending data where the timing and delivery are precise and predictable.

Redundancy - a safety feature that uses backup systems or components so that if the main system fails, the backup can take over.

Bit - the smallest unit of data (a 0 or 1) used in a vehicle's electronic communication systems.

Arbitration - the process used in a vehicle's network to decide which message can use the communication Bus when two or more devices try to send data at the same time.

Protocol - a set of rules that devices in a vehicle follow to communicate and exchange data with each other.

Principles of Parallel & Serial Communication

Before explaining what CAN Bus is and how it works, it's important to understand two basic ways that electronic devices can send and receive information: **parallel communication** and **serial communication**.

In parallel communication, many wires are used to send multiple bits of data at the same time. *[see Figure 2.2]*.

You can imagine this like a multi-lane highway:

- Each lane (wire) carries one part of the information.
- All lanes move together at the same time, delivering the full message all at once.

For example, if we need to send an 8-bit piece of data, we use 8 wires, one wire for each bit, and all 8 bits are sent simultaneously.

Chapter 2 Introduction to CAN Bus Systems

Parallel communication Advantages

- Fast, because all bits can arrive at the same time.
- Simple to understand for short distances.

Parallel communication Disadvantages

- Needs many wires, which take up space and cost more.
- Not reliable for longer distances. The signals on different wires can get slightly out of sync, causing errors.
- Heavy wiring is a problem in vehicles, where space and weight are critical.

In serial communication, data is sent one bit at a time over a single wire (or pair of wires). *[see Figure 2.3]*.

You can imagine this like a single-lane road:

- Each bit travels one after the other, in a stream, down the same wire.
- The receiving device puts the bits back together to form the full message.

Serial communication Advantages

- Needs fewer wires, making it lighter, cheaper, and easier to install.
- More reliable over longer distances; no risk of bits arriving at different times.
- Reduces weight and clutter in the vehicle wiring harness.

Serial communication Disadvantages

- Slower than parallel communication if the same **clock speed** is used (but this can be overcome by increasing the data rate).

These two principles are the foundation of how data moves between control units and sensors in a vehicle.

Modern vehicles have dozens of electronic control units (ECUs), for the engine, brakes, airbags, lighting, and more, that need to talk to each other all the time.

If parallel communication was used, the wiring would be huge and heavy. Instead, serial communication allows all these ECUs to share information quickly and reliably over a few wires.

This is where CAN Bus comes in:
- CAN (Controller Area Network) is a serial communication protocol designed specifically for vehicles.
- It lets all the ECUs communicate efficiently on a shared pair of wires.
- It saves weight, reduces cost, and is very reliable even in the harsh environment of a car.

Chapter 2 Introduction to CAN Bus Systems

Clock speed - the rate at which the vehicle's electronic control units (ECUs) or other digital components operate, typically measured in megahertz (MHz) or gigahertz (GHz). It indicates how quickly these electronic systems process data and perform tasks within the vehicle.

Multiplexing Network Architecture

A multiplexed network is one where many signals share the same wiring, saving weight and cost. How these devices (or nodes) are connected to each other depends on the network architecture.
This section describes the three common network layouts: Star, Ring (or Daisy Chain), and Bus to help you understand how they are designed and operate.

Star Network (Server or Master/Slave)

The Star Network is arranged like a wheel with spokes:

- One central device (called the server, master, or hub) sits in the middle.
- All other devices (slaves) connect directly to the master.
- The slaves do not talk to each other directly; they only communicate through the master.

Layout and Design:

- Each node has its own dedicated wire to the master.
- The master controls and coordinates communication.
- It can decide who talks and when (master/slave communication).

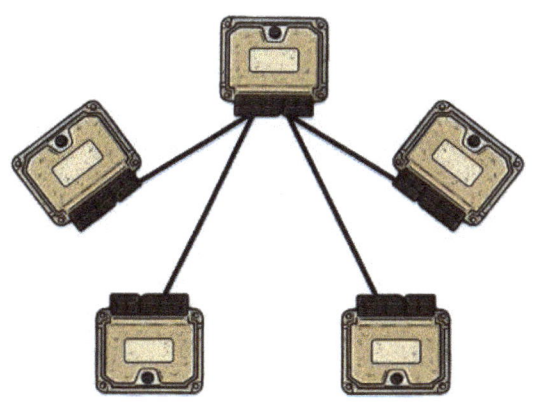

Figure 2.4 Star network

Star Network (Server or Master/Slave) Advantages	Star Network (Server or Master/Slave) Disadvantages
• Easy to understand and troubleshoot. Problems are often at the master or a single spoke. • A failure in one spoke does not affect the others.	• Requires more wiring, which can be heavy and expensive. • If the master fails, the whole network stops working.

Star networks are sometimes used for diagnostics or small subsystems, but not common for CAN Bus because of the wiring cost.

Chapter 2 Introduction to CAN Bus Systems

Ring Network (Daisy Chain)

The Ring Network, also called a Daisy Chain, is arranged in a loop:

- Each node connects to the next node, and the last node connects back to the first, forming a ring.
- Data travels around the loop, passing through each node.

Layout and Design:

- Each device has two connections: one in and one out.
- Messages circulate around the ring until they reach the right node.
- Messages travel in both directions at once.

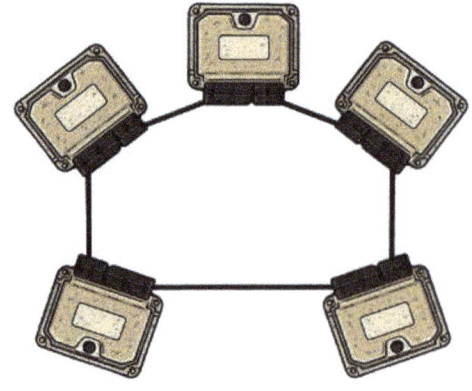

Figure 2.5 Ring network

Ring Network (Daisy Chain) Advantages	Ring Network (Daisy Chain) Disadvantages
• Less wiring than a star network. • Can still function even if one node fails (in some designs).	• More complex to troubleshoot; a break in two places could stop communication. • Data takes longer to travel, as it must pass through each node.

 Ring networks are rarer than other types, but sometimes used in body, infotainment or fibre-optic systems like MOST (Media Oriented Systems Transport).

Bus Network

The Bus Network is the most common layout in vehicles, and the one used by CAN Bus.

- All nodes are connected to the same pair of wires (the Bus).
- Every node can listen to messages and decide if the message is meant for it.

Layout and Design:

- Two main wires run through the vehicle, with each ECU connected (or tapped) to these wires.
- The Bus is terminated at both ends with resistors to prevent signal reflection.

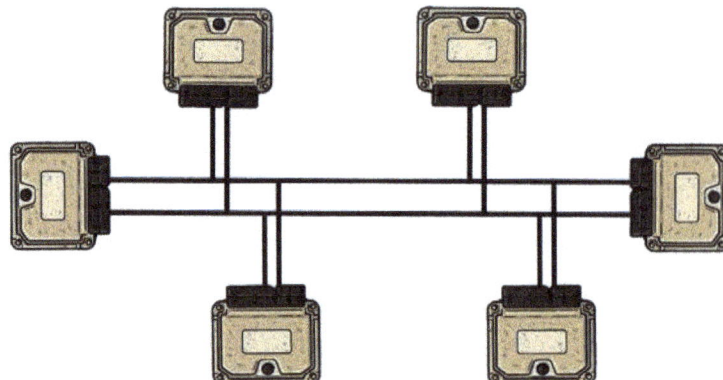

Figure 2.6 Bus network

Chapter 2 Introduction to CAN Bus Systems

Bus Network Advantages

- Very efficient; only two wires serve many nodes.
- Lightweight and cost-effective.
- Easy to add or remove nodes without changing the whole network.

Bus Network Disadvantages

- If the Bus wires are cut or shorted, the entire network can stop working.
- Troubleshooting wiring faults can be time consuming.

Bus cut relays

Bus cut relays are essential components within a vehicle's Controller Area Network Bus system, designed to protect and secure the vehicle's critical operations. In the event of a catastrophic network failure, these relays act as safety buffers by isolating vital systems such as brakes and steering, ensuring they continue to function independently and maintain vehicle control.
Beyond safety considerations, Bus cut relays serve an important security role. They isolate vulnerable components that could be targets for hackers, reducing the risk of unauthorised access and potential vehicle theft. By cutting off access to the rest of the network for these sensitive parts, Bus cut relays help maintain the integrity and security of the vehicle's electronic systems; they play a dual role in safeguarding both the vehicle's functionality and protecting it from external threats.

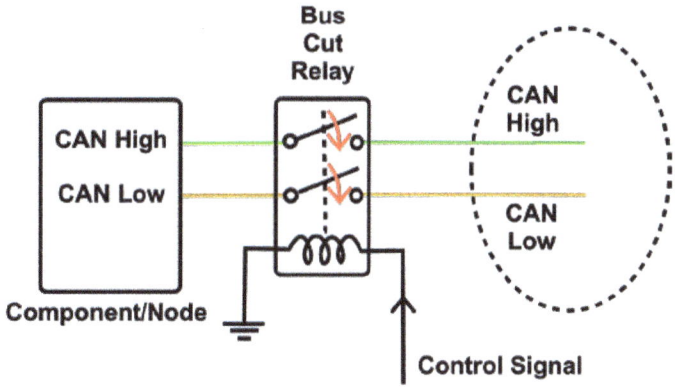

Figure 2.7 Bus cut relays

Bus networks are the standard for most vehicle communication systems, including CAN, LIN, and FlexRay.
CAN Bus was designed specifically to use a Bus architecture. This minimises wiring, is reliable enough for critical vehicle systems, and allows many ECUs to share the same two wires efficiently; that's why almost all modern vehicles rely on this layout.

Table 2.2 Summary of network architectures

Feature	Star	Ring	Bus
Wiring	Most wires	Moderate	Least wires
Central device	Yes (master)	No	No
Reliability	Depends on master	Can tolerate some faults	Single point of failure
Use in vehicles	Rare (small systems)	Rare (infotainment)	Common (CAN, LIN)

Chapter 2 Introduction to CAN Bus Systems

This analogy, which we'll call 'String Theory' will help you picture how CAN Bus and similar networks communicate, and what can go wrong.

The Setup: A Circle of People Holding a String
Imagine a group of people standing in a circle. Everyone is holding on to the same loop of string, and the string is pulled tight between them. This string represents the network wiring in the vehicle.
Now, everyone closes their eyes. No one can see each other, but they can feel the string.

How They Communicate: Tugs on the String
When someone wants to send a message, they give the string a quick, clear tug.
- Everyone holding the string feels the tug at the same time.
- Each person then decides if the tug was meant for them or not.

This is just like how ECUs (electronic control units) on a CAN Bus send a message:
- One ECU sends a signal.
- All the other ECUs 'hear' the message at the same time.
- Only the ECU that needs the information acts on it, the rest ignore it.

What Happens if Two People Tug at Once?
But there's one rule: only one person can tug at a time.
- If two people tug at the same time, the string feels messy, and the tugs overlap.
- On a CAN Bus, this is called a **collision**, and the network has a way to sort out who gets to send their message first and this is called arbitration.

So as long as everyone takes turns and respects the rules, communication works smoothly.

If the String Breaks…
Now imagine part of the string breaks, maybe someone lets go, or the string snaps.
- The people still holding the string can keep communicating with each other.
- But anyone who has lost connection to the string is now cut off from the group.

This is like a wiring fault in a vehicle network: devices still connected can keep working, but any disconnected device can't receive or send messages.

What if Someone Misbehaves?
Finally, imagine one person decides to hold the string so tightly that no one else can tug it.
- This blocks everyone else from communicating properly.
- On a CAN Bus, this is like a faulty or rogue ECU that dominates the Bus or holds it 'silent,' disrupting communication for the whole network.

This simple string circle explains a lot about vehicle networks:
- ☑ Everyone listens all the time.
- ☑ Only one message can go through cleanly at a time.
- ☑ Everyone gets the message at the same time and decides if it applies to them.
- ☑ Breaks and faults can isolate devices.
- ☑ One bad node can disrupt communication.

Chapter 2 Introduction to CAN Bus Systems

Components of a CAN Network

To understand how a CAN Bus system works in a vehicle, it's important to know about the main components that make up the network.

This section will explain the key parts:

- Electronic Control Units (ECUs) — also called nodes
- Sensors
- Actuators
- Wiring Harness

Each of these plays an important role in allowing the vehicle's systems to talk to each other and work together.

Think of the human body as a complex communication network, just like a vehicle's CAN Bus system.
- **ECUs (Electronic Control Units)** are like different organs and body parts such as the brain, heart, and limbs, each with its own specific function.
- **The CAN Bus cable** is like the nervous system, especially the spinal cord and nerves, that connect all these organs and parts.
- **Messages (Data)** are like nerve signals or electrical impulses that travel between the brain and the rest of the body, telling muscles to move or organs to function.
- **The Message Controller** is like the brain, deciding which signals to send and when, ensuring that the right commands reach the right parts without confusion.

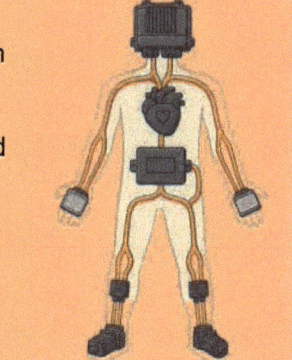

Electronic Control Units (ECUs) — The brains of the network

At the heart of every CAN network are the Electronic Control Units, often called ECUs or simply nodes. Each ECU is a small computer that controls and monitors a specific part of the vehicle.

For example:

- The Engine Control Module (ECM) manages fuel injection and ignition.
- The ABS Module controls the anti-lock braking system.
- The Airbag Control Module monitors crash sensors and deploys airbags when needed.

On a CAN Bus, all these ECUs are connected to the same pair of wires (the Bus) and can communicate with each other. Each ECU can send messages (like a status update or command) and listen for messages from other ECUs. Each ECU decides for itself if a message is relevant. You can think of ECUs as the 'brains' of the network.

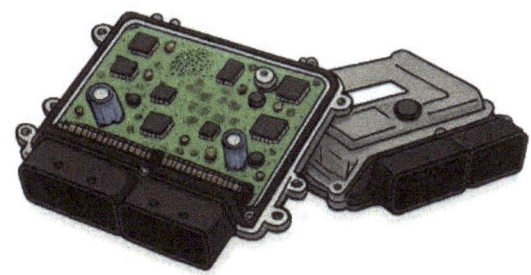

Figure 2.8 Electronic Control Unit ECU

Chapter 2 Introduction to CAN Bus Systems

Sensors — The eyes and ears of the system

Sensors collect information from the vehicle and send it to the ECUs.

For example:

- A wheel speed sensor sends data to the ABS ECU.
- An oxygen sensor reports exhaust gas oxygen levels to the Engine ECU.
- A crash sensor alerts the Airbag ECU to a collision.

Sensors are usually simple devices that detect a physical condition (like speed, temperature, or pressure) and convert it into an electrical signal. This signal is then read by the ECU and can also be shared on the CAN Bus for other ECUs to use if needed.
Sensors help the network know what's happening in the vehicle in real time.

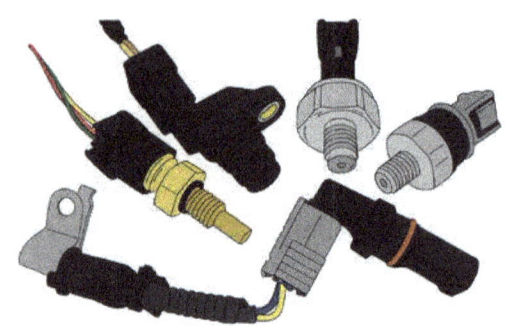

Figure 2.9 Sensors

Actuators — The hands of the system

Actuators are the devices that actually make things happen in the vehicle based on commands from an ECU.

For example:

- Fuel injectors spray fuel into the engine.
- Airbags deploy to protect passengers.
- Dashboard lights turn on to alert the driver.

Actuators take electrical signals from the ECUs and turn them into mechanical movement or another physical action.
While sensors gather information, actuators carry out the decisions of the ECUs.

Figure 2.10 Actuators

Wiring Harness — The nerves of the system

The wiring harness is the bundle of wires that connects all the ECUs, sensors, and actuators together.

- In a CAN network, only two wires (CAN High and CAN Low) run through the vehicle to carry communication signals between all the ECUs.
- These two wires form the Bus, which all the ECUs tap into.
- The wiring harness also includes power and ground wires to supply electricity to the components.

The wiring harness is like the nervous system of the vehicle, carrying messages and power wherever they're needed.

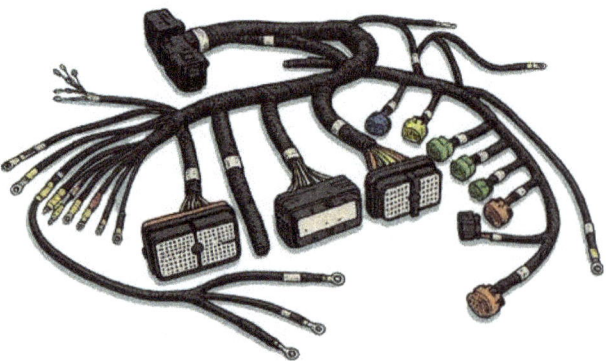

Figure 2.11 Wiring harness

Chapter 2 Introduction to CAN Bus Systems

How these components interact

Step 1: A *sensor* detects that the vehicle is skidding.

Step 2: The *sensor* sends this information to the ABS *ECU*.

Step 3: The *ECU* processes the data and sends a command over the CAN Bus.

Step 4: The *actuators* at the ABS modulator adjust pressure to help regain traction.

Step 5: At the same time, the *ECU* sends a message to the dashboard to light up the skid warning.

All of this happens in milliseconds thanks to the CAN network.

CAN Protocol Basics

The CAN protocol defines the rules that all the ECUs (nodes) follow when they send and receive messages. This ensures that everyone speaks the same language, takes turns properly, and avoids collisions.

Standard and extended CAN formats

Every message sent on the CAN Bus includes an identifier; a number that tells the other ECUs what the message is about and how important it is.

There are two formats of CAN message identifiers:

Standard Format (CAN 2.0A)
- Uses an 11-bit identifier.
- Can represent up to 2048 unique message IDs.
- Shorter and slightly faster than the extended format.
- Still the most commonly used format in vehicles today.

Extended Format (CAN 2.0B)
- Uses a 29-bit identifier.
- Can represent over 500 million unique message IDs.
- Used when a system needs more IDs, like in very complex networks.

Chapter 2 Introduction to CAN Bus Systems

 In most vehicles, the standard 11-bit format is enough, but some networks (like trucks or buses with many systems) might use the extended format.

Bit rates — How fast CAN Bus sends data

The bit rate is the speed at which bits of data travel on the CAN Bus.
You can think of it as the network's 'speed limit.' It's measured in kilobits per second (kbps) or megabits per second (Mbps).

Some common bit rates in vehicles include:

- 125 kbps: Often used for body electronics, like windows, locks, and climate control.
- 250 kbps: Used for medium-speed networks.
- 500 kbps: Common for powertrain and chassis systems where quick response is needed.
- 1 Mbps: Maximum standard CAN speed, used in some high-performance applications.

 Higher speeds allow more data to move quickly, but they're more sensitive to noise and require shorter cable lengths.
Lower speeds are more reliable over longer distances but slower to transmit data.

Arbitration — How ECUs take turns on the Bus

Since all the ECUs share the same two wires on the CAN Bus, only one ECU can send a message at a time. But what happens if two or more ECUs try to send a message at the exact same moment?
This is where arbitration comes in.

How Arbitration Works:

- Each ECU sends its message's identifier bit by bit.
- All ECUs listen to the Bus while sending.
- If an ECU sees that another ECU's identifier is lower (higher priority), it stops transmitting and waits its turn. *[see note]*.

 In CAN, the message with the <u>lowest identifier number</u> has the highest priority and wins arbitration.
The losing ECUs simply try again when the Bus is free.
This process happens very fast, in microseconds, and ensures that critical messages (like brake or airbag signals) always get through first.

Chapter 2 Introduction to CAN Bus Systems

Table 2.3 Protocol summary

Feature	What it means
Standard Format	11-bit ID, up to 2048 messages, common in cars.
Extended Format	29-bit ID, over 500 million messages, used in more complex networks.
Bit Rate	Network speed (e.g., 125 kbps – 1 Mbps). Faster for critical systems.
Arbitration	Process to decide who sends when. Lower ID = higher priority.

These rules, formats, speeds, and arbitration are what make CAN Bus such a reliable, efficient way to connect lots of ECUs in a vehicle.

Common CAN Bus Architectures

CAN Bus is used in many different ways to connect electronic systems. Depending on what the system needs to do, manufacturers choose different types of CAN Bus setups.

The three most common CAN Bus **architectures** you'll find in vehicles include:

- High-Speed CAN
- Low-Speed CAN (also called fault-tolerant CAN)
- Single-Wire CAN

Each one is designed for a specific purpose, and knowing the difference will help you understand what you're working with when diagnosing or repairing a vehicle.

High-Speed CAN

High-Speed CAN is the most common type used in vehicles, especially for systems that are safety-critical or need fast response.

Where it's used:

- Engine/EV management
- Transmission control
- Anti-lock brakes (ABS)
- Airbags and crash sensors
- Electric power steering

Speed:

- Typically runs at 500 kbps (kilobits per second) or even up to 1 Mbps (megabit per second).

Why use it:

- High-speed CAN is able to send a lot of data very quickly, which is important for systems like braking and airbags where milliseconds matter.
- It is also reliable for short to medium distances within the vehicle.

Wiring:

- Uses two wires: CAN High (CAN H) and CAN Low (CAN L) twisted together to reduce interference.

Chapter 2 Introduction to CAN Bus Systems

Low-Speed CAN (Fault-Tolerant CAN)

Low-Speed CAN, also called **fault-tolerant** CAN, is designed for systems where speed isn't as important, but reliability is. It is fault-tolerant because it can keep working even if one of the two wires is damaged.

Where it's used:

- Power windows and door locks
- Climate control
- Interior lights
- Seat modules

Speed:

- Typically runs at 125 kbps or slower.

Why use it:

- Many body and comfort systems don't need fast communication.
- The wiring can be longer and more robust against faults.
- Can still operate (at reduced capability) if one wire breaks.

Wiring:

- Also uses two wires (CAN H and CAN L), but with special fault-tolerant **transceivers**.

Single-Wire CAN

Single-Wire CAN is a simpler, lower-cost version of CAN used mostly in older vehicles or for diagnostics.

Where it's used:

- Diagnostics (like GM's GMLAN)
- Simple body electronics on older vehicles

Speed:

- Usually much slower, around 33.3 kbps or similar.

Why use it:

- Reduces wiring cost and complexity in simple systems.
- Good enough for low-priority, low-speed communication.

Wiring:

- Only uses a single wire and the vehicle's chassis ground.

Chapter 2 Introduction to CAN Bus Systems

Table 2.4 Bus architecture summary

Type of CAN	Speed	Wires	Typical Use
High-Speed CAN	Up to 1 Mbps	2	Engine, brakes, airbags
Low-Speed CAN	Up to 125 kbps	2 (fault-tolerant)	Windows, seats, lights
Single-Wire CAN	~33 kbps	1	Diagnostics, simple systems

Architecture - the overall design and layout of how all the electronic control units (ECUs), sensors, actuators, and communication networks (like CAN, LIN, or Ethernet) are connected and work together in a vehicle.

Fault-tolerant - the ability of a system or network to keep working even if part of it fails or gets damaged.

Transceivers - an electronic chip or circuit that connects an ECU to a communication network (like CAN or LIN). It works as both a transmitter and receiver, sending signals from the ECU onto the network, and receiving signals from the network into the ECU.

Digital Signals

CAN Bus networks operate using digital communication, which means they send and receive data as a series of electrical signals that represent only two possible states: high or low voltage.

In a CAN network, every message is made up of bits. A bit is the smallest piece of data, and it can have one of two values:

- 1 (one) — represented by a high voltage level
- 0 (zero) — represented by a low voltage level

These high and low signals are sent very quickly over the two CAN wires. The ECUs on the network 'read' the changing voltages and translate them into useful information, like wheel speed, engine RPM, or brake pressure.

Think of it as a light switch: it can only be on (1) or off (0). The CAN Bus rapidly switches between these two states to spell out messages.

You can think of the CAN Bus as a kind of Morse code, but instead of short and long beeps, it uses quick changes in voltage — high and low — to spell out the message. Every ECU listens to these changes and decodes the message into meaningful data it can use.

Chapter 2 Introduction to CAN Bus Systems

How does CAN use these signals?

CAN uses two wires: CAN High (CAN H) and CAN Low (CAN L) that carry opposite signals.
When a message bit is sent:
- For a 1, CAN H and CAN L stay close together (called 'recessive' state).
- For a 0, CAN H goes higher and CAN L goes lower (called 'dominant' state).

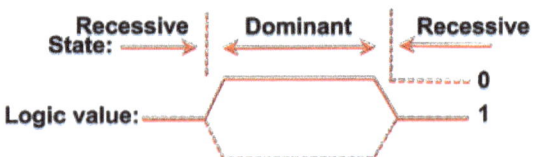

Figure 2.12 Dominant and recessive state

Why binary

There are only two voltage states because:

- It's simple and fast to detect a high or low signal.
- It's very reliable, even in noisy electrical environments like a car.
- It makes it easier for multiple ECUs to share the same wires without confusion.

By switching quickly between high and low voltages, the CAN Bus sends thousands of bits per second, allowing the vehicle's systems to communicate smoothly and efficiently.

Timing & Synchronisation

The CAN Bus sends data as a stream of bits, high and low voltage signals, very quickly. Each bit is sent in a tiny, fixed amount of time, called a bit time.
Every ECU needs to know exactly when each bit starts and ends, so they can read and understand the message correctly.
If one ECU runs too fast or falls behind, it won't be able to make sense of the data.
This is why all the ECUs on the network must stay in sync with each other's timing.

How do nodes stay in sync

CAN networks use a clever technique called **bit timing** and **synchronisation**:

- Every ECU has an internal clock that keeps track of time.
- When a message is sent, the ECUs adjust their clocks slightly by detecting the edges of the bits (the changes between high and low voltage).
- This way, even if their clocks drift a little, they re-align (synchronise) to the correct timing every time a new message comes in.

Bit timing - the process of defining the time segments for each bit transmitted in a CAN Bus network. It ensures that data is transmitted accurately and synchronously between different Electronic Control Units (ECUs) in a vehicle.

Synchronisation - the process of aligning the timing of data transmission between various Electronic Control Units (ECUs) in a vehicle.

Chapter 2 Introduction to CAN Bus Systems

Imagine a busy train station where trains (messages) arrive and depart on a precise schedule.
Each train represents a bit of data being sent on the CAN Bus.

The station has multiple platforms (nodes or ECUs), and each one is expecting a train to arrive at exactly the right time. If the timing is off, passengers (data) might:

- Miss their train.
- Get on the wrong one.
- Or arrive at the wrong destination.

In a CAN network:

- The train is the data (bit).
- The schedule is the bit timing.
- The platforms (ECUs) must stay synchronised with the schedule to correctly receive the data.

If even one platform's clock is running a little fast or slow, it might think the train (bit) has already passed or hasn't arrived yet causing it to misread the data.
To prevent timing drift, all the train platforms constantly monitor signals like clock towers or synchronisation beacons to keep their watches aligned.
Likewise, ECUs on the CAN Bus use signal edges (when the voltage changes from 0 to 1 or 1 to 0) to fine-tune their internal clocks.

This keeps every ECU 'on schedule' so they can read each bit at the exact right time.

If a platform doesn't follow the train schedule:

- It might open the train doors too early or too late.
- It could let the wrong passengers off or pick up the wrong ones.

In CAN Bus, this means:

- Incorrect bits are read.
- Messages become garbled or are ignored.
- Communication fails between ECUs.

Voltage Levels

In a CAN Bus system, data is sent using electrical signals that change voltage levels on two wires.

The two wires: CAN High and CAN Low

- CAN High — this wire's voltage goes up when a message bit is active.
- CAN Low — this wire's voltage goes down when a message bit is active.

These wires always work as a pair, and their voltage levels move in opposite directions to represent data.

Chapter 2 Introduction to CAN Bus Systems

Table 2.5 shows approximate voltages on CAN High and CAN Low and their dominant and recessive states.

Table 2.5 Dominant and recessive states

State	CAN High Voltage	CAN Low Voltage	What It Means
Recessive	~2.5 volts	~2.5 volts	Bus is idle or sending a 1
Dominant	~3.5 volts	~1.5 volts	Bus is active, sending a 0

Recessive means no ECU is trying to control the Bus; it's quiet.
Dominant means an ECU is actively sending a bit, and this state wins over recessive ones during arbitration (when ECUs try to talk at the same time).

What you might see on a multimeter or oscilloscope

If you measure the wires:

- On a healthy, quiet Bus (recessive), both CAN H and CAN L will be about 2.5 volts.
- When data is being transmitted (dominant), CAN H will jump up to about 3.5 volts, and CAN L will drop to about 1.5 volts.

When using an oscilloscope, you'll see the CAN High and CAN Low lines 'mirror' each other, one goes up while the other goes down, forming square waves that represent the bits being sent.

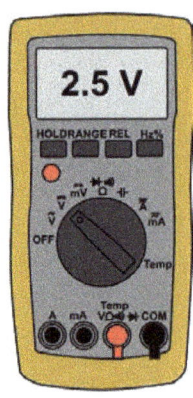

Figure 2.13 CAN signals on a multimeter

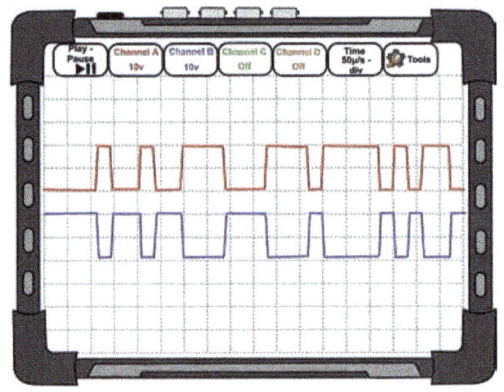

Figure 2.14 CAN signals on an oscilloscope

Conclusion

This chapter has explored the fundamental concepts of the CAN Bus system, which serves as the backbone for modern vehicle communication. Understanding the terminology, architecture, and basic protocols is essential for diagnosing, troubleshooting, and maintaining the intricate network of communication between the various Electronic Control Units (ECUs) in today's vehicles. By grasping these core principles, you are equipped to work effectively with sophisticated network systems, ensuring smooth interaction between vehicle components. This knowledge will help you build the expertise needed to keep vehicles running reliably and efficiently.

Circuit Theory

Chapter 3 Circuit Theory

To diagnose and repair vehicles confidently, it is essential to understand how in-vehicle networks, particularly the Controller Area Network (CAN Bus), support communication between electronic systems. This chapter will help you develop a solid understanding of the key principles behind how CAN Bus enables reliable communication between the many electronic control units (ECUs) found in today's vehicles. You will also be introduced to essential concepts of how digital signals are transmitted across a shared network, how messages are prioritised, and how different control systems exchange critical information to ensure the safe and efficient operation of the vehicle.

Contents

Bus Topology	56
Terminating Resistors	58
Differential Voltage in CAN Bus Communication	60
Decimal, Binary and Hexadecimal	61
Construction & Operation of Electric, Electronic, & Semiconductor Components	65
Boolean Logic & Logic Gates	69
The Physical Layer of CAN Bus Systems	71
CAN Message Structure	74
Bit Timing in CAN Bus Systems	76

When working on CAN Bus systems and vehicle networks, always remember that these circuits are part of the vehicle's critical control systems. Disconnecting, shorting, or applying the wrong voltage to CAN wiring can cause damage to electronic control units (ECUs), erase data, or even disable safety systems like airbags and ABS.
Before testing or repairing any CAN circuits:

- Always disconnect the battery if specified by the manufacturer's procedures.

- Use the correct diagnostic tools and avoid using standard test lights on CAN wires, as they can overload sensitive circuits.

- Never cut, splice, or tap into CAN wiring without proper guidance, as this can introduce faults and communication errors.

- Be aware that CAN systems operate even when the ignition is off; some ECUs stay awake for a short time after key-off.

Work methodically, follow the vehicle manufacturer's repair information, and always observe health and safety regulations. Taking care around CAN networks will help prevent costly damage and keep vehicle systems operating safely and reliably.

Circuit Theory

Bus Topology

Understanding the different types of network topologies and signalling methods is key when working with modern vehicles. While CAN Bus with its twisted-pair differential signalling is the standard for many vehicle systems, other networks like LIN, FlexRay, Ethernet, and SENT are used for specific needs. Each has its strengths and trade-offs, depending on speed, cost, and complexity.

The signal highway of CAN Bus

One of the most widely used network structures in automotive electronics is Bus **Topology**. In a Bus network, all electronic control units (ECUs) are connected along a single communication line or 'Bus.' This shared data path allows messages to be sent from one ECU to another without needing individual wiring between every device. This reduces weight, complexity, and cost.

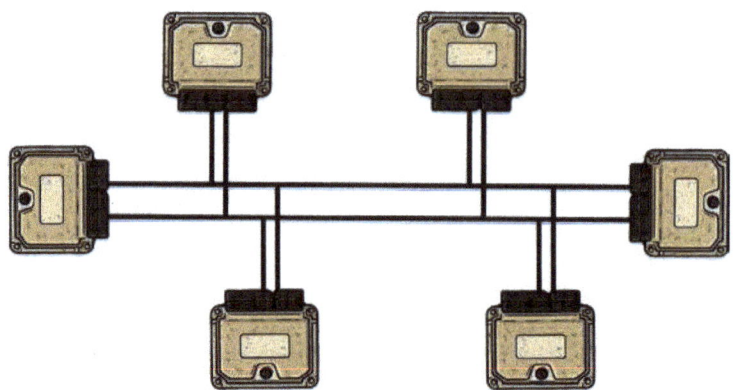

Figure 3.1 Bus network

CAN Bus and differential signalling

The Controller Area Network (CAN) uses a Bus topology combined with a two-wire **twisted pair** system for communication. The two wires are called CAN High and CAN Low.

Here's how it works:

- Both wires carry the same signal, but one is the **inverse** of the other.
- This is known as **differential signalling**.
- The voltage difference between the two wires represents the **binary data** being transmitted (1s and 0s).
- For example, when CAN H is 3.5V and CAN L is 1.5V, the Bus is in a **dominant** state (logical 0).
- When both wires are at about 2.5V, it's a **recessive** state (logical 1).

Because the wires are twisted together, any **electromagnetic interference (EMI)** picked up from the outside environment will affect both wires equally. Since the system only reads the difference in voltage between the two, outside noise is effectively cancelled out. This makes CAN Bus highly reliable, even in electrically noisy environments like vehicles.

Figure 3.2 Twisted pair wiring

Other automotive network topologies and types

Many vehicles don't just rely on CAN. Depending on the type of system, speed, complexity, or safety requirements, manufacturers use a range of network technologies. Each uses a different topology and signalling method.

Circuit Theory

Table 3.1 describes some other automotive types and topologies.

Table 3.1 Alternative automotive topology types

Name	Topology	Use	Notes
LIN (Local Interconnect Network)	Single-wire Bus, typically master-slave.	Low-speed systems like mirrors, windows, seat motors.	Communication: One master ECU controls multiple slave devices. Cost-effective and simple for non-critical systems.
FlexRay	Often dual-channel Bus or star topology.	High-speed, time-critical applications like brake-by-wire or advanced driver assistance systems (ADAS).	Features: Offers redundancy and deterministic communication, very predictable timing.
VAN (Vehicle Area Network)	Bus.	Older PSA (Peugeot-Citroën) vehicles.	Predecessor to CAN in some systems. Mostly obsolete now.
MOST (Media Oriented Systems Transport)	Typically ring or star.	Multimedia systems, audio, video, GPS.	Uses **optical fibre** or electrical wiring for high-speed data.
BEAN (Byteflight Enhanced Automotive Network)	Proprietary, mostly Bus.	Older BMW models, mainly for body electronics.	Now mostly replaced by LIN and CAN.
Volcano	Runs on CAN Bus.	Mainly found in Volvo and Saab vehicles.	Not a protocol itself, but a design framework using CAN.
SENT (Single Edge Nibble Transmission)	Point-to-point.	Digital sensors to ECUs (e.g., throttle position or pressure sensors).	Transmits data as a sequence of timed pulses. Very accurate and cheap for sensor communication.
Ethernet	Typically, star.	High-bandwidth needs: infotainment, cameras, over-the-air updates.	Much faster than CAN. Increasingly used in electric and autonomous vehicles.
K-Line	Single-wire.	Diagnostics (OBD), especially in older vehicles.	Very simple and slow. Mostly replaced by CAN.
CAN FD (Flexible Data-rate)	Same as traditional CAN Bus topology with twisted pair.	Improved CAN with faster speeds and more data per message.	Backward compatible with standard CAN.
CAN XL	Bus-based, (early adoption stage).	Designed for future applications needing more **bandwidth** up to 20 Mbps.	Support for autonomous driving and large data streams.
UART (Universal Asynchronous Receiver/Transmitter)	Typically, point-to-point.	Internal communication within modules, diagnostics, and development tools.	Very basic and commonly used in microcontroller communication.

Circuit Theory

Topology - the way electronic control units (ECUs) and communication lines are physically and logically arranged in a vehicle's network system.

Twisted pair - two insulated wires that are twisted together to carry electrical signals in a vehicle's communication system, such as CAN Bus.

Inverse - two electrical signals that are opposite to each other at any given time. When one signal is high (positive voltage), the other is low (negative or zero voltage), and vice versa.

Differential signalling - a method used to send electrical signals over two wires, where each wire carries the same signal but in opposite (inverse) voltage levels.

Binary data - information that is represented using only two values: 0 and 1.

Dominant - a CAN Bus signal that represent a logical 0.

Recessive - the bits in a CAN Bus signal that represent a logical 1.

Electromagnetic interference (EMI) - unwanted electrical noise or signals that can interfere with the proper operation of a vehicle's electronic systems.

Optical fibre - a type of cable that uses strands of glass or plastic that carry light to send data instead of electrical signals.

Bandwidth - the amount of data that can be sent through a vehicle's communication network in a certain amount of time. It is usually measured in bits per second (bps).

Terminating Resistors

Without proper **termination**, the CAN Bus wiring acts like a long, open-ended cable that causes signals to 'bounce' back and forth; this is known as **signal reflection**. These reflections distort the signal and cause errors in communication between ECUs. Proper termination absorbs these signal reflections by matching the **impedance** of the Bus wiring, ensuring that the data signals remain clean and stable.

Imagine a vehicle driving down a bumpy road. Without shock absorbers, every bump and jolt would be transferred directly to the occupants, making the ride uncomfortable and difficult to control. Shock absorbers play a crucial role by smoothing out these bumps, ensuring a stable and comfortable ride.

In a similar way, termination resistors in a CAN Bus network act like shock absorbers for electrical signals. Without termination resistors, the electrical signals could bounce back and forth along the wiring, causing data reflections and potential communication errors, very much like the jarring ride without shock absorbers. These resistors absorb the excess energy at the end of the transmission lines, allowing for seamless communication between the vehicle's electronic components.

Circuit Theory

Terminating resistors are special electrical components used at the ends of a communication Bus, such as a CAN Bus, to improve signal quality. They are typically fixed resistors with a specific resistance value, commonly 120 ohms in automotive CAN systems. Their main role is to match the electrical characteristics of the Bus wiring to prevent unwanted effects.

In a CAN Bus network, the two-wire twisted pair cable carries signals between electronic control units. To ensure clean and reliable communication, a terminating resistor is placed in parallel at each end of the CAN Bus cable. This means there are usually two terminating resistors in total, one at the first node and one at the last node of the network.

Terminating resistors are often built into the ECU at either end of the CAN Bus line or sometimes provided as separate physical components connected to the Bus wiring. You might find them integrated on circuit boards inside the vehicle's control modules or occasionally as standalone parts inside a type of junction box.

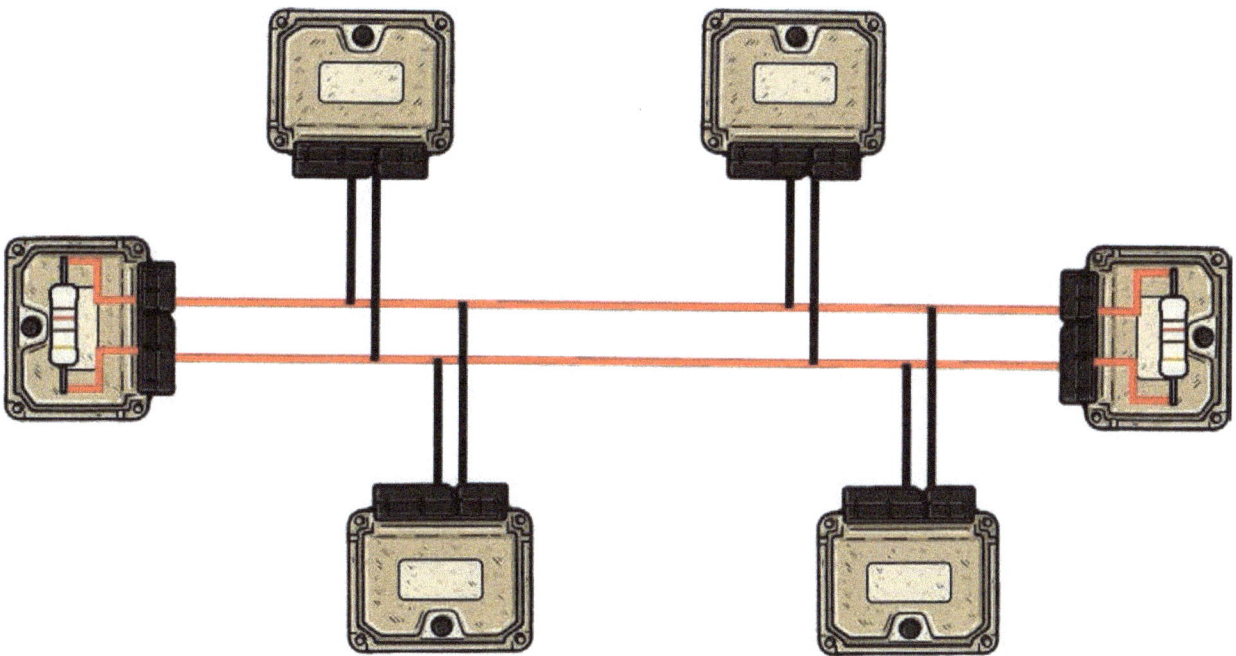

Figure 3.3 Terminating resistors

Termination - the use of resistors placed at both ends of a CAN Bus wiring network to prevent signal reflection and interference.

Signal reflection - an electrical signal sent through a wire bouncing back instead of being absorbed at the end of the line.

Impedance - the total resistance to the flow of electrical current in a circuit, especially in wires that carry signals. It combines regular resistance with the effects of frequency and signal timing.

Circuit Theory

Differential Voltage in CAN Bus Communication

Differential voltage is at the heart of how CAN Bus works. By transmitting data using the voltage difference between two wires, rather than one wire and ground, the system ensures strong, accurate communication between ECUs.

The same data is sent on both of these communication wires as an on and off voltage signal.
One signal is sent as a positive switch and one is sent as a negative switch, providing a mirror image on each network wire.
The potential difference between the voltages on the two lines produces a digital signal that can be processed into information.

Data transmission - high speed

The transmitting ECU sends switched voltage through the CAN H and CAN L Bus.

It sends 2.5 to 3.5 volt signals to the CAN High line and 2.5 to 1.5 volt signals to the CAN Low line.

The receiving ECU reads the data from the CAN lines as a potential difference of between 3.5 and 1.5 volts.

In **Figure 3.4**, 'Recessive' refers to the state where both CAN H and CAN L are at the 2.5 volt state, and 'Dominant' refers to the state where CAN H is at the 3.5 volt state and CAN L is at the 1.5 volt state. These values correspond to a binary value of either 1 or 0.

Recessive = Logic value of 1
Dominant = Logic value of 0

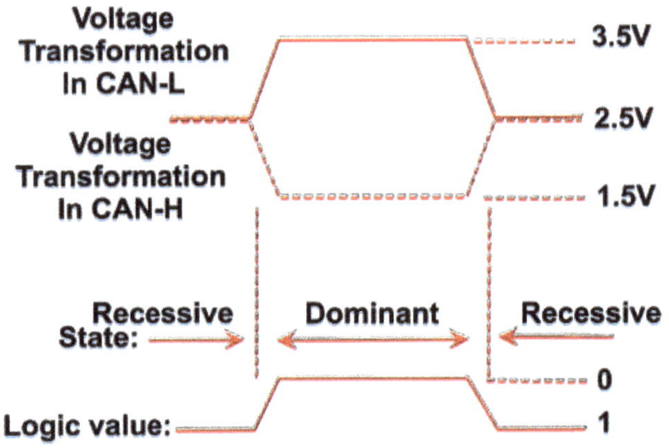

Figure 3.4 Data Transmission High Speed

Data transmission - low speed

The transmitting ECU sends switched voltage through the CAN H and CAN L Bus.

It sends 0 to 4 volt signals to the CAN High line and 1 to 5 volt signals to the CAN Low line.

The receiving ECU reads the data from the CAN High and CAN Low as a potential difference of between 5 and 0 volts.

In **Figure 3.5**, 'Recessive' refers to the state where CAN H is at 0 volt and CAN L is at 5 volt, and 'Dominant' refers to the state where CAN H is at 4 volt and CAN L is at 1 volt.

Recessive = Logic value of 1
Dominant = Logic value of 0

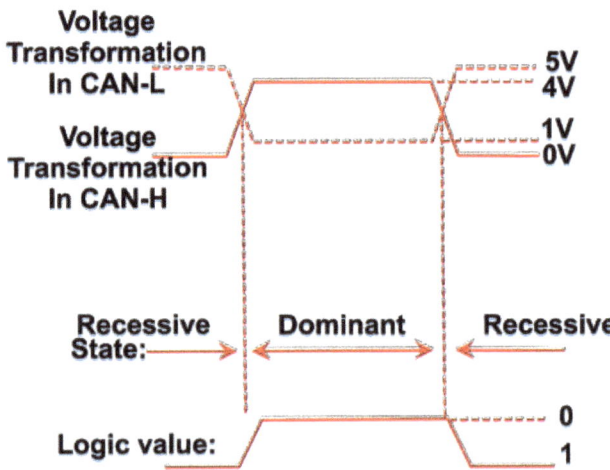

Figure 3.5 Data Transmission Low Speed

Circuit Theory

Decimal, Binary & Hexadecimal

In automotive diagnostics and network systems like CAN Bus, numbers are not always shown the way we are used to seeing them. Computers, control units, and scan tools often use different number systems to process and display data, especially **binary**, **decimal**, and **hexadecimal**. Understanding these numbering systems will help you interpret scan tool data, diagnostic trouble codes, and network messages more effectively.

Decimal - The everyday number system

The decimal system is the one we use in daily life; it's based on ten digits (0 through 9). That's why it's called the **base-10** system.

How the decimal system works

Each place in a decimal number represents a power of 10.

For example, the number **256** means:

- 2 hundreds (2 × 100)
- 5 tens (5 × 10)
- 6 ones (6 × 1)

To count to 256, you simply keep increasing the rightmost digit until it reaches 9. It then resets to 0 and the digit to its left increases by 1, just like the odometer in a car. This continues until you reach 256.

So, 256 = 2×100 + 5×10 + 6×1

In base 10:

- Each position is 10 times larger than the one to its right.
- The far-right digit is called the least significant digit (LSD).
- The far-left digit is called the most significant digit (MSD).

Digit	Position (from right)	Place Value	Value
1	3rd	2 × 100	200
2	2nd	5 × 10	50
3	1st	6 × 1	6
		Total	256

In the context of CAN Bus and automotive electronics, 256 is a very important number because:
- It represents the number of values that can be held in 8 bits (1 byte), ranging from 0 to 255.
- CAN Bus messages are structured using bytes. Each byte can store 256 different values.
- Many data fields, sensor readings, and control signals are encoded using 1 byte of data.
- Understanding the range from 0–255 helps technicians interpret scan tool data, sensor outputs, and control unit messages more accurately.

So, 256 is not just a random number, it's the upper limit of what can be stored in a single byte, making it fundamental to how data is structured and understood in automotive network systems.

Circuit Theory

Decimal is easy for people to understand, but it's not the language that computers use.

Vehicle computers often convert data between decimal, binary, and hexadecimal formats. Scan tools frequently display decimal values for sensor readings, diagnostic trouble codes, or module parameters. Understanding how decimal values work helps you decode and interpret this information more confidently.

Binary - The language of computers

In automotive electronics and CAN Bus systems, understanding binary numbers is essential. Computers and control units (ECUs) don't 'think' in decimal (base 10) like humans do, they use binary, which is **base 2**. The binary system only uses two digits: 0 and 1. That's why it's called base-2.
Each digit in a binary number is called a **bit**. A single bit can represent two values: on (1) or off (0). When we line up multiple bits, we can represent larger numbers. Computers and vehicle ECUs process everything from sensor readings to CAN Bus messages as streams of bits.

Think of electrical switches, where each symbol visually represents an electrical state: a switch with a 1 is ON and a switch with a 0 is OFF; if the switch is simply a push button ON and OFF the symbols/numbers are often combined.
These symbols are simple visual codes, similar to how digital signals use 1s and 0s to indicate different states.
In digital terms, the ON position corresponds to a 1, meaning the circuit is closed and electricity flows. The OFF position is like a 0, where the circuit is open and no current passes.
Just as these symbols give a quick visual understanding of the switch's state, in digital systems, 1s and 0s quickly communicate whether a device is on or off.

For example:

Binary 1101 = (1 × 8) + (1 × 4) + (0 × 2) + (1 × 1) = 13 in decimal

Here's a quick comparison:

In binary, each digit position (bit) represents a power of 2, increasing from right to left:

To find the decimal value of a binary number, add up the values of the bit positions where a 1 appears. For example:

- Binary 00000001 = Decimal 1
- Binary 00000101 = 4 + 1 = 5
- Binary 11111111 = 128 + 64 + 32 + 16 + 8 + 4 + 2 + 1 = 255

Decimal	Binary
0	0000
1	0001
2	0010
3	0011
4	0100
5	0101
6	0110
7	0111
8	1000
9	1001
10	1010

Bit Position	7	6	5	4	3	2	1	0
Value	128	64	32	16	8	4	2	1

The highest value you can represent with 8 bits (1 byte) is 255, and the total number of combinations is 256 (from 0 to 255).

Circuit Theory

Why Binary Matters in CAN Bus:
- CAN Bus data frames carry data in bytes (8 bits).
- Each sensor reading, diagnostic trouble code, or control signal is transmitted in binary form.
- Technicians working with scan tools, data decoders, or diagnostics need to understand how binary values relate to real-world numbers like speed, temperature, or voltage.

Binary is the language of the CAN Bus and learning how it counts is like learning the alphabet of digital communication in a vehicle.

Binary count table (0 to 255)

Here's a table showing how to count from 0 to 255 in binary (in increments of 16).

Table 3.2 Binary (Decimal Steps of 16) and Bit Position Headers

128	64	32	16	8	4	2	1	Decimal
0	0	0	0	0	0	0	0	0
0	0	0	1	0	0	0	0	16
0	0	1	0	0	0	0	0	32
0	0	1	1	0	0	0	0	48
0	1	0	0	0	0	0	0	64
0	1	0	1	0	0	0	0	80
0	1	1	0	0	0	0	0	96
0	1	1	1	0	0	0	0	112
1	0	0	0	0	0	0	0	128
1	0	0	1	0	0	0	0	144
1	0	1	0	0	0	0	0	160
1	0	1	1	0	0	0	0	176
1	1	0	0	0	0	0	0	192
1	1	0	1	0	0	0	0	208
1	1	1	0	0	0	0	0	224
1	1	1	1	0	0	0	0	240
1	1	1	1	1	1	1	1	255

Because binary numbers get long very quickly, engineers often use hexadecimal to simplify them.

Hexadecimal - A shortcut for binary

When working with vehicle electronics and CAN Bus systems, you will often see data represented in hexadecimal format. This system is widely used because it provides a more compact and readable way to express binary numbers, which are the foundation of all digital communication.

The word hexadecimal comes from two parts:
- Hexa- meaning 'six' in Greek (representing the base-16 number system).
- Decimal meaning 'ten' in Latin.

So, hexadecimal literally means 'sixteen.'

Circuit Theory

Hexadecimal (or **hex** for short) is a number system based on 16 digits. It uses numbers 0–9 and letters A–F:

- A = 10
- B = 11
- C = 12
- D = 13
- E = 14
- F = 15

Each hex digit represents 4 binary bits (also called a nibble). That means a single byte (8 bits) can be neatly represented as two hexadecimal digits. This is why hexadecimal is commonly used in CAN Bus diagnostics, scan tool readouts, and DTC (Diagnostic Trouble Code) definitions.
Each hex digit represents four binary bits. That makes it a compact (shorthand) way to write binary values.

For example:

Binary 1101 0110 = Hex D6 (1101 = D, 0110 = 6)

This is especially useful when reading CAN IDs or data bytes in scan tools, where values like 0x1A or 0x3F appear (the '0x' prefix means the number is in hexadecimal).

In CAN Bus communication, data frames are typically 8 bytes long.
When viewing this information on a scan tool or diagnostic display, hexadecimal simplifies the output:

- A single byte of data like 11110000 (binary) becomes F0 (hex).
- This helps technicians quickly read and interpret sensor values, command messages, or error codes.

Dec v Hex	0x0	0x1	0x2	0x3	0x4	0x5	0x6	0x7	0x8	0x9	0xA	0xB	0xC	0xD	0xE	0xF
0	00	01	02	03	04	05	06	07	08	09	0A	0B	0C	0D	0E	0F
16	10	11	12	13	14	15	16	17	18	19	1A	1B	1C	1D	1E	1F
32	20	21	22	23	24	25	26	27	28	29	2A	2B	2C	2D	2E	2F
48	30	31	32	33	34	35	36	37	38	39	3A	3B	3C	3D	3E	3F
64	40	41	42	43	44	45	46	47	48	49	4A	4B	4C	4D	4E	4F
80	50	51	52	53	54	55	56	57	58	59	5A	5B	5C	5D	5E	5F
96	60	61	62	63	64	65	66	67	68	69	6A	6B	6C	6D	6E	6F
112	70	71	72	73	74	75	76	77	78	79	7A	7B	7C	7D	7E	7F
128	80	81	82	83	84	85	86	87	88	89	8A	8B	8C	8D	8E	8F
144	90	91	92	93	94	95	96	97	98	99	9A	9B	9C	9D	9E	9F
160	A0	A1	A2	A3	A4	A5	A6	A7	A8	A9	AA	AB	AC	AD	AE	AF
176	B0	B1	B2	B3	B4	B5	B6	B7	B8	B9	BA	BB	BC	BD	BE	BF
192	C0	C1	C2	C3	C4	C5	C6	C7	C8	C9	CA	CB	CC	CD	CE	CF
208	D0	D1	D2	D3	D4	D5	D6	D7	D8	D9	DA	DB	DC	DD	DE	DF
224	E0	E1	E2	E3	E4	E5	E6	E7	E8	E9	EA	EB	EC	ED	EE	EF
240	F0	F1	F2	F3	F4	F5	F6	F7	F8	F9	FA	FB	FC	FD	FE	FF
256	100	—	—	—	—	—	—	—	—	—	—	—	—	—	—	—

In summary:

- Decimal is what we use every day (base-10).
- Binary is how computers and ECUs think (base-2).
- Hexadecimal is a shorthand for binary used in diagnostics (base-16).

Circuit Theory

Why Technicians Should Know These Systems
Understanding these number systems is important when:

- Reading diagnostic codes (DTCs) that include hex values.
- Interpreting CAN Bus messages.
- Looking at raw data in diagnostic software.
- Programming or flashing ECUs.
- Working with sensor signals and control logic.

For example, a diagnostic tool might show a value of 0x0F, which you should recognise as 15 in decimal or 00001111 in binary.

Being familiar with all three systems helps you better understand how data is stored, transmitted, and displayed in vehicle electronics. With this foundation, you'll be better equipped to troubleshoot, decode messages, and interpret what your scan tool, oscilloscope or CAN Bus analyser is really showing.

Binary - a number system that uses only two values: 0 and 1. It is the basic language that vehicle computers and electronic control units (ECUs) use to process and communicate data.

Decimal - the standard number system we use every day, based on ten digits (0 to 9). It's also called the base-10 system.

Hexadecimal (hex) - a number system based on 16 digits:
0, 1, 2, 3, 4, 5, 6, 7, 8, 9, A, B, C, D, E, F (where A = 10, B = 11, and so on up to F = 15).

Base-10 - the number system we use in everyday life. It uses 10 digits:
0, 1, 2, 3, 4, 5, 6, 7, 8, and 9.

Base-2 - also known as the binary system, is the number system that uses only two digits: 0 and 1.

Bit - (short for binary digit) is the smallest unit of data used in automotive electronics. It can have only two possible values: 0 (off) or 1 (on).

Construction & Operation of Electric, Electronic, & Semiconductor Components

To help make sense of the physical processes taking part with in-vehicle networks, it's important to have a basic overview of components used in vehicle electrical and electronic systems. Understanding these parts is essential for diagnosing and repairing automotive circuits, especially with systems like CAN Bus that rely heavily on electronics.

Circuit Theory

Resistors

Electrical resistors are components that provide resistance to the flow of electric current in a circuit. Resistors can be used for various purposes, such as limiting the current, dividing the voltage, and biasing active circuit elements. Most resistors are made from a ceramic rod coated in a material like carbon or metal film. The thickness and material determine how much resistance they provide.

There are several types of resistors, including fixed resistors and variable resistors. Fixed resistors have a constant resistance value that does not change with temperature, time, or voltage.

In automotive use

- Used to reduce voltage for sensors.
- Help with timing in circuits.
- Provide biasing for transistors.

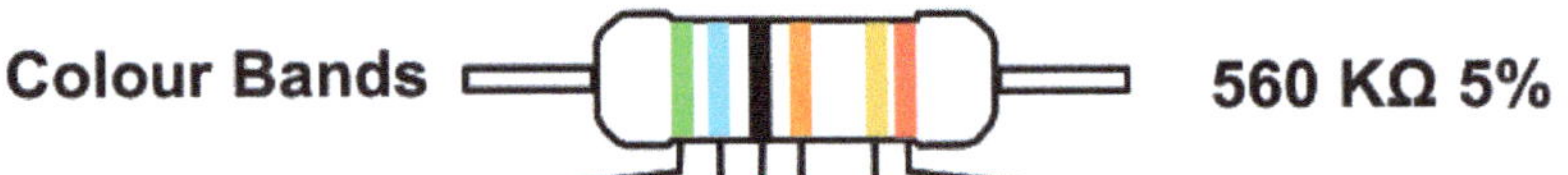

Colour	First Digit	Second Digit	Third Digit	Multiplier	Tolerance	Temperature Coefficient (ppm/K)
Black	0	0	0	1		
Brown	1	1	1	10	1%	100 ppm
Red	2	2	2	100	2%	50 ppm
Orange	3	3	3	1K		15 ppm
Yellow	4	4	4	10K		25 ppm
Green	5	5	5	100K	0.5%	
Blue	6	6	6	1M	0.25%	
Violet	7	7	7	10M	0.1%	
Grey	8	8	8		0.05%	
White	9	9	9			
Gold				0.1	5%	
Silver				0.1	10%	

560 KΩ 5%

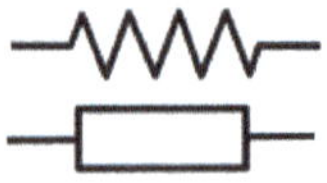

1K=1000
1M=1000000

Figure 3.6 Fixed Resistor Colour Codes

Circuit Theory

Diodes

A diode is an electronic component that only allows electric current to flow in one direction. It is made of two types of semiconductor material, called P-type (positive) and N-type (negative), that are joined together to form a PN junction. The P-type material is engineered to have fewer electrons than the N-type and is often described as having 'holes.' The PN junction creates a barrier known as a depletion layer, which prevents an easy flow of electrons between the two semiconductor elements.

How diodes work:

Imagine a road with a one-way sign. If current tries to flow the wrong way, the diode blocks it. This is useful for protecting circuits from accidental reverse connections.

When a diode is connected to a voltage source, the potential difference can push electrons from the negative side to the positive side across the depletion layer, as there is space (holes) for the electrons to fill, and current flows. However, if the polarity is reversed, the negative side is full, and the holes cannot be pushed across the depletion layer.

Figure 3.7 Diode Symbol

Diodes can be damaged by over-voltage. A voltage potential higher than the design capability with reverse polarity will cause an issue known as the breakdown voltage. At this point, the diode's ability to prevent current flow fails and allows a large current to flow in the reverse direction. This can damage the diode if not controlled.

There are several types of diodes that have different characteristics and applications. Some of the common types are:

- Zener diode - A diode that is designed to break down at a set voltage value and allow current flow in the reverse direction.
- Light-emitting diode (LED) - A diode that emits light when connected to a circuit in one direction only.
- Photodiode - A diode that generates current when exposed to light.
- Schottky diode - A diode that has a metal-semiconductor junction instead of a PN junction and has a lower forward voltage drop and faster switching speed.
- Tunnel diode - A diode that has a very thin PN junction and exhibits negative resistance in the forward direction, meaning that the current decreases as the voltage increases.

In automotive use

- Protect ECUs from reverse polarity.
- Prevent back-feed in relay circuits.
- Rectify AC to DC.

Circuit Theory

Transistors

Transistors are semiconductor electronic components that can control the flow of electrical current in a circuit. They use semiconductor materials composed of P-type and N-type materials in a similar manner to diodes. They are arranged so that they generally have three parts, which are joined to create either PNP (positive-negative-positive) junctions or NPN (negative-positive-negative) junctions. These arrangements will either block the flow of current or allow the flow of current depending on their design. A transistor will be joined to a circuit with an input current connection, often known as the collector or source, an output current connection, often known as the emitter or drain, and a voltage connection in the middle semiconductor component, often called the base or gate. By switching a small voltage on and off, the base/gate section can be changed between two states:

- A conductor, which will allow current to flow between the collector/source and the emitter/drain.
- An insulator, which prevents the flow of current between the collector/source and the emitter/drain.

In this way, a small voltage can be used to determine or regulate the flow of current in an electrical circuit, allowing it to act as a switch or amplifier.

A good way of imagining a transistor's operation is to think of it like a farmer opening and closing a gate to allow sheep into a field.
On one side of the gate, the sheep are waiting to enter the field; this corresponds to the collector or source.
On the other side of the gate is the field, where the sheep will graze; this corresponds to the emitter or drain.
The farmer can control the flow of sheep into the field by opening and closing the gate, which is similar to applying a voltage at the transistor's base or gate.

There are two main types of transistors: bipolar junction transistors (BJTs) and metal-oxide-semiconductor field-effect transistors (MOSFETs).

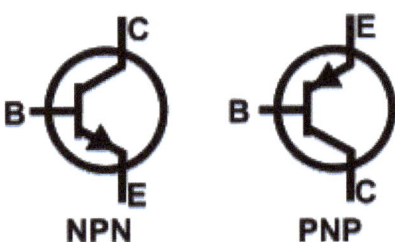

- A BJT has three terminals: the base, the collector, and the emitter. The base is the input terminal that controls the current flow between the collector and the emitter.
- A MOSFET has four terminals: the gate, the source, the drain, and the body. The gate is the input terminal that controls the current flow between the source and the drain. The source is the terminal that supplies the current. The drain is the terminal that receives the current. The body is the terminal that connects to the reactive section of the semiconductor.

Figure 3.8 Transistor Symbols

In automotive use

- Power control in ECUs.
- Switching relays.
- Signal amplification for sensors.
- ECU output stages.
- Electronic throttle control.
- CAN Bus systems (to switch nodes on/off).
- Smart relays and power modules.

Circuit Theory

Bus cut relays

A Bus cut relay is a special type of relay used to isolate parts of a vehicle's communication network (like the CAN Bus) or power system. This helps save battery power or protect the network from faults.

Bus cut relays act like a switch. When the vehicle goes to sleep or is shut off, the ECU can open the relay to disconnect certain circuits. This is especially important for battery management in vehicles.

It is normally a standard relay controlled by the ECU but designed with careful timing and noise filtering, so it doesn't interrupt communication or cause voltage spikes.

Figure 3.9 Bus cut relays

Use

- Disconnecting parts of the CAN Bus when not in use.
- Cutting power to infotainment or telematics modules.
- Used in energy-saving strategies.

Summary Table:

Component	Main Function	Automotive Use Example
Resistor	Limits current flow	Sensor circuits, timing
Diode	One-way current flow	Reverse polarity protection
Transistor	Switches or amplifies current	ECU output stages
MOSFET	High-efficiency switching	Power control modules
Bus Cut Relay	Isolates circuits	Power-saving in CAN systems

Each of these components plays a crucial role in vehicle electronics. Whether it's limiting current, protecting circuits, or switching high-current loads with low control effort, understanding how these parts work will make you more effective at diagnosing and repairing advanced automotive systems.

Boolean Logic & Logic Gates

In automotive systems, especially in CAN Bus networks and electronic control units (ECUs), digital **logic** plays a crucial role in how decisions are made. At the heart of digital logic is something called Boolean logic, named after mathematician George Boole.
Boolean logic is a way of making decisions using just two possible states:

- ON or OFF
- 1 or 0
- TRUE or FALSE

These binary choices are ideal for electronic systems, where a voltage (e.g., 5V) represents ON (or 1), and 0V represents OFF (or 0). Every logical decision made by a microcontroller or ECU is based on combining these states in predictable ways.

Circuit Theory

Logic Gates – The building blocks

Logic gates are small digital circuits inside ECUs that perform specific decisions based on input signals. Each type of gate follows a simple rule. Here are the most common ones used in automotive electronics:

AND Gate

- Function: All inputs must be ON for the output to be ON.
- Example: A cooling fan might only turn on if both the engine temperature is high and the ignition is on.

Input (A)	Input (B)	Output (X)
0	0	0
0	1	0
1	0	0
1	1	1

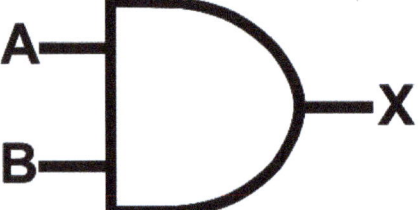

Figure 3.10 AND Gate

OR Gate

- Function: If any input is ON, the output is ON.
- Example: A warning light may come on if either the oil pressure is low, or the coolant level is low.

Input (A)	Input (B)	Output (X)
0	0	0
0	1	1
1	0	1
1	1	1

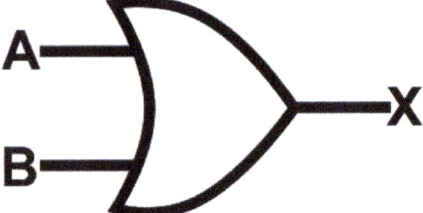

Figure 3.11 OR Gate

NOT Gate (Inverter)

- Function: Reverses the input. If the input is ON, the output is OFF.
- Example: A system that triggers when a sensor is not active, such as an open-door circuit.

Input	Output
0	1
1	0

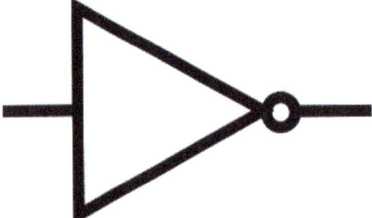

Figure 3.12 NOT Gate

Circuit Theory

NAND Gate (NOT + AND)

- Function: Like an AND gate, but with the output reversed.
- Example: Used in safety systems where a circuit only allows power when a fault condition is not present.

Input (A)	Input (B)	Output (X)
0	0	1
0	1	1
1	0	1
1	1	0

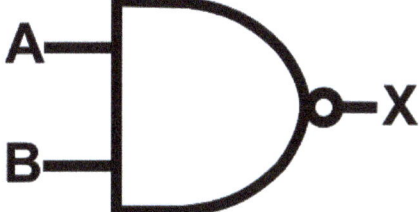

Figure 3.13 NAND Gate

NOR Gate (NOT + OR)

- Function: Like an OR gate but reversed. Output is only ON when all inputs are OFF.
- Example: Could be used in systems where action is only needed when no inputs are triggered (e.g. all sensors at rest).

Input (A)	Input (B)	Output (X)
0	0	1
0	1	0
1	0	0
1	1	0

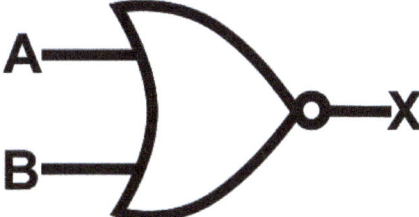

Figure 3.14 NOR Gate

Understanding logic gates helps explain why an ECU behaves a certain way. For example, a fuel pump relay might not energise even if you think it should, because a logic condition isn't met (e.g. crankshaft position signal missing AND immobiliser not cleared). With this knowledge, you can use wiring diagrams and scan data more effectively.

 Logic gates are how electronic systems decide what to do, based on input conditions. As a technician, learning to 'think like a gate' helps you predict ECU behaviour, trace signal paths, and diagnose why outputs are (or aren't) activated.

The Physical Layer of CAN Bus Systems

The physical layer of a CAN Bus system refers to the actual hardware and wiring that allows all the electronic control units (ECUs) in a vehicle to communicate with each other. This includes the wires, connectors, resistors, and network topology. Understanding this layer is essential for diagnosing communication faults and performing electrical repairs.

Circuit Theory

Basic components of the physical Layer

The CAN physical layer includes:

- Wiring (Twisted Pair): CAN uses two wires, CAN High and CAN Low, typically twisted together to reduce electrical interference. These wires carry voltage signals that allow ECUs to send and receive messages.
- Nodes: A node is any device or ECU connected to the CAN Bus. Examples include the engine control module (ECM), transmission control unit (TCU), body control module (BCM), ABS module, and more.
- Connectors: Nodes are connected to the CAN Bus through connectors and terminals. Each node taps into the CAN H and CAN L wires and must have a transceiver that converts digital signals into voltage changes on the wires, and vice versa.

Communication wires

The wiring for network communication can be constructed from three main methods:

- Twisted copper wiring.
- Coaxial wiring.
- Fibre optical.

It is possible to use a mixture of layout types and communication wires for different vehicle systems (i.e. powertrain, chassis, body and entertainment). These systems can then be connected to each other through individual electronic control units known as 'gateways'.

Figure 3.15 Network wires

Bus topology - How the network is laid out

CAN systems typically use a linear Bus topology, meaning the CAN wires run in a straight line with nodes connected along the way.

Think of it like a backbone with many branches:

- The main twisted-pair wire is the backbone.
- Each ECU connects to this backbone via short branches (called stubs or drop lines).

It's important to keep these branches as short as possible, usually under 30 cm, to reduce signal reflection and ensure reliable communication.

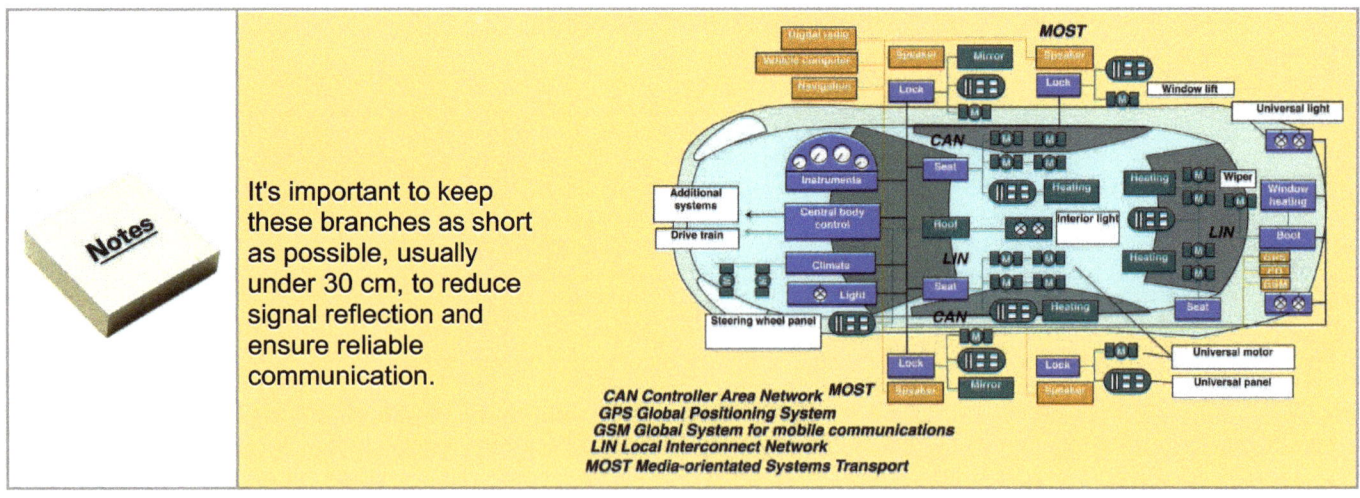

Circuit Theory

Termination resistors

At each end of the CAN Bus backbone, there must be a termination resistor, typically 120 ohms each, connected in parallel between CAN H and CAN L.

Figure 3.16 Termination resistors

Gateways

In vehicles, not all ECUs are on the same CAN network. Instead, multiple CAN networks exist, for example, high-speed CAN (e.g., powertrain), medium-speed CAN (e.g., body systems), and low-speed CAN (e.g., convenience features).

- A gateway module connects these different networks and manages communication between them.
- For example, the BCM or a dedicated Gateway Control Module might allow the engine ECU (on high-speed CAN) to share data with the instrument cluster (on medium-speed CAN).
- Gateways help reduce traffic and improve reliability by isolating different parts of the network.

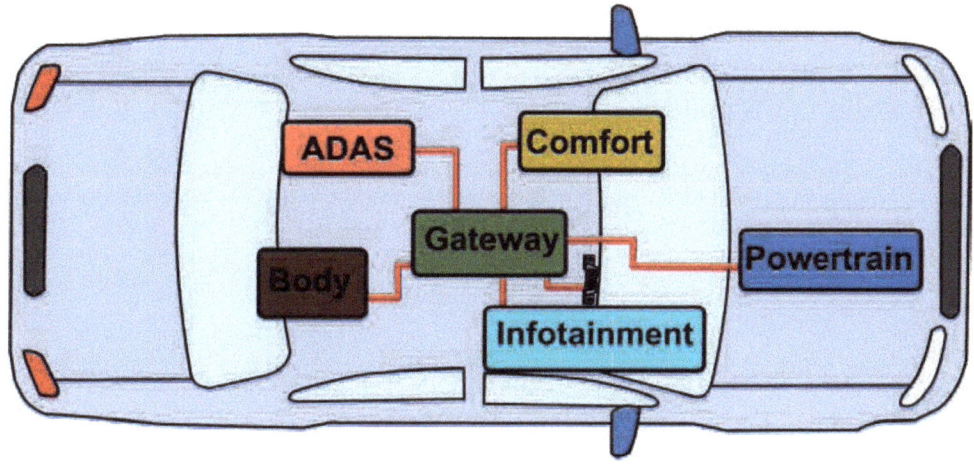

Figure 3.17 Gateways

Diagnostic connection - DLC - Data Link Connector

The **diagnostic port** (usually located under the dashboard) is how technicians connect a scan tool to the vehicle's CAN system.

- The standard connector is called the OBD-II DLC (On-Board Diagnostics – Data Link Connector).
- On this connector, Pin 6 is for CAN High, and Pin 14 is for CAN Low.
- The scan tool reads data, sends requests, and may even initiate module reprogramming or actuation tests through the CAN Bus.

When diagnosing a fault, you can measure voltages or resistance at the DLC to help identify wiring issues or Bus faults *[see Chapter 6]*.

Circuit Theory

It is often possible to conduct an initial diagnosis of network systems at the pins of the vehicle data link connector. Due to the standardised layout of the 16-pin connector the terminals can be identified from the image shown below:

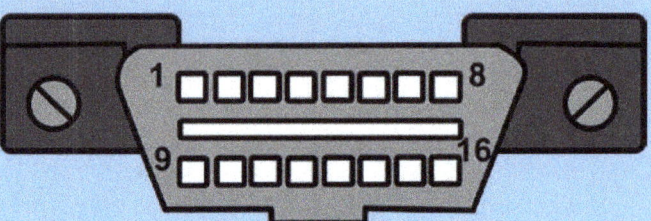

1. Manufacturer specific [sometimes used for network communication].
2. Bus positive SAE J1850 PWM and VPW.
3. Manufacturer specific [sometimes used for network communication].
4. Chassis ground.
5. Signal ground.
6. CAN High.
7. K-Line of ISO9141-2 and ISO14230-4.
8. Manufacturer specific [sometimes used for network communication].
9. Manufacturer specific [sometimes used for network communication].
10. Bus negative SAE J1850 PWM.
11. Manufacturer specific [sometimes used for network communication].
12. Manufacturer specific [sometimes used for network communication].
13. Manufacturer specific [sometimes used for network communication].
14. CAN Low.
15. L-Line of ISO9141-2 and ISO14230-4.
16. Battery voltage.

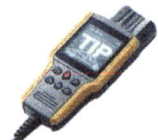

CAN Message Structure

Each ECU communicates with the CAN Bus periodically, sending information from several sensors. This information is circulated on the Bus as a data packet. Each ECU needing data on the Bus can receive these data frames sent from each ECU simultaneously. A single ECU transmits multiple data frames. When data packets conflict with one another (when more than one ECU transmits signals at the same time), data is prioritised for transmission by a process called '**mediation**'.

If mediation is required:

1. The data frame with high priority is transmitted first according to ID codes embedded in the data packet.
2. Transmission of low-priority data is suspended by the issuing ECU until the Bus clears (when no transmission data exists on the CAN Bus).
3. The ECU containing suspended data frames transmits when the Bus becomes available.

Circuit Theory

Think of CAN Bus like a group chat for vehicle components.
- Each participant (ECU or sensor) can send messages, like reporting speed, fuel levels, or airbag status.
- Instead of every person having to text each other individually, CAN Bus acts as a shared group chat, where messages are sent once and everyone listens in.
- The chat moderator (arbitration/mediation process) ensures that urgent messages—like braking commands—get posted first, while less critical updates—like window position—wait their turn.
- Unlike older systems where components needed dedicated wires for communication (like texting separately), CAN Bus reduces wiring complexity by letting everyone use the same network, making vehicle communication faster, more efficient, and less cluttered.

Communication data of in-vehicle network system

When an ECU receives a signal from a vehicle sensor, it processes it and places the information on the network Bus as a data packet. The data packet is usually made up of the following components:

- A header, **SOF (Start of Frame)**: the equivalent of 'hello, I am transmitting a message.'
- The priority **ID (Identifier)** region: how important this message is.
- Remote transmission request **RTR**: indicates whether a message is a data frame or a remote request frame. A data frame contains actual data, while a remote request frame asks for data from another ECU.
- Flexible data frame **FDF**: indicates whether a message is a CAN FD frame or a Classical CAN frame. CAN FD is an extension of the CAN protocol that allows for higher data rates and longer data fields.
- Data length **Control region DLC**: this tells the receiver how many bytes of data are in the packet.
- Data type **Data region**: this indicates what type of information is contained, e.g. voltage, speed, temperature, etc.
- Data **Data region**: the actual information itself.
- An error detection code **Cyclic Redundancy Check (CRC)** region: this verifies that all the information has been received correctly.
- Finally, a request for a response from the receiving ECU **ACK (Acknowledge) region**: this says, 'thank you, I got your message'.
- End of message **EOF (End of Frame)**: 'goodbye'.

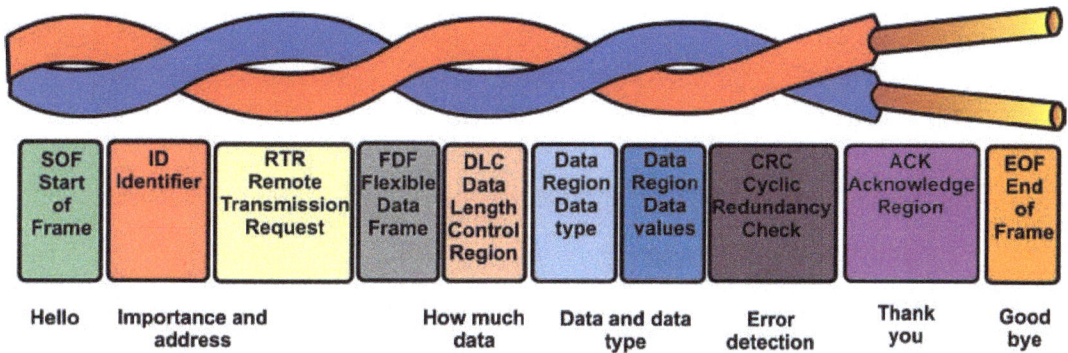

Figure 3.18 CAN Bus communication data packet

Circuit Theory

Bit Timing in CAN Bus Systems

In a CAN Bus system, the communication between ECUs depends on accurate timing. The CAN protocol sends data in the form of bits, 1s and 0s, and these bits must be sent and received at exactly the right time for the system to work correctly. This section explains the key elements of **bit timing**: **synchronisation**, **bit stuffing**, and **baud rates**.

Bit timing

Bit timing refers to the way the CAN Bus system controls the precise timing of each bit sent over the network. It ensures that every ECU on the Bus understands when a bit starts and ends so that data is not misread or corrupted.

 Imagine a group of people clapping in rhythm, they need to clap at exactly the same time, or the pattern falls apart. Bit timing works in the same way: it keeps every node in sync.

Synchronisation - Staying in step

Each ECU has its own **oscillator** (a kind of internal clock) that controls how fast it sends and receives bits. Since no two clocks are exactly the same, CAN uses a technique called synchronisation to keep every ECU working together.

How it works

Step 1
- When a message begins, the first bit (a start-of-frame bit) signals all nodes to synchronise their timing.

Step 2
- Each ECU adjusts its internal clock slightly to match the incoming message.

Step 3
- This way, all ECUs stay 'in step' with each other, even if their clocks are not perfectly accurate.

 Think of it like a drummer counting in and setting the beat at the start of a song. Everyone else listens, starts and plays along at the same pace.

Circuit Theory

Baud rate - How fast bits travel

The baud rate is the speed at which bits are transmitted on the CAN Bus. It's measured in bits per second (bps).

Common automotive CAN baud rates include:

- 500 kbps (kilobits per second): used in high-speed systems like engine or ABS control.
- 250 kbps: often used in medium-speed body control systems.
- 125 kbps or lower: seen in low-speed networks like convenience systems.

Higher baud rates allow faster data transfer but are more sensitive to wiring length and interference. Lower speeds are more reliable for longer wires or less-critical systems.

Time segments of a bit

Each bit is divided into several **time segments**. These help the ECU know when to sample the bit (read it) and when to make adjustments:

- Sync Segment: The first part of the bit, used to synchronise nodes.
- Propagation Segment: Compensates for signal delays across the wiring.
- Phase Segment 1 (PS1) and Phase Segment 2 (PS2): These allow for small corrections in timing, helping ECUs stay in sync even if there's slight clock drift.

Together, these segments form what's called a Bit Time. The precise configuration of these segments is handled automatically by the CAN controller but understanding that bits are made up of smaller time blocks helps explain how the system stays accurate.

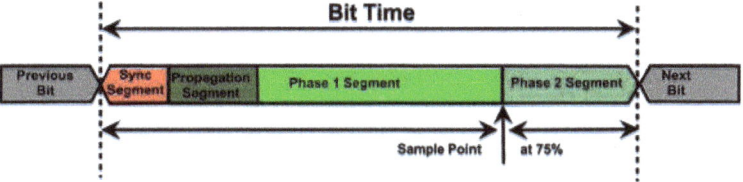

Figure 3.19 Bit time

Bit stuffing - Avoiding confusion

The CAN Bus uses a clever trick called bit stuffing to help ECUs stay synchronised and to avoid false messages.

Here's what happens:

- If 5 consecutive bits of the same value (all 1s or all 0s) are sent, the system automatically inserts a sixth bit of the opposite value.
- This 'stuffed' bit breaks up long runs of identical bits, which could otherwise confuse the receiving ECUs or disrupt timing.
- The receiving ECU knows to ignore these stuffed bits during message interpretation.

Example:
- Data to send: 111110
- After bit stuffing: 1111100 (a 0 is inserted after five 1s)

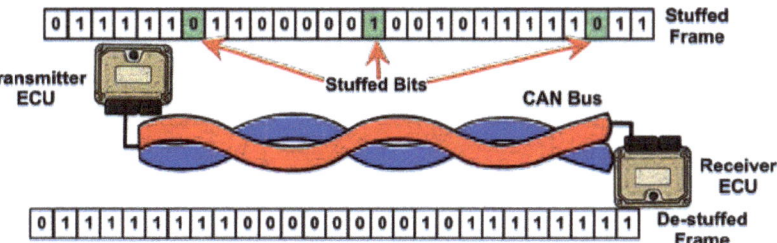

Figure 3.20 Bit stuffing

This process keeps the voltage levels on the CAN lines changing often enough to help receivers maintain accurate timing.

Circuit Theory

Why bit timing matters in diagnostics

Understanding bit timing helps you when diagnosing communication problems:

- Mismatched baud rates between modules can cause total communication failure.
- Bit timing errors may appear as intermittent or random faults.
- Problems with clock speed, wire lengths, or resistance can cause timing mismatches and data corruption.
- Oscilloscope checks can be used to verify timing and baud rate accuracy during diagnosis.

Bit timing is like the rhythm section of the CAN Bus and keeps every ECU playing in time, so the system works as a unified network. Synchronisation keeps clocks aligned, bit stuffing ensures clean data signals, and the baud rate controls how fast messages travel.
While these details happen behind the scenes, with a basic understanding of bit timing you are better prepared to solve communication faults and keep vehicle networks running smoothly.

Mediation - the process or system that manages communication between different electronic systems or networks within a vehicle, especially when they use different protocols, speeds, or formats.

Bit timing - the precise control of when each bit (1 or 0) is sent and received on a vehicle's communication network, like the CAN Bus.

Synchronisation - the process of making sure that all electronic control units (ECUs) on a vehicle's communication network, like CAN Bus, are working in time with each other.

Bit stuffing - a technique used in vehicle communication networks, like CAN Bus, to help keep data accurate and in sync. It means automatically adding an extra bit after five identical bits (all 1s or all 0s) to prevent errors and help modules keep track of the timing. The receiver then removes the extra bit when reading the message.

Baud rates - the speed at which data is sent on a vehicle's communication network, like the CAN Bus.

Oscillator - an electronic component inside a control module that creates a steady timing signal, like a clock.

Time segments - parts of a single bit time used in vehicle communication networks like CAN Bus. They divide each bit into smaller time blocks to help control when data is sent, checked, and adjusted.

Conclusion

As technology advances, network systems will only become more important, especially with the rise of electric and autonomous vehicles. Knowing how these networks work and how they talk to each other will help you diagnose, repair, and understand vehicles at a deeper level.

Electromagnetic Principles

Chapter 4 Electromagnetic Principles

To understand how data moves reliably through vehicle networks, it is essential to grasp the basic principles of electromagnetism and how they affect electronic communication systems. In the context of CAN Bus and other in-vehicle networks, electromagnetic fields can either support or interfere with signal transmission. This chapter will introduce you to the fundamental electromagnetic concepts that underpin data communication in vehicles, including how signals travel along wires, how interference is generated, and how systems are designed to minimise signal disruption. You will also learn how design features such as twisted pair cables, shielding, and termination resistors help maintain clear and stable communication between electronic control units (ECUs).

Contents

Understanding Electromagnetism	80
Electromagnetic Interference (EMI)	81
Capacitance & Inductance	83
Sources of EMI in Vehicles	85
Common-Mode vs Differential-Mode Noise	86
Suppression of Common-Mode Noise	88
Shielding & Grounding Principles	89
Cross-Talk & Interference Between Networks	90

When working on CAN Bus systems and vehicle networks, always remember that these circuits are part of the vehicle's critical control systems. Disconnecting, shorting, or applying the wrong voltage to CAN wiring can cause damage to electronic control units (ECUs), erase data, or even disable safety systems like airbags and ABS.
Before testing or repairing any CAN circuits:

- Always disconnect the battery if specified by the manufacturer's procedures.

- Use the correct diagnostic tools and avoid using standard test lights on CAN wires, as they can overload sensitive circuits.

- Never cut, splice, or tap into CAN wiring without proper guidance, as this can introduce faults and communication errors.

- Be aware that CAN systems operate even when the ignition is off; some ECUs stay awake for a short time after key-off.

Work methodically, follow the vehicle manufacturer's repair information, and always observe health and safety regulations. Taking care around CAN networks will help prevent costly damage and keep vehicle systems operating safely and reliably.

Electromagnetic Principles

Understanding Electromagnetism

Electromagnetism is a fundamental principle of physics that explains the relationship between electricity and **magnetism**. In simple terms, whenever an electric current flows through a wire, it creates a **magnetic field** around that wire. Whenever a moving magnetic field moves around a wire it **induces** a current in that wire. These invisible magnetic fields can interact with other nearby components and wires, sometimes in helpful ways, but most of the time it can cause problems if not properly managed.

A brief history of electromagnetism

The link between electricity and magnetism was first discovered in 1820 by a Danish physicist named Hans Christian Ørsted. During a classroom demonstration, Ørsted noticed that a compass needle moved when placed near a wire carrying electric current. This showed that electric current could produce a magnetic effect, and it marked the beginning of what we now call electromagnetism.

Later scientists like Michael Faraday and James Clerk Maxwell expanded on this idea. Faraday discovered that changing magnetic fields could create electric currents, a principle now used in alternators, sensors, and many other automotive systems. Maxwell developed mathematical equations that described how electric and magnetic fields interact, forming the basis for modern electrical and electronic engineering.

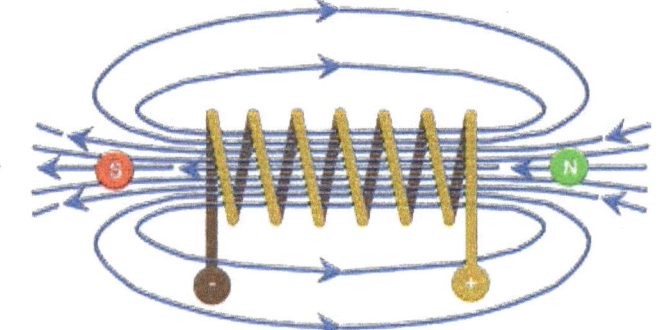

Figure 4.1 Magnetic fields and electric current

What creates electromagnetism

Electromagnetism is created when:

- An electric current flows through a conductor (such as a copper wire).
- The current changes direction or strength (as in alternating current or pulse signals).
- Electric charges move, such as electrons flowing through a circuit.

In vehicle systems, every time a current flows through a wire or electronic component, it generates a small magnetic field. If this field interacts with other signals or components, it can cause unwanted effects like **interference** or noise.

Why electromagnetism happens

Electromagnetism occurs because electric charges in motion naturally create a magnetic field around them. This is a law of nature described by physics, and it happens every time current moves, even in the smallest circuits inside a vehicle control module.

Understanding this is important because:

- Poor wiring or grounding can increase unwanted electromagnetic interference (EMI).
- Improper shielding can allow signals from one wire to disturb another (called **crosstalk**).
- Twisted pair wiring and termination resistors help cancel out these effects.

Electromagnetic Principles

Magnetism - a force exerted by magnets or magnetic materials, where like poles repel and opposite poles attract, due to the movement of electric charges within atoms.

Magnetic field - the magnetic force or area of influence created by magnetic components in a vehicle.

Induces - the process of generating an electric current or voltage in a vehicle's system by changing magnetic fields, often in components like sensors or generators. It involves the creation of electrical energy through electromagnetic induction.

Interference - unwanted electrical or radio signals within a vehicle that can disrupt the operation of electronic systems, sensors, or communication.

Crosstalk - unwanted signal interference between different electronic or electrical wires or circuits in a vehicle, which can cause communication errors or malfunctions.

In CAN Bus and other in-vehicle networks, managing electromagnetism is critical to keep signals clean and data communication reliable.

Electromagnetic Interference (EMI)

Understanding noise and shielding in vehicle networks

Electromagnetic Interference, or EMI, is a type of electrical noise that can disrupt signals in a vehicle's electronic systems. Just like background noise in a conversation can make it hard to hear someone speaking, EMI can interfere with the digital messages being sent between vehicle control units on systems like CAN Bus, LIN, or FlexRay.

EMI occurs when unwanted electromagnetic energy enters a signal line and causes disruption. This energy can come from many sources, both inside and outside the vehicle.

Common causes include:

- Alternators and ignition systems.
- Electric motors (like EV drive motors, window regulators or fuel pumps).
- Mobile phones and radio transmitters.
- Poor grounding or damaged shielding.

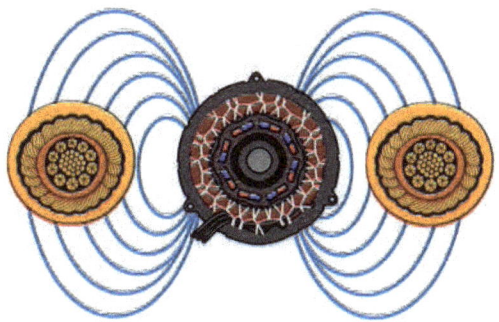

Figure 4.2 Causes of electromagnetic interference EMI

Electromagnetic Principles

In vehicles, dozens of Electronic Control Units (ECUs) constantly send and receive messages to manage EV drive, engine operation, braking, lighting, and much more. If these messages are distorted by EMI, the system may fail to operate correctly, or communication errors may occur on the network.

How EMI affects data transmission

CAN Bus and similar vehicle networks use precise digital signals to transfer information. These signals are made up of high and low voltages, often switching very quickly.

EMI can alter or interrupt these signals in several ways:

- Data corruption: A message may be misread due to interference.
- Communication loss: The receiving ECU may miss or reject the message.
- Bit errors: A '0' may be mistakenly read as a '1', causing faults or triggering DTCs (Diagnostic Trouble Codes).

In severe cases, EMI can cause the CAN Bus to go into **Bus off** mode, where communication stops entirely until the error is cleared.

Shielding techniques and how they work

To reduce EMI, vehicles are designed with several layers of protection.

Some of the most common **shielding** and prevention techniques include:

1. Twisted Pair Wiring: CAN High and CAN Low wires are twisted together. This layout helps cancel out EMI because the noise affects both wires equally, and the **differential signal** compares the difference between the two lines. Since both wires pick up the same noise, the difference stays the same, keeping the signal clean.
2. Shielded Cable: Some high-speed data lines are wrapped in a metallic braid or foil (called a shield). This shield blocks external EMI from entering the signal wires. One end of the shield is usually grounded to safely drain any interference.
3. Proper Grounding: A good electrical **ground** allows excess electromagnetic energy to safely exit the system. Bad or corroded grounds can increase EMI problems, especially in older vehicles.
4. Filtering Components: Capacitors, **ferrite beads**, or special EMI filters can be added to circuits to block or absorb high-frequency noise before it affects communication.

Figure 4.3 Twisted pair

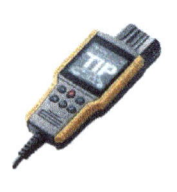

As vehicles become more electronically controlled, understanding EMI is more important than ever. Communication faults caused by EMI can be difficult to diagnose because they may come and go or only appear under certain conditions (e.g., engine running, certain accessories on).
You should be aware of:
- Wire routing and repair: Avoid running data wires near noisy components like ignition coils or high-voltage components.
- Using proper replacement parts: Always match the shielding and layout of factory wiring.
- Checking grounds: A bad ground can mimic EMI symptoms or make them worse.

Electromagnetic Principles

Bus-off - a safety state that a CAN controller enters when it detects too many communication errors. In this state, the device completely disconnects from the network and stops all communication until it's reset, either automatically or with a scan tool.

Shielding - the use of special materials, usually metal or conductive layers, wrapped around wires or electronic components to block unwanted electrical noise or interference.

Differential signal - a way of sending data using two wires instead of one. One wire carries the normal signal (called CAN Low, for example), and the other carries the opposite signal (called CAN High). These two signals are always mirror images of each other.

Ground - the reference point for all electrical circuits. It is usually connected to the vehicle's metal chassis or body.

Ferrite beads - small components used in automotive electrical systems to reduce electromagnetic interference (EMI) and high-frequency noise in wiring and circuits. They are made from a type of ceramic material called ferrite and are often shaped like small cylinders or rings that fit around wires or are built into circuit boards.

Capacitance & Inductance

Effects on signal integrity and wiring in CAN Bus systems

In vehicle electronics, especially in CAN Bus and other in-vehicle networks, it's important to understand how the physical properties of wiring can affect signal quality. Two key electrical properties, **capacitance** and **inductance**, can have a major influence on how signals behave as they travel through wires.

Capacitance

Capacitance is the ability of two conductors (such as wires) to store electrical **charge** between them when separated by an insulator, like plastic or air. In automotive wiring, every wire naturally has some capacitance, especially when it runs alongside another wire.

Why it matters in CAN Bus systems:

- Capacitance can slow down voltage changes, which affects how quickly a signal can switch between its high and low states (0s and 1s). This can cause delays or distortions in the signal, particularly at higher data rates.
- High capacitance can also blur the edges of the signal waveform, reducing clarity and increasing the chance of communication errors.

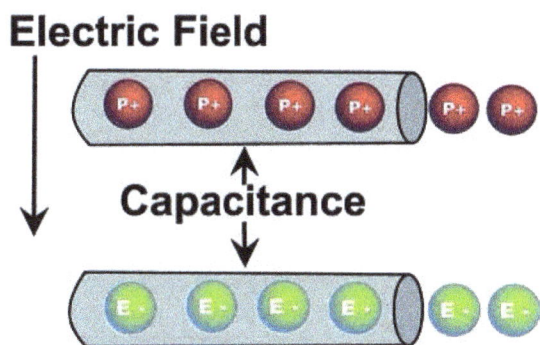

Figure 4.4 Capacitance

Electromagnetic Principles

Inductance

Inductance is the property of a wire or coil that resists changes in **current flow**. When current flows through a wire, it creates a magnetic field. If the current suddenly changes, the magnetic field also changes, and this creates a voltage that opposes the change.

Why it matters in CAN Bus systems:

- Inductance can resist fast current changes, which affects how clean and sharp a digital signal looks.
- Long wires or coils (like those in harnesses) can increase inductance.
- Inductance can lead to **ringing** or unwanted **oscillations** in the signal, especially when switching on or off quickly.

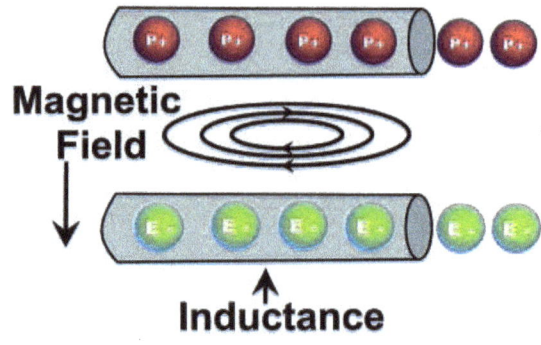

Figure 4.5 Inductance

Combined impact on signal integrity

Both capacitance and inductance affect **signal integrity**, which is the accuracy and shape of electrical signals as they travel.

When capacitance or inductance levels are too high:

- Signals may arrive too late or distorted.
- Errors can occur in data communication.
- **Interference** or **reflections** can be more severe.

Capacitance and inductance are natural physical properties of all wiring, and while they can't be eliminated completely, they can be managed. To reduce the negative effects of capacitance and inductance, vehicle designers:

- Use twisted pair wires for CAN Bus, which helps cancel out inductive effects and reduce EMI.
- Keep wire lengths and harness layouts controlled to maintain consistent electrical properties.
- Terminate the CAN Bus with resistors to match impedance and reduce reflections caused by inductive and capacitive mismatches.
- Use shielded cables and ferrite beads to manage unwanted high-frequency effects.

Capacitance - the ability of two electrical parts (like wires) to store electrical energy between them when they're separated by an insulator (like plastic).

Inductance - the property of a wire or coil that resists changes in electrical current.

Charge - the amount of electricity stored or carried by a component.

Electromagnetic Principles

Current flow - the movement of electrical charge (electrons) through a wire or circuit.

Ringing - unwanted electrical oscillations or ringing waves that occur on a signal line after a sudden change in voltage. It's like a vibration or echo in the wiring caused by the wiring's inductance and capacitance.

Oscillations - repeated up-and-down or back-and-forth changes in an electrical signal or current.

Signal integrity - the quality and accuracy of electrical signals as they travel through wiring and networks like CAN Bus.

Interference - unwanted electrical noise or signals that disrupt the normal communication between electronic components.

Reflections - when an electrical signal traveling along a wire hits a break, end, or improper connection and bounces back.

Sources of EMI in Vehicles

EMI in vehicles arises mainly from high-current electric motors, power electronics with rapid switching, ignition and fuel systems, and wireless communication modules. Proper CAN Bus design, shielding, filtering, and grounding are crucial to protect vehicle networks from these interference sources and maintain stable, reliable communication between electronic control units (ECUs).

Table 4.1 describes some potential sources of EMI for different vehicle types.

Table 4.1 Potential sources of EMI for different vehicle types

Vehicle Type	EMI Source	Description
Conventional Propulsion	Ignition Systems	Spark plugs and ignition coils generate strong electrical pulses causing EMI.
	Alternators	Rotating electrical machines produce electrical noise.
	Starter Motors	High current and mechanical switching cause magnetic interference (especially when old or worn-out).
	Fuel Injectors	Rapid on/off switching creates bursts of electromagnetic noise.
	Electric Cooling Fans & Pumps	Motor operations produce fluctuating magnetic fields.
	Relays and Solenoids	Mechanical switches cause voltage spikes and switching noise.
	Voltage Regulators	Power electronics emit high-frequency signals.
	Lighting Systems	Xenon and LED headlights may introduce electrical noise.
	Audio/Infotainment Systems	Radio frequency signals can interfere with vehicle networks.

Electromagnetic Principles

Table 4.1 Potential sources of EMI for different vehicle types

Vehicle Type	EMI Source	Description
Hybrid Propulsion	High-Voltage Battery Packs	Rapid current and voltage changes produce EMI.
	DC-DC Converters	High-frequency switching in power converters generates noise.
	Inverters	Convert DC to AC with switching transistors that emit EMI.
	Electric Traction Motors	Motors generate magnetic fields inducing interference.
	Regenerative Braking Systems	Power electronics switching causes electromagnetic noise.
	Onboard Chargers	Charging power electronics introduce EMI.
	Electric Pumps & Fans	High-speed motors produce fluctuating electromagnetic fields.
Electric Vehicles (EV)	High-Power Inverters & Converters	Frequent switching at high frequencies creates EMI.
	Battery Management Systems (BMS)	Monitoring and balancing circuits can emit electromagnetic noise.
	Traction Motors	Large currents and rotating magnetic fields generate EMI.
	Fast Charging Systems	High currents during charging lead to transient interference.
	Electric HVAC Systems	Motors and compressors contribute to electromagnetic noise.
	Wireless Communication Modules	Bluetooth, Wi-Fi, and cellular phones may produce RF interference.
	Onboard DC-DC Converters	Switching power supplies cause EMI.
Hydrogen Fuel Cell (HFC)	Fuel Cell Stack	Electrical conversion with power electronics emitting EMI.
	Hydrogen Pumps & Compressors	Electrically driven components produce electromagnetic noise.
	Power Electronics (Inverters, Converters)	High-frequency switching noise similar to EVs.
	Cooling Systems	Electric pumps and fans contribute to EMI.
	High-Voltage Wiring	Large current flows and switching cause electromagnetic fields.
	Communication Modules	RF transmitters for telemetry and diagnostics can cause interference.

Common-Mode vs Differential-Mode Noise

In automotive electronics, especially in network systems like CAN Bus, noise is one of the main challenges when transmitting data reliably. Two major types of electrical noise that can interfere with signal integrity are **common-mode noise** and **differential-mode noise**.

Common-mode noise

Common-mode noise occurs when the same electrical interference appears on both wires of a two-wire system (such as CAN High and CAN Low) relative to the vehicle's ground.
- Think of it as 'shared' noise that affects both lines equally.
- It can be caused by electromagnetic interference (EMI) from sources like electric motors, ignition systems, or radio-frequency signals.
- Even though both wires are noisy, the CAN system may still work because the difference between them remains the same (and it's the difference that matters in differential signalling).

Electromagnetic Principles

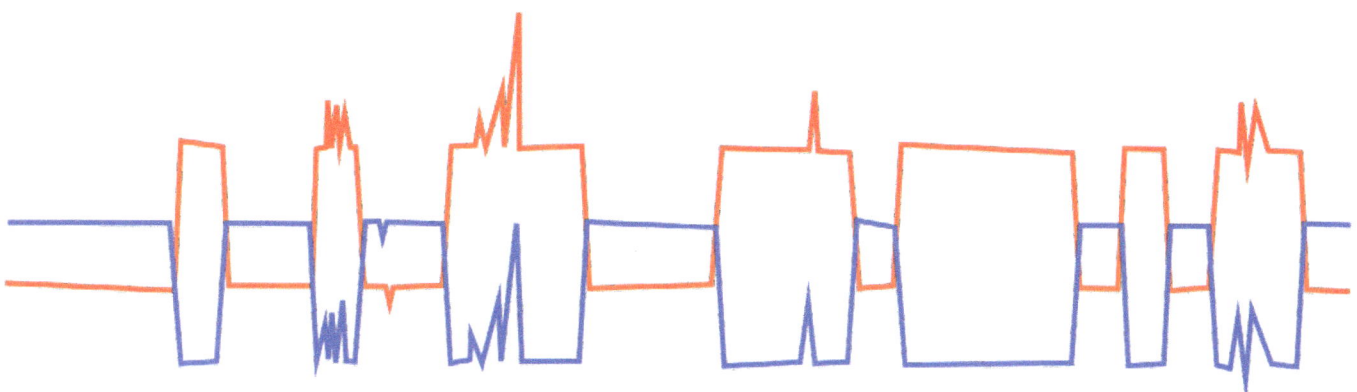

Figure 4.6 Common mode noise

Example:

If both CAN H and CAN L wires are affected by a 2V noise spike at the same time, the system might still function correctly because the voltage difference between the two wires hasn't changed.

Differential-mode noise

Differential-mode noise occurs when interference affects the two wires in opposite or unequal ways. Since CAN Bus uses differential signalling, where data is transmitted by the difference in voltage between CAN H and CAN L, this type of noise can cause serious problems.

- It alters the voltage difference that carries the data.
- It is more dangerous for data integrity because the receiver sees the change as part of the message.
- Causes can include poor cable shielding, unbalanced wiring, or nearby fast-switching power devices.

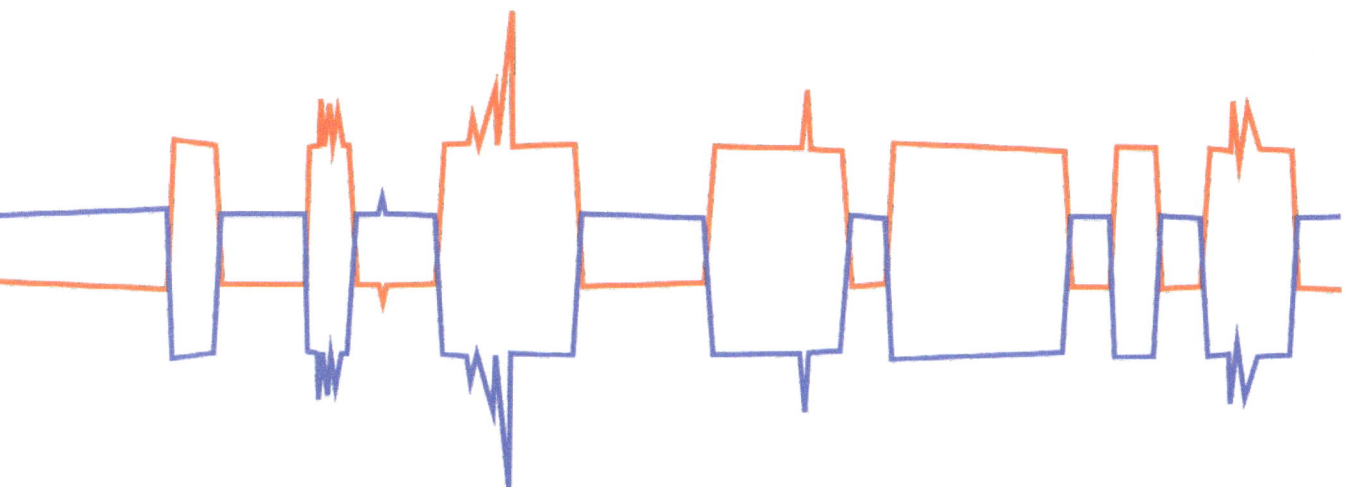

Figure 4.7 Differential mode noise

Example:

If one wire picks up more noise than the other, the intended voltage difference is distorted. This can result in corrupted messages or communication errors.

Electromagnetic Principles

Summary			
Type of Noise	Affects	Source Examples	Impact on CAN Bus
Common-Mode Noise	Both wires equally (relative to ground).	Motors, relays, power lines, EMI from radio signals.	Often tolerated; differential signalling cancels it.
Differential-Mode Noise	One wire more than the other.	Unbalanced cables, poor shielding, nearby switching devices.	Dangerous; can corrupt messages.

Suppression of Common Mode Noise

Reliable communication between electronic control units (ECUs) is essential. The Controller Area Network is one of the most widely used communication systems in automotive electronics. One of the key reasons for CAN's reliability is its use of differential signalling, which helps suppress the specific type of electrical interference: common-mode noise.

Differential signalling

Differential signalling means that the data is sent across two wires, instead of just one. The message is carried not by the voltage on either wire alone, but by the difference in voltage between the two wires.

- When a dominant bit (logical 0) is transmitted, CAN H goes higher (about 3.5V) and CAN L goes lower (about 1.5V), creating a strong voltage difference.
- When a recessive bit (logical 1) is sent, both CAN H and CAN L settle around the same level (about 2.5V), meaning there's very little voltage difference.

Common-mode noise affects both wires equally. For example, if an electric motor or ignition system generates electromagnetic interference (EMI), it may raise the voltage on both CAN H and CAN L by the same amount. For example, let's say a 1V noise spike occurs:

- CAN H rises from 3.5V to 4.5V.
- CAN L rises from 1.5V to 2.5V.
- The voltage difference between the two is still 2V, so the signal is still valid.

This is the core advantage of differential signalling: noise that affects both wires in the same way is cancelled out.

Summary Example				
Scenario	CAN_H	CAN_L	Voltage Difference (CAN_H - CAN_L)	Result
Normal dominant signal	3.5V	1.5V	2.0V	Interpreted as '0'
With common-mode noise (+1V spike)	4.5V	2.5V	2.0V	Interpreted as '0'
With noise only on CAN H (rare case)	4.5V	1.5V	3.0V	Still valid, but less ideal
With equal noise on both wires	+1V	+1V	No change in difference	No effect on data

Electromagnetic Principles

Shielding & Grounding Principles

CAN Bus and in-vehicle network systems must operate reliably in the presence of electromagnetic interference (EMI), which can distort or corrupt the data being exchanged. To protect sensitive signals, engineers use shielding and grounding, two key design strategies that help block and control EMI.

Shielding

Shielding is the use of a conductive material (usually metal) placed around signal-carrying wires or components to block external electromagnetic energy. Shielding works much like a protective barrier, reflecting or absorbing unwanted interference before it can affect the signal.

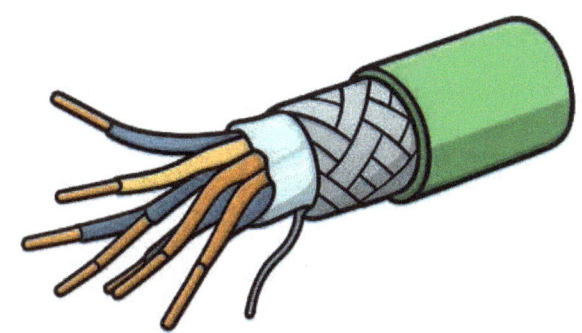

Figure 4.8 Shielding and grounding

Table 4.2 describes some common shielding types used in automotive design.

Table 4.2 Common types of shielding in automotive design

Shield Type	Construction	Where It's Used
Foil Shield	A thin layer of aluminium foil wrapped around the wire or cable.	Low-frequency signal cables.
Braided Shield	A woven mesh of copper or tinned copper wires surrounding the cable.	High-frequency CAN or Ethernet cables.
Spiral Shield	A coiled wire wrapped along the cable length.	Flexible harnesses where moderate shielding is needed.
Combination Shield	Foil and braid used together for improved performance.	High-speed or safety-critical data lines.
Shielded Twisted Pair (STP)	Two signal wires twisted together and surrounded by a shield.	Differential data lines like CAN or FlexRay.

Grounding

Grounding means connecting a component or shield to a common reference voltage, typically the vehicle chassis or battery ground. This allows unwanted EMI to safely **discharge** away from the signal lines and into the **earth** or chassis, rather than affecting communication.

There are two main grounding strategies in vehicle electronics:

1. Single-Point Grounding
   - All grounds connect back to one central location (ideal for low-noise systems).
   - Used in sensitive diagnostic or infotainment systems.
2. Multi-Point Grounding
   - Grounds are connected at multiple locations to reduce resistance and voltage differences.
   - Common in high-current or safety-critical systems like airbags or braking.

Electromagnetic Principles

How shielding and grounding work together

Shielding alone is not enough; it must be properly grounded to be effective. If a shield is left **floating** (not grounded), it may act like an antenna and actually increase noise.

When the shield is grounded:

- Interference is captured by the shield.
- The interference flows harmlessly to ground instead of into the signal lines.

This combination greatly improves signal integrity and reduces the chances of communication errors, bit corruption, or Bus faults.

While standard CAN Bus is quite robust due to its use of differential signalling, shielded twisted pair (STP) cables are often used in:
- High-speed CAN (up to 1 Mbps)
- CAN FD (Flexible Data-Rate)
- Noise-sensitive environments, such as hybrid or electric powertrains

Shielding is especially important when CAN wires run near:
- Ignition coils
- Alternators
- Power inverters
- Electric motors
- High-voltage battery lines (in EVs and hybrids)

Cross-talk & Interference Between Networks

As vehicles become more advanced, the number of electronic systems and networks has increased dramatically. Multiple in-vehicle networks such as CAN, LIN, FlexRay, MOST, and Ethernet now operate alongside each other, often within the same wiring harness.
While these systems allow for precise control and communication, they also introduce a new challenge: cross-talk and electromagnetic interference (EMI) between the networks.

Cross-talk

Cross-talk is a type of unintentional electrical interference that occurs when a signal traveling in one wire or circuit creates a signal in another nearby wire. This happens because electric and magnetic fields surrounding the wire carrying the signal can leak into adjacent wires.

Imagine two people in separate phone calls standing close to each other if one person speaks loudly, their voice may be picked up by the other phone. This is similar to what happens in cross-talk.

Electromagnetic Principles

Cross-talk usually occurs when:

- Wires are too close together, especially over long distances.
- Signal frequencies are high, such as in CAN FD or automotive Ethernet.
- Improper or missing shielding allows signals to radiate outward.
- Grounding is poor or inconsistent, allowing stray current paths.
- Signal and power lines share the same harness without proper separation.
- Long, unbalanced wire runs amplify capacitive and inductive coupling.

Table 4.3 describes the two main types of cross-talk that can occur in vehicle wiring.

Table 4.3 The two main types of cross-talk that can occur in vehicle wiring

Type	Description
Capacitive Coupling	Caused by electric fields between nearby wires; more common at high frequencies.
Inductive Coupling	Caused by magnetic fields from current changes in one wire inducing voltage in another.

Cross-talk in hybrid and electric vehicles

Electric and hybrid vehicles are especially prone to EMI and cross-talk because of:

- High-voltage battery systems.
- Inverter switching (used in traction motors).
- DC/DC converters and onboard chargers.

Special care must be taken to isolate high-voltage cables from low-voltage signal lines, and to use shielded, twisted-pair cables for network communication.

Summary

Cause of Cross-talk	Prevention Technique
Wires too close together	Cable separation and routing discipline
High-frequency signals	Twisted pair wiring and shielding
No or poor shielding	Use of foil or braid shields
Long cable runs	Termination resistors and impedance matching
Inverter and motor switching noise	Physical isolation and ferrite filters

Electromagnetic Principles

Common-mode noise - unwanted electrical noise that appears equally on both wires of a communication pair (such as CAN High and CAN Low) with respect to ground.

Differential-mode noise - unwanted electrical noise that appears differently on each wire of a signal pair, such as CAN High and CAN Low.

Discharge - the release or flow of stored electrical energy from a component, such as a battery, capacitor, or other energy storage device into a circuit.

Earth - a low resistance electrical return path to source.

Floating - a component, wire, or circuit that is not connected to ground (earth) or a defined voltage level. This means it has no fixed electrical reference point, which can cause unpredictable or unstable behaviour.

Conclusion

This chapter has explored the fundamental principles of electromagnetism and its impact on vehicle network systems. Understanding key concepts such as electromagnetic interference (EMI), capacitance, inductance, and the differences between common mode and differential mode noise is essential for diagnosing and mitigating potential electromagnetic issues in vehicles. By comprehending these principles, along with techniques like shielding and minimising cross-talk, you are equipped to develop the necessary skills to maintain the reliability and efficiency of modern automotive systems.

Communication Protocol & Voltage Regulation

Chapter 5 Communication Protocol & Voltage Regulation

To effectively diagnose, service and repair vehicles, you must understand the communication protocols that allow electronic control units (ECUs) to exchange information seamlessly. This chapter focuses on the key communication protocols used in automotive networks, with a special emphasis on the Controller Area Network (CAN) system. It also covers the essential principles of voltage regulation that ensure stable power delivery to these networks. By exploring how data signals are managed and how voltage levels are maintained, you will gain a solid foundation for working with in-vehicle networks and troubleshooting related electrical issues.

Contents

The Origins of CAN Bus	94
CAN Bus Frame Structure	95
Error Detection	99
Arbitration	100
Self-diagnosis	102
Power Supply	115
Safety & High-Voltage Handling	116
Isolation Techniques	118
Protective Measures for Automotive Network Components	121

When working on CAN Bus systems and vehicle networks, always remember that these circuits are part of the vehicle's critical control systems. Disconnecting, shorting, or applying the wrong voltage to CAN wiring can cause damage to electronic control units (ECUs), erase data, or even disable safety systems like airbags and ABS.
Before testing or repairing any CAN circuits:

- Always disconnect the battery if specified by the manufacturer's procedures.

- Use the correct diagnostic tools and avoid using standard test lights on CAN wires, as they can overload sensitive circuits.

- Never cut, splice, or tap into CAN wiring without proper guidance, as this can introduce faults and communication errors.

- Be aware that CAN systems operate even when the ignition is off; some ECUs stay awake for a short time after key-off.

Work methodically, follow the vehicle manufacturer's repair information, and always observe health and safety regulations. Taking care around CAN networks will help prevent costly damage and keep vehicle systems operating safely and reliably.

Communication Protocol & Voltage Regulation

The Origins of CAN Bus

As vehicles became more complex over time, the amount of wiring needed to control electrical and electronic systems increased dramatically. In older vehicles, each electrical component was often connected with its own dedicated wiring, resulting in heavy wiring looms that were difficult to manage, added weight, and increased the chances of faults or wiring failures.

By the 1980s, vehicle manufacturers were looking for better ways to reduce wiring complexity while improving the speed and reliability of communication between components like sensors, actuators, and control units. The idea was to allow different electronic control units to talk to each other over a shared network, rather than through separate wires.

In response to this growing need, the Controller Area Network (CAN) protocol was developed in 1983 by Robert Bosch GmbH, a leading German engineering and electronics company. The goal was to create a robust communication system that could operate reliably in the electrically noisy environment of a vehicle. By 1991, CAN had become widely adopted in production vehicles, and it was later standardised as ISO 11898.

Unlike traditional wiring systems, CAN Bus allows multiple ECUs to communicate over a two-wire network. Instead of point-to-point wiring, CAN uses a Bus topology, where each ECU or node is connected to the same shared communication lines. This reduces weight, cost, and complexity while increasing reliability.

Figure 5.1 Bus arrangement (topology)

CAN was designed with several important features:

- Priority-based messaging, so critical data (like braking signals) get through quickly.
- Error detection and handling, so corrupted messages can be spotted and corrected.
- **Multi-master** capability, allowing more than one ECU to start communication.

As the number of ECUs in vehicles continued to grow, other communication protocols were also developed to suit different applications, including:

- LIN (Local Interconnect Network) for simple, low-speed communication.
- SENT (Single Edge Nibble Transmission), a digital communication standard used for transmitting sensor data.
- FlexRay for safety-critical and high-speed systems.
- MOST (Media Oriented Systems Transport) for infotainment and multimedia data.
- Ethernet for large data loads and high bandwidth requirements.

CAN remains the most widely used protocol in the automotive world due to its balance of speed, simplicity, and reliability. Enhanced versions like CAN FD (Flexible Data-Rate) and CAN XL are being introduced to meet the growing demands of modern vehicles, particularly in electric and autonomous vehicle designs.

Communication Protocol & Voltage Regulation

Understanding CAN Bus Protocols

Imagine you and some friends are seated around a table, ready to dive into a card game. Everyone is excited to play, and the goal is clear, to win by playing your cards according to the rules. Just like this card game, the CAN Bus protocol enables communication within a vehicle's network, ensuring all components play by the rules to maintain harmony and efficiency.

The Game Rules: Protocol Guidelines

The game's flow is governed by specific rules: you can only play a card that matches the colour or number of the one on top of the discard pile, and special cards have unique actions. Similarly, the CAN Bus protocol has its own set of rules that dictate how electronic control units (ECUs) within a vehicle communicate.

1. **Game Turns and Priority**: In the game, players take turns, and sometimes a card lets a player skip ahead or get another turn. In the CAN Bus system, messages are like cards, and the protocol sets the priority. Here, devices send messages based on priority rather than waiting in line, much like choosing which card to play based on the game scenario.

2. **Message Frames as Cards**: Each card contains specific information, colour, number, or a special function. In the CAN Bus network, each message contains a data frame that carries ID and data to identify the sender and convey the message content. Just like you need to pick the right card to play, message frames ensure the correct data is exchanged as needed.

3. **Rules Enforcement: Error Handling**: If someone tries to play an invalid card, the rules dictate that it's not allowed, and often the player must draw more cards. Similarly, CAN Bus uses error detection and handling mechanisms to prevent transmission errors, ensuring the network only accepts valid messages.

CAN Bus Frame Structure

In any communication system, information must be organised in a way that both the sender and receiver can understand. In the case of the CAN Bus, this information is transmitted using a specific format known as a **frame structure**. The frame acts like a data envelope that wraps up all the information needed for successful communication across the network.

A **CAN frame** is the basic unit of communication on the Controller Area Network. Each frame carries not just the actual data, but also important control information that tells the receiving ECUs what the data is, where it came from, and how to handle it.

Communication Protocol & Voltage Regulation

Table 5.1 describes the key components of a standard CAN data frame.

Table 5.1 Key components of a standard CAN data frame

Field Name	Function / Description
Start of Frame (SOF)	A single dominant bit that signals the beginning of a new frame. All nodes on the network start listening as soon as they detect this bit. This is the equivalent of 'hello, I am transmitting a message.'
Arbitration Field	This includes the **Identifier**, which defines the message priority. The lower the binary number, the higher the priority. This field may also include a Remote Transmission Request (RTR) bit that distinguishes data frames from request frames.
Control Field	Indicates the length of the data and includes bits that help control the flow of information. It indicates whether a message is a CAN FD frame or a Classical CAN frame and tells the receiver how many bytes of data are in the packet.
Data Field (Payload)	This indicates what type of information is contained and contains the actual message content being sent. In standard CAN (also known as Classical CAN), this can carry up to 8 bytes (64 bits) of data.
CRC Field (Cyclic Redundancy Check)	A mathematical **checksum** used for error checking. If the data has been corrupted, the receiver will detect it using this CRC.
ACK Field (Acknowledge)	Once a node successfully receives the message, it sends an acknowledgment bit so the sender knows the frame was received correctly.
End of Frame (EOF)	Marks the conclusion of the message and is the equivalent of saying 'goodbye'.

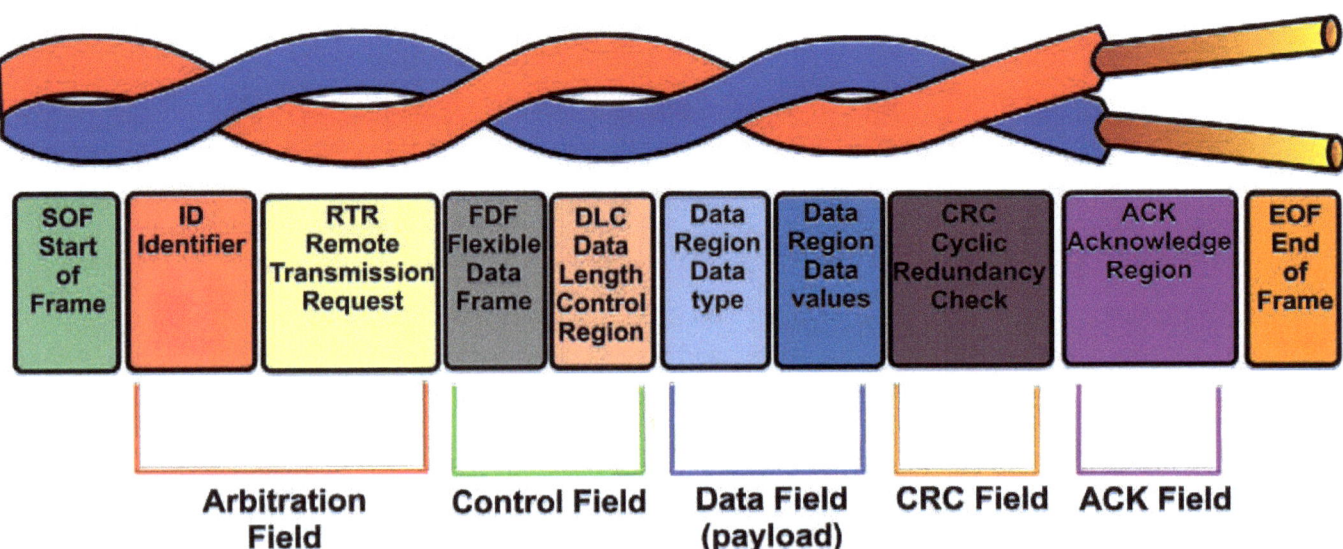

Figure 5.2 CAN Bus data frame

Communication Protocol & Voltage Regulation

Understanding how a CAN Bus data packet works can be much easier if we compare it to something more familiar, like sending a letter through the post. Just like a letter has to be prepared and packaged properly before being sent, a CAN message must be formatted in a specific way so that it can travel across the network and arrive at the right destination.

Let's imagine a CAN frame as a multi-page letter placed inside an envelope. Each part of the CAN frame has a job to do, just like each part of a mailed letter.

Start of Frame (SOF) → The Stamp on the Envelope
Before your letter can be sent, you need to attach a stamp. This tells the postal service that the letter is ready to go. In CAN, the Start of Frame bit is like the stamp, it marks the very beginning of the message and tells all the devices on the network, 'Here comes a new message!'

Arbitration Field → The Address and Class of Post
Next, you write the recipient's address on the envelope. This tells the postal system where the letter should go. You also choose if you're sending it first class or second class, which determines how urgent or high-priority it is.

In a CAN frame, the arbitration field includes the Identifier, which sets the priority of the message. The lower the identifier, the higher the priority, just like first-class mail gets sorted before second-class. This field makes sure that the most important messages go through first if two messages are sent at the same time.

Control Field → Page Numbering
Inside the envelope is your multi-page letter. At the top of each page, you write 'Page 1 of 8,' 'Page 2 of 8,' and so on. This helps the receiver know how many pages to expect and in what order.

The control field in a CAN frame does a similar job. It tells the receiver how many bytes of data are included in the message so that it knows how much to expect.

Data Field → The Content of the Letter
This is the actual information you want to send. It could be instructions, a list of values, or any kind of useful message.

In the CAN data frame, the data field carries the payload, the real message content that one ECU is sending to another.

CRC Field → Page Count Check
Before sealing the envelope, you quickly double-check that all the pages are present and in the correct order. This helps ensure that the letter won't be misunderstood when it's opened. The CRC (Cyclic Redundancy Check) does the same thing in a CAN message. It verifies that the data hasn't been damaged or changed while being sent.

ACK Field → Proof of Delivery
Once your letter arrives, the recipient will sign a delivery slip to prove they got it. This confirmation will then be returned to you.

The ACK (Acknowledgement) field in CAN is like that delivery slip. It lets the sender know that at least one ECU received the message correctly.

End of Frame (EOF) → Sealing the Envelope
Finally, you seal the envelope, knowing everything is inside and properly packaged. It's now ready to move through the system.

The End of Frame marks the end of the message in a CAN transmission. It tells the network that the message is complete, and no more data follows.

Enhanced frame structures: CAN FD and CAN XL

As automotive networks became more data-heavy, newer versions of CAN were developed to handle larger payloads and faster communication.

CAN FD (Flexible Data Rate)

CAN FD builds on the original CAN protocol but adds key enhancements:

- Data Payload: Up to 64 bytes of data (compared to 8 in standard CAN).
- Flexible Data Rate: Allows faster transmission speeds during the data phase (up to 8 Mbps or more).
- Bit Rate Switching (BRS): Speeds up communication by allowing different speeds in the arbitration and data sections of the frame.

CAN FD retains much of the original frame structure but modifies the control field to support longer payloads and higher speeds.

CAN XL

CAN XL is the next evolution of CAN, designed to support future applications that require even higher data throughput:

- Payload Size: Up to 2048 bytes.
- Improved Protocol Control: Includes new fields to manage larger and more complex messages.
- Hybrid Compatibility: Designed to operate alongside Ethernet in certain applications.

CAN XL uses a more advanced frame structure, with additional control and protocol information to manage the increased data capacity.

Table 5.2 CAN XL Frame Fields and Their Functions

Field Name	Function / Description
Start of Frame (SOF)	Marks the beginning of the CAN XL frame; tells all nodes to start listening.
Priority ID (PID)	Identifies the message and sets its priority; lower values have higher priority.
Extended Data Length (EDL)	Indicates that this is a CAN XL frame and not a classical or CAN FD frame.
XL Data Length Code (XLC)	Tells how many bytes of data are in the message (up to 2048 bytes).
SDT (Service Data Unit Type)	Specifies the type of message: user data, control data, or system information.
VCI (Virtual CAN Interface)	A virtual channel ID used when multiple **virtual networks** are running on the same Bus.
Data Field	Carries the actual message content (payload) from one ECU to another.
CRC Sequence	A special check code to make sure the data wasn't damaged during transmission.
Acknowledgement (ACK)	Confirms that at least one ECU on the network received the message without errors.
End of Frame (EOF)	Marks the end of the message; tells ECUs that no more data is coming.
Intermission	A short pause that separates messages; gives ECUs time to prepare for the next frame.

Communication Protocol & Voltage Regulation

Multi-master - more than one control unit (ECU) on a network, such as a CAN Bus, can send messages at any time. There isn't just one 'master' in charge; instead, all ECUs have equal rights to talk on the network, as long as they follow the rules to avoid speaking over each other.

Frame structure - the organised format of a message sent between control units (ECUs). It acts like a digital envelope that carries important data.

CAN frame - a complete message sent on a Controller Area Network (CAN) in a vehicle. It includes all the parts needed to deliver data between electronic control units (ECUs), such as the message ID, the actual data, and error-checking bits.

Identifier - a special code used in a CAN Bus message to label or name the message. It tells all the electronic control units (ECUs) what kind of data is in the message and how important it is.

Virtual networks - a software-based communication system that allows different parts of a vehicle to talk to each other as if they were on the same physical network, even if they are not.

Checksum - a small value or code calculated from a message or block of data to check for errors.

Error Detection

It is crucial that the data being shared between control units is accurate and free from errors. Vehicle systems rely on this information to make real-time decisions. To ensure that messages arrive without errors, CAN Bus protocols include robust error detection mechanisms. One of the most important of these is called a Cyclic Redundancy Check (CRC).

Error detection is the process of identifying if a message has been corrupted during transmission. In a vehicle, electrical noise, faulty wiring, or other disturbances can cause bits in a message to flip from 1 to 0 or vice versa. Error detection methods help identify when this happens so that the faulty message can be ignored or resent.

How CRC works

Before a message is sent on the CAN Bus, the sender runs a special maths formula on the contents of the message to create a short code; this is the CRC value. This value is then attached to the message and sent out. When the receiving control unit (ECU) gets the message, it runs the same formula on the received data and checks if its result matches the CRC value that came with the message. If it matches, the data is accepted as correct. If it doesn't, the receiver knows an error occurred and discards the message.

Communication Protocol & Voltage Regulation

Imagine you are an equipment supplier sending a toolbox full of tools to a workshop across town using a courier. To make sure nothing goes missing or gets damaged, you do something smart:
Before closing the toolbox, you count every tool inside; spanners, screwdrivers, sockets, and write the total number (let's say 371 tools) on a checklist taped to the lid. This checklist acts like a checksum.

Now, when the workshop receives the toolbox, the mechanic there opens it up and counts the tools too. If they also count 371 tools, they know everything likely arrived safely; nothing lost, nothing added. But if they count only 369, or find 372 for example, they know something went wrong during the trip. That triggers a check or a request to resend a new toolbox.

This is how a Cyclic Redundancy Check (CRC) works in a CAN Bus system. The CRC creates a mathematical checksum based on the exact bits in the message. The receiving ECU recalculates the checksum using the data it got. If both values match, the data is good. If not, there's an error, and the message is either rejected or requested again.

Other types of error detection in CAN

In addition to CRC, CAN Bus uses several other error-checking methods:

- Bit Monitoring: Each node checks what it sends and listens to what's actually on the Bus. If there's a mismatch, it means an error has occurred.
- Bit Stuffing: To avoid too many repeated bits in a row (which can confuse timing), CAN adds an opposite bit after five of the same bits. The receiver checks for this and flags an error if the rule is broken.
- Frame Check: CAN checks the overall format of the message frame. If any part is malformed, it's treated as an error.
- Acknowledgement Check (ACK): After a message is received, at least one node must acknowledge it. If no one does, the sender knows the message failed.

Error detection keeps in-vehicle communication reliable and safe. Without it, corrupted data could lead to malfunctioning systems, such as airbags deploying at the wrong time or engine misbehaviour. CAN Bus automatically handles these errors, making the network robust even in electrically noisy automotive environments.

Arbitration

In a CAN Bus system, many electronic control units (ECUs), or nodes, share the same communication line; but what happens when more than one ECU wants to send a message at the same time?
This is where **arbitration** comes into play.

Arbitration is the method used by CAN Bus to decide which ECU gets to send its message first, without any data getting mixed up or lost. It's a clever and automatic system that ensures messages don't collide on the Bus.

Communication Protocol & Voltage Regulation

How It works

Each CAN message frame has a part called the identifier (ID). This ID not only tells other ECUs what kind of message it is, but it also plays a key role in arbitration.

- When two or more ECUs try to send messages at the same time, the CAN Bus checks the IDs of the messages.
- The message with the lowest numerical ID (which is seen as the highest priority) wins.
- The other ECUs stop transmitting immediately and wait for the next chance to try again.

This happens so quickly that you don't even notice a delay.

Why it works so well

The CAN Bus uses something called non-destructive bitwise arbitration. This means that even when multiple ECUs start talking at once, none of their messages get damaged or lost. The 'losers' simply back off and wait their turn, while the 'winner' sends its full message without interruption.

Think of the CAN Bus like a shared meeting room in a company where multiple employees want to speak. Everyone from the Managing Director (MD) to the intern uses the same room (the Bus) to deliver their messages (data).

Each person has a rank number that reflects their importance in the company. The MD is ranked number 1, the department manager is number 2, the supervisor is number 3, and so on, down to the intern at number 10. In this system, the lower the number the higher their priority.

Now, imagine they all walk into the meeting room and start to talk at the same time. To keep things organised and prevent people from talking over one another, they follow a rule:
The person with the lowest rank number (highest priority) gets to speak first.

So, even if the intern and the MD start speaking at exactly the same time, everyone listens to the rank numbers:

The MD (rank 1) has the lowest number and wins the chance to speak.
The others (ranks 2–10) immediately stop and wait for their turn.

This is exactly how CAN Bus arbitration works.

Each electronic control unit (ECU) on the Bus has an identifier number, just like the employee ranks. When multiple ECUs want to send messages at once, the one with the lowest identifier wins the arbitration and continues sending. The others stop and try again shortly after, usually within milliseconds.

Because this process is non-destructive, no data is lost. It's like the other staff members didn't start shouting, they simply paused and let the higher-ranked person go first.

Communication Protocol & Voltage Regulation

Self-Diagnosis

Because in-vehicle networks and CAN Bus are so critical to vehicle operation, they must also be able to monitor their own health. This is where self-diagnosis comes in.
Self-diagnosis in CAN Bus systems helps to detect faults and act when something goes wrong. Two important parts of this process are timeouts and the bus-off state.

Timeout – waiting too long for a message

In a healthy CAN network, ECUs regularly send and receive messages. Many systems rely on timing; they expect to receive certain messages at fixed intervals.

A **timeout** happens when an ECU is waiting for a message that doesn't arrive in time. This could be a sign that:

- The sending ECU has failed.
- There is a wiring or connection issue.
- Interference or noise is disrupting communication.

When a timeout occurs, the receiving ECU might:

- Trigger a warning light on the dashboard.
- Log a diagnostic trouble code (DTC).
- Enter a default or safe mode until the issue is resolved.

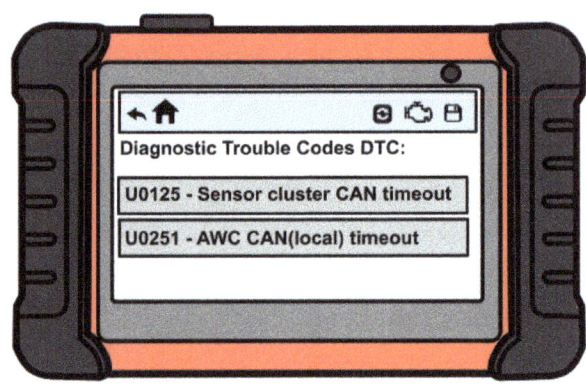

Figure 5.3 Time out message

You can diagnose this by using a scan tool or checking the CAN message flow with an oscilloscope or diagnostic software *[see Chapter 6]*.

Bus-off – too many errors, ECU shuts down

Each ECU on the CAN Bus keeps track of how many **transmission errors** it experiences. These errors might be caused by wiring faults, incorrect voltage levels, interference, or internal faults.

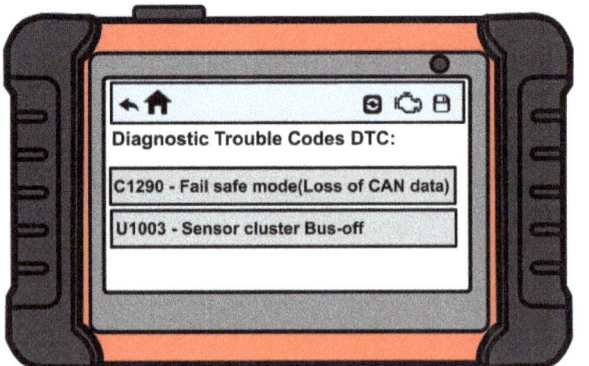

To prevent a faulty ECU from disrupting the whole network, the CAN protocol includes an automatic error handling mechanism. If an ECU sees too many errors in a short time, it will go into **Bus-off** mode.

When an ECU enters Bus-off state, it disconnects itself from the network. It stops sending and receiving messages completely. This protects the rest of the system from the faulty ECU and avoids corrupt data.
The ECU can recover from Bus-off, but only after certain conditions are met; usually after a cool-down period or manual reset, depending on the system.

Figure 5.4 Bus-off message

Communication Protocol & Voltage Regulation

Differentiating Between Time-Out and Bus-Off Codes

Time-Out Codes: These occur when a device on the CAN network doesn't receive a message within a specified time frame.
Think of it as a missed message warning—it's usually caused by a slow or inactive device, or a temporary glitch in communication.

Focus: Check the specific sensor or module reported in the code. Verify if it's powered, properly connected, and functioning correctly. Often, the issue is with that device or its wiring.

Bus-Off Codes: These happen when a device detects too many errors on the network and shuts itself down to prevent damage.
It's like a device saying, 'I can't communicate reliably, so I'm disconnecting.'

Focus: Look for high error rates on the entire network or the device that caused the bus-off. Check for wiring issues, short circuits, or faulty modules that may be causing excessive errors.

Time-out: Device missed messages → check that specific device/module.
Bus-off: Device disconnected due to errors → check network errors and wiring integrity.

By knowing whether the code indicates a time-out or bus-off, you can target your testing more effectively.

Arbitration - the process used to decide which electronic control unit (ECU) is allowed to send a message on the network when multiple ECUs try to send at the same time.

Transmission errors - mistakes that occur when data is sent between electronic control units (ECUs) in a vehicle.

Bus-off - a safety state in a CAN Bus system where an electronic control unit (ECU) temporarily disconnects itself from the network after it detects too many communication errors.

SENT network protocol

As vehicles become more complex, the demand for fast and reliable digital communication between sensors and control units has increased. One solution used in some powertrain systems is the **SENT** protocol, which stands for **Single Edge Nibble Transmission**.

Communication Protocol & Voltage Regulation

What is SENT?

SENT is a **unidirectional** digital communication protocol developed specifically for use in automotive applications. It was designed to transmit data from simple sensors (like pressure or temperature sensors) to engine control units (ECUs) in a low-cost and high-accuracy way.

Unlike more complex protocols such as CAN or LIN, SENT is meant for **point-to-point** connections, where one sensor sends data to one receiver; typically used where high-resolution sensor data is required, but a full communication Bus isn't necessary.

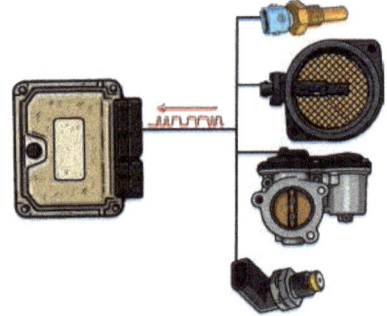

Figure 5.5 SENT arrangement (topology)

SENT transmits data using **pulse width modulation (PWM)**, where the time between signal edges represents data values. Each message is made up of small chunks of information called **nibbles** (a nibble is 4 bits of binary data).

Table 5.3 describes the message structure of a SENT message.

Table 5.3 SENT message structure

Message Structure	Function / Description
Sync pulse	Helps the receiver align its timing to the incoming data.
Status nibble	Contains extra information like diagnostics or sensor health.
Data nibbles	Usually 6 nibbles (24 bits) carrying the main sensor data.
CRC nibble	A checksum used for error checking.
Pause pulse	Optional; allows the system to space out the messages if needed.

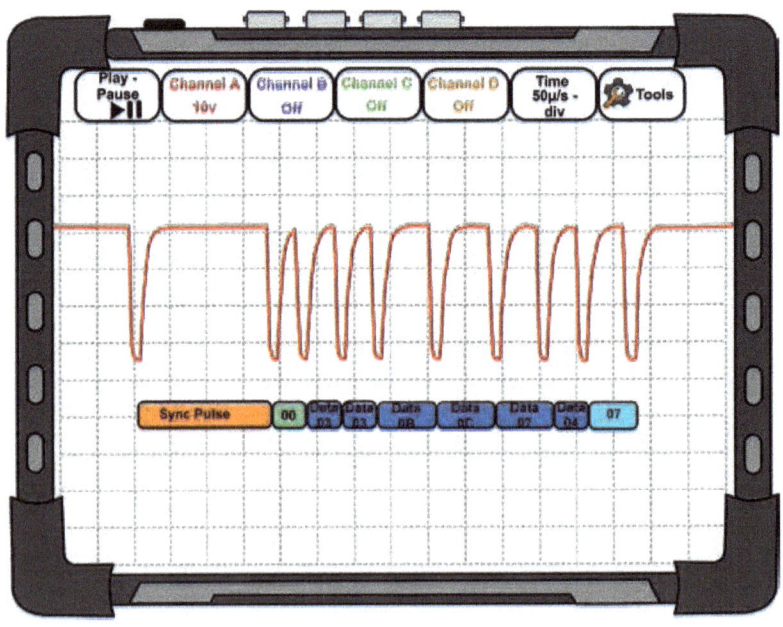

Figure 5.6 SENT waveform

Communication Protocol & Voltage Regulation

 SENT does not use a **clock signal**, unlike some serial protocols, so timing is extremely important. The receiving ECU measures the length of each pulse to determine the value being sent.

SENT is commonly used in:

- Throttle position sensors
- Pressure sensors (such as fuel rail pressure)
- Temperature sensors
- Air mass meters

Its use is especially popular in engine and transmission systems, where **high-resolution**, **low-latency** data is required, but where the sensor itself is relatively simple and doesn't need to send or receive complex messages.

Benefits	Limitations
SENT has several benefits for vehicle designers:	While SENT is very useful, it does have some limitations:
<ul><li>High resolution: Can send very detailed sensor data.</li><li>Simple wiring: Only requires a single wire for data transmission, reducing cost and weight.</li><li>Noise immunity: Designed to resist electrical noise, making it reliable even in harsh automotive environments.</li><li>Cost-effective: Ideal for sensors that don't need full two-way communication.</li></ul>	<ul><li>Unidirectional: Data flows only from the sensor to the ECU. It cannot receive commands.</li><li>Short distance: Best suited for short cable runs within the engine compartment.</li><li>Timing-sensitive: Both the sensor and ECU must be precisely timed, which can be challenging in noisy environments.</li></ul>

LIN network protocol

Not every function in a vehicle needs the speed and complexity of a CAN Bus system. That's where **LIN (Local Interconnect Network)** comes in.

LIN is a low-cost, single-wire communication protocol developed specifically for use in vehicles, particularly for non-critical systems like interior electronics. LIN is often used as a companion network to CAN, handling simpler tasks while CAN manages the more critical, high-speed operations.

LIN is commonly used in systems such as:

- Electric window and mirror controls
- Seat adjustments
- Climate control flaps and sensors
- Sunroof and convertible roof motors
- Door locks and lighting controls

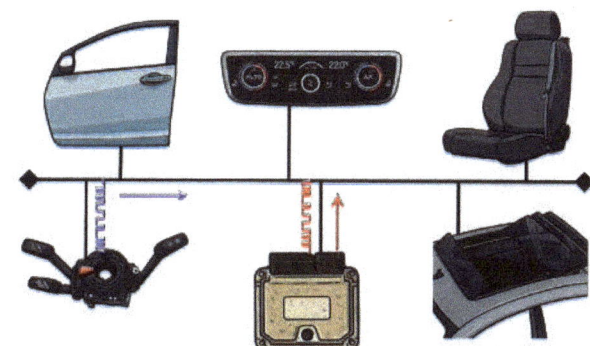

Figure 5.7 LIN arrangement (topology)

Communication Protocol & Voltage Regulation

A LIN network consists of:

- One master node (often a small ECU or a gateway connected to the CAN network).
- One or more slave nodes (simple devices like switches, motors, or sensors).

Communication on the LIN Bus is always controlled by the master. The master sends out a schedule of messages, and slaves respond only when requested. This method is called **master-slave polling**.

Unlike CAN, which is multi-master and allows messages to be sent by any ECU at any time (with arbitration), LIN uses a single master, ensuring there are no message collisions.

The LIN protocol was developed by a group of automotive manufacturers and suppliers under the LIN Consortium, which is now part of the Domestic Automotive Control (DAC) alliance. While the protocol itself is standardised and publicly documented, companies or manufacturers do not have to pay royalties or licensing fees to use the LIN protocol. They can implement the protocol in their electronic control units (ECUs) freely, provided they adhere to the standards.

Key Features of LIN

- Single-wire communication (plus ground).
- Speed up to 20 kbps (sufficient for non-critical systems).
- Low cost (ideal for simple electronics).
- Self-synchronising using a sync byte.
- Checks for data errors using checksums and **parity bits.**

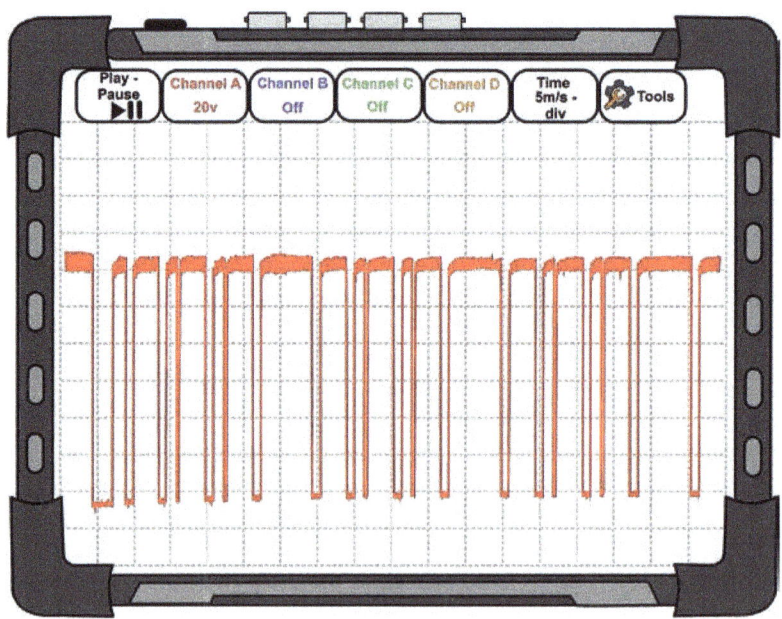

Figure 5.8 LIN waveform

Communication Protocol & Voltage Regulation

Message structure in LIN

Table 5.4 describes the message structure of LIN.

Table 5.4 LIN message structure

Message Structure	Function / Description
Break Field	Signals the start of a new message (master-generated).
Sync Field	Allows slave nodes to synchronise their timing.
Identifier	Tells which node should respond and what kind of data is expected.
Data Bytes	The actual data (up to 8 bytes).
Checksum	Used to check for errors in transmission.

How CAN and LIN work together

In many vehicles, LIN is connected to the main CAN Bus via a **gateway** ECU. This allows data to be shared between simple devices on the LIN network and the more complex ECUs on the CAN Bus. For example, a button press on a LIN-connected switch (like a window control) may be relayed to the body control module (BCM) over CAN.

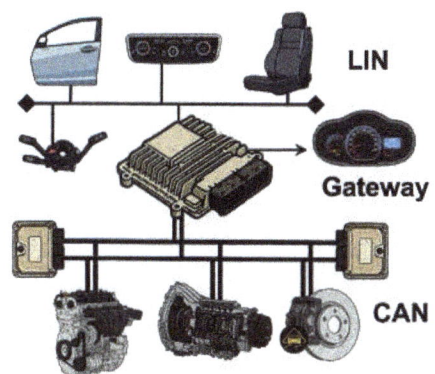

Figure 5.9 LIN – CAN gateway arrangement (topology)

Single Edge Nibble Transmission (SENT) - a digital communication protocol used in vehicles to send sensor data from devices like pressure, position, or temperature sensors to an electronic control unit (ECU).

Unidirectional - data or signals flow in only one direction—from a sender to a receiver. The receiver does not send anything back.

Point-to-point - a direct connection between two devices, such as one sensor and one control unit (ECU).

Pulse Width Modulation (PWM) - a method of controlling power to devices like motors, lights, or sensors by switching a signal on and off very quickly. The amount of time the signal is 'on' versus 'off' (called the duty cycle) determines how much power the device receives.

Nibbles - a group of 4 bits (half a byte) used to represent small amounts of digital data.

Clock signal - a timing signal used to synchronise data transmission between electronic components.

High-resolution - the ability to measure or display very small changes in signals, data, or images with great accuracy.

Low-latency - very little delay between sending and receiving data.

Communication Protocol & Voltage Regulation

Local Interconnect Network (LIN) - a low-cost, simple communication protocol used in vehicles to connect devices like window controls, mirrors, and seat motors.

Master-slave polling - a communication method used in vehicle networks like LIN, where one main controller (the master) controls when other devices (slaves) are allowed to talk.

Parity bits - extra bits added to data in vehicle communication to help check for errors.

Gateway - a device or module in a vehicle that connects different networks or communication systems, allowing data to be shared and translated between them.

FlexRay network protocol

As vehicles have become more advanced, with features like adaptive cruise control, electric power steering, and automated driving, manufacturers needed a communication system that's faster and more reliable than traditional CAN Bus. **FlexRay** was developed to meet these demands.

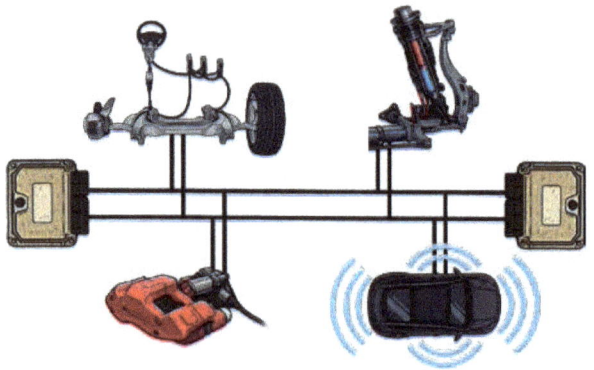

FlexRay is an advanced, high-speed, and fault-tolerant communication protocol used in automotive networks. It was designed to handle critical systems that require precise timing and fast data exchange, such as braking, steering, and driver-assist technologies.

FlexRay can transmit data at speeds of up to 10 Mbps, which is significantly faster than the standard CAN Bus (typically 500 Kbps to 1 Mbps). This speed, combined with a very reliable and predictable timing system, makes FlexRay ideal for time-sensitive applications.

Figure 5.10 FlexRay arrangement (topology)

CAN Bus is ideal for many vehicle systems, but it wasn't originally designed to handle the strict timing requirements of real-time control systems. For example, if an automated braking system needs to activate in milliseconds, any delay or data loss can be critical.

FlexRay was introduced to:

- Improve speed and bandwidth.
- Provide deterministic communication (where timing is predictable).
- Offer **redundancy** for critical systems.
- Work alongside CAN, LIN, and Ethernet in a multi-network vehicle architecture.

FlexRay uses two communication channels, called Channel A and Channel B. These channels can work together for increased data speed or separately to provide backup in case one channel fails.
FlexRay operates in **time cycles**, where each cycle is split into two parts:

1. **Static Segment**: Predefined time slots assigned to each node. This ensures that messages from critical systems always arrive on time.
2. **Dynamic Segment**: Flexible time slots used by less critical messages, similar to how CAN Bus handles data.

Communication Protocol & Voltage Regulation

This structure allows both **deterministic communication** for safety systems and **flexible communication** for non-critical data.

Deterministic communication is like traffic lights for data; each message knows exactly when it can go, so there are no delays or surprises. This is crucial for safety features like braking or airbags that need reliable, on-time responses.

Flexible communication is like walkie-talkie systems that talk when they need to, which is useful for non-critical tasks like entertainment or navigation updates.

Message structure in FlexRay

Table 5.5 describes the message structure of FlexRay.

Table 5.5 FlexRay message structure

Message Structure	Function / Description
Header Segment	Contains metadata about the frame.

Field	Size (bits)	Description
Reserved	1	Reserved for future use.
Payload Preamble Indicator	1	Indicates if a **preamble** exists.
Null Frame Indicator	1	Indicates a null frame.
Sync Frame Indicator	1	Indicates a synchronisation frame.
Startup Frame Indicator	1	Indicates a startup frame.
Frame ID	11	Unique ID for scheduling the frame.
Payload Length	7	Number of 2-byte words in the payload.
Header CRC	11	CRC for detecting errors in the header.
Cycle Count	6	Counter for the communication cycle.

Message Structure	Function / Description
Payload Segment	Carries the actual application data.

Field	Size	Description
Data	0–254 bytes (127 words)	Payload data

- The size is determined by the Payload Length in the header.
- Maximum size is 254 bytes.

Message Structure	Function / Description
Trailer Segment	Used for error detection of the payload.

Field	Size (bits)	Description
CRC	24	Cyclic Redundancy Check for header + payload

Communication Protocol & Voltage Regulation

Key Features of FlexRay	
Feature	Description
High Speed	Up to 10 Mbps—suitable for fast control systems.
Dual Channels	Two physical channels offer redundancy and reliability.
Time-Triggered Communication	Messages are sent at precise times, essential for real-time control.
Fault Tolerance	Built-in error detection and backup paths enhance safety.
Determinism	Ensures messages arrive exactly when they're supposed to.

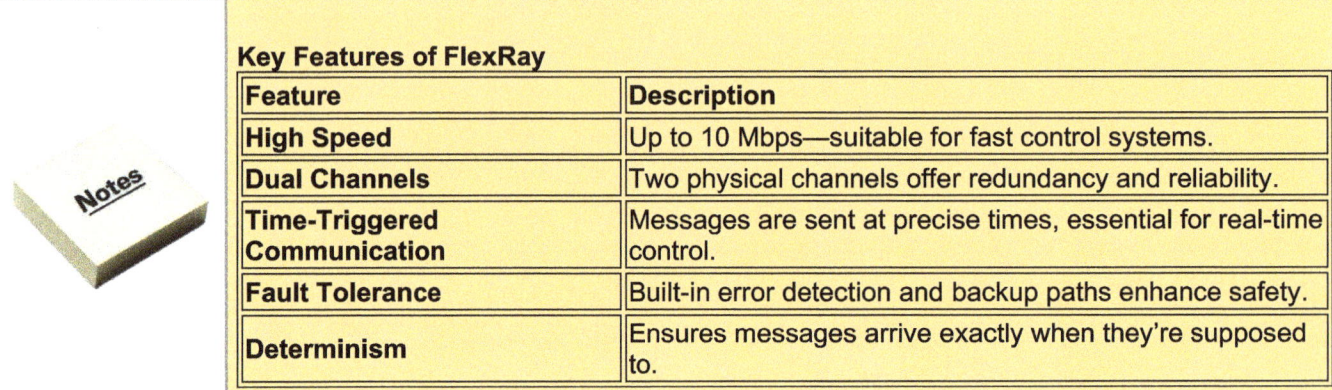

FlexRay - a high-speed, reliable communication protocol used in automotive design to connect electronic control units (ECUs).

Redundancy - having backup systems or components in a vehicle to ensure safety and continued operation if the main system fails.

Deterministic communication - messages between vehicle systems are delivered at exact, predictable times.

Flexible communication - messages between vehicle systems can be sent as needed, without a strict schedule.

Preamble - a special bit pattern sent at the start of a FlexRay frame to help receivers detect and prepare for incoming data.

Payload - the part of a FlexRay message that carries the actual data being sent between vehicle systems.

Ethernet network protocol

Ethernet is a communication protocol originally developed for computers and office networks; Automotive Ethernet is a version of this protocol designed to connect vehicle systems quickly and efficiently.
As cars have become more like computers on wheels, they need to transfer large amounts of data. Traditional protocols like CAN or LIN are reliable but slower. That's where Ethernet comes in, it offers much faster data speeds, which are essential for features like cameras, sensors, **infotainment** systems, and **advanced driver assistance systems (ADAS)**.

Figure 5.11 Ethernet arrangement (topology)

Communication Protocol & Voltage Regulation

Think of Ethernet like a multi-lane highway where messages (data packets) travel from one system to another. Each message knows its destination and follows the rules of the road to get there without crashing into others.

In simple terms:
- Each car system (like a camera or ECU) is a driver.
- The Ethernet cable is the road.
- The protocol is the traffic rules.

Messages are broken into **packets** and sent across the network. Ethernet ensures that they arrive at the right place, in the correct order, and without being corrupted.

Message structure in Ethernet

Table 5.6 describes the message structure of Automotive Ethernet.

Table 5.6 Automotive Ethernet message structure

Message Structure	Function / Description
Preamble	A short sequence at the start that tells other devices a frame is coming.
Destination Address	Who the message is for.
Source Address	Who sent the message.
Type/Length Field	What kind of data is inside.
Payload	The actual data being sent (like camera images or commands).
CRC (Cyclic Redundancy Check)	An error check to make sure the data isn't damaged or corrupted.

Why Ethernet matters in modern vehicles

- Speed: Ethernet can transfer data at speeds of 100 Mbps, 1 Gbps, or even more.
- Capacity: More data from more sensors means Ethernet can handle the load better than older systems.
- Flexibility: Ethernet can support many types of applications; everything from backup cameras to **over-the-air (OTA) updates**.

Voltage and wiring

- Automotive Ethernet typically uses differential signalling on twisted pair cables.
- It often runs on **100BASE-T1**, a single twisted pair that supports 100 Mbps.
- It's designed to work with the vehicle's 12V or 48V electrical system, and withstand harsh conditions like heat, vibration, and electromagnetic interference (EMI).

Communication Protocol & Voltage Regulation

Ethernet comparison with CAN Bus

Feature	CAN Bus	Ethernet
Speed	Up to 1 Mbps	100 Mbps to 1 Gbps
Data Size	Small (8 bytes typical)	Large (up to 1500 bytes per frame)
Use Case	Engine, brakes, airbags	Cameras, radar, infotainment
Priority	Built-in message priority	Uses network switching
Cost	Lower	Higher (but decreasing)

Ethernet - a high-speed communication system used in modern vehicles to connect electronic components like cameras, sensors, and control units.

Infotainment - the system in a vehicle that combines information and entertainment features for the driver and passengers.

Advanced driver assistance systems (ADAS) - smart features in vehicles that help the driver stay safe and make driving easier.

Packets - small bundles of data sent between electronic systems in a vehicle.

Over-the-air (OTA) updates - wireless software updates sent to a vehicle, similar to how smartphones receive updates.

100BASE-T1 - a special cable system that lets car parts talk to each other at high speed using just two wires, saving space and weight.

UART network protocol

UART stands for **Universal Asynchronous Receiver/Transmitter**. It is a simple, widely used communication protocol that allows two electronic devices to talk to each other by sending **serial data** one bit at a time.
In automotive systems, UART is often used for communication between microcontrollers, sensors, and diagnostic tools. While it's not as common as CAN or Ethernet for complex vehicle networks, UART is important for simpler data exchanges and debugging.

Figure 5.12 UART arrangement (topology)

Communication Protocol & Voltage Regulation

 Imagine UART as a one-lane road where cars (bits of data) travel one after another, without needing a traffic light or stop signs to keep them in sync.

With UART:

- Information is **asynchronous,** meaning there is no shared clock signal between sender and receiver.
- Both devices agree on a fixed speed (called baud rate), such as 9600 or 115200 bits per second.
- Data is sent in a start-bit, data bits, optional parity bit, and stop-bit format.

Message structure in UART

Table 5.7 describes the message structure of UART.

Table 5.7 UART message structure

Message Structure	Function / Description
Start Bit	Signals the beginning of data transmission (usually a low voltage).
Data Bits	The actual information (usually 7 or 8 bits) sent one at a time.
Parity Bit (optional)	Used for simple error checking (can be even, odd, or none).
Stop Bit(s)	Marks the end of the data frame (usually one or two bits).

Voltage and wiring in UART

- UART typically uses two wires: one for transmitting (TX) and one for receiving (RX).
- It works on simple voltage levels, often 5V or 3.3V in automotive electronics.
- Unlike CAN, UART does not use differential signalling, so it is more susceptible to electrical noise and interference.
- Because UART is point-to-point (one sender, one receiver), it does not support multi-node networks without additional hardware.

UART is used in vehicles for:

- **Diagnostics and Programming:** Many scan tools and ECU programming devices use UART interfaces to communicate with vehicle modules.
- **Simple Sensor Communication:** Some sensors or modules send data via UART to control units.
- **Bootloading** and **Debugging**: Engineers use UART to upload software or troubleshoot systems during development.

UART is a straightforward serial communication protocol used in vehicles for simple, direct data exchange between two devices. While not suitable for complex networks, it remains essential for diagnostics, programming, and basic sensor communication.

Communication Protocol & Voltage Regulation

MOST network protocol

MOST stands for **Media Oriented Systems Transport** and is a specialised automotive network protocol built for high-quality **multimedia** communication. It's ideal for infotainment systems where smooth audio and video performance is essential. Although newer vehicles are gradually moving toward Automotive Ethernet for similar roles, MOST is still found in many existing systems, especially in luxury and high-end models.

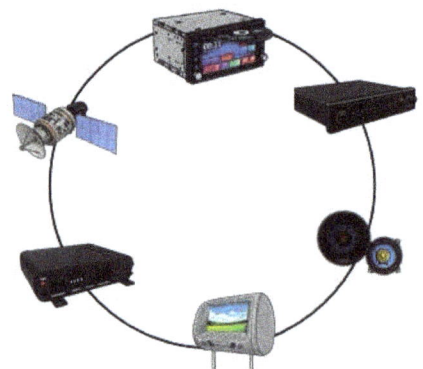

Figure 5.13 MOST arrangement (topology)

As vehicles became more advanced, vehicle manufacturers needed a network that could handle high-quality audio and video streams between components like:

- Radios and media players
- Rear-seat entertainment systems
- Navigation units
- Amplifiers and speakers
- Bluetooth and hands-free modules
- Displays and control panels

How MOST works

MOST is different from other protocols like CAN or LIN. It is not designed for real-time control or safety systems. Instead, it's optimised for continuous, **high-bandwidth** data, especially streaming.

- It works like a **ring network**: Devices (nodes) are connected in a circle. Data flows in one direction around the ring.
- Each node (such as a media player or display) receives the data, checks if it's for them, and either uses it or passes it on.
- MOST supports synchronous data transmission, perfect for audio and video that must stay in sync.

MOST can carry three types of data:

1. **Synchronous data**: For time-critical streams like audio and video.
2. **Asynchronous data**: For less time-sensitive information, like software updates or control commands.
3. Control messages: For managing and configuring devices on the network.

MOST physical layers: Fiber and copper

MOST has several versions, depending on how the data travels physically and these are shown in **Table 5.8**.

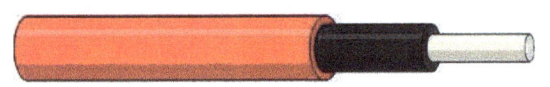

Figure 5.14 POF plastic optical fibre

Table 5.8 MOST versions

Version	Medium Used	Speed
MOST25	Plastic Optical Fiber (POF)	25 Mbps
MOST50	Plastic Optical Fiber (POF)	50 Mbps
MOST150	Optical Fiber or Copper	150 Mbps

- **Optical fibre** is immune to electrical noise, which is great for clear signal transmission in the noisy automotive environment.
- Newer versions can use **unshielded twisted pair (UTP)** copper wires, which lowers cost and simplifies manufacturing.

Communication Protocol & Voltage Regulation

Universal Asynchronous Receiver/Transmitter (UART) - a simple communication method that lets two electronic devices send data back and forth one bit at a time without needing a shared clock.

Asynchronous - means data is sent without a shared timing signal (clock) between devices.

Bootloading - the process of updating or loading software into a vehicle's electronic control unit (ECU) when the device starts up.

Debugging - finding and fixing problems or errors in a vehicle's electronic or software systems.

Media Oriented Systems Transport (MOST) - a communication network in cars designed to send high-quality audio and video between entertainment and multimedia devices.

Multimedia - the audio, video, and interactive entertainment features in a vehicle.

High-bandwidth - the ability to transfer a large amount of data quickly between vehicle systems.

Ring network - a type of communication setup where vehicle devices are connected in a circular loop, passing data around the ring from one device to the next.

Synchronous data - data that is sent and received at precise, regular time intervals, synced between devices.

Asynchronous data - data sent without needing devices to be perfectly timed or synchronised.

Optical fibre - a thin, flexible glass or plastic cable that uses light to transmit data quickly and without interference.

Unshielded twisted pair (UTP) - a type of cable made of two wires twisted together to reduce electrical interference, commonly used for data communication in vehicles.

Power Supply

In any vehicle communication network, whether it's CAN Bus, FlexRay, Ethernet, or others, a stable power supply voltage is crucial for reliable operation.

- Power supply integrity means the vehicle's electronic control units (ECUs) and communication modules receive a consistent voltage level within their required range.
- If the voltage is too low or fluctuates too much, the modules may misinterpret signals, lose communication, or even shut down unexpectedly.
- Stable voltage ensures that all parts of the network work together smoothly, maintaining accurate data exchange essential for vehicle performance and safety.

Communication Protocol & Voltage Regulation

A voltage drop happens when the voltage level at a device's power input is lower than at the source (battery or power supply).

In vehicles, voltage drops can be caused by:

- Long or thin wiring with high electrical resistance.
- Loose or corroded connections and terminals.
- High current draw from multiple devices operating simultaneously.
- Poor grounding or shared ground paths.
- Battery issues or alternator problems.

Voltage drops can cause several issues in vehicle networks:

- Data Corruption: Electronic modules may misread signals or data bits because the voltage is not strong enough to represent the correct logic levels.
- Communication Loss: Modules may temporarily lose connection with the network or fail to respond.
- Component Damage: Repeated undervoltage or voltage spikes can damage sensitive ICs (integrated circuits) or reduce their lifespan.
- Intermittent Faults: Voltage instability often causes intermittent issues that are hard to diagnose, leading to unreliable vehicle behaviour.

To prevent voltage-related problems, vehicles use:

- Voltage regulators: These keep the voltage supplied to modules steady, despite changes in battery voltage or load conditions.
- Fuses and circuit breakers: Protect wiring and modules from overcurrent or short circuits.
- Proper wiring design: Using the correct wire gauge and routing to minimise resistance and interference.
- Good grounding practices: Ensuring clean, solid ground connections for reliable return paths.

Checking Power Supply Integrity
- Always inspect wiring and connectors for corrosion, looseness, or damage.
- Use a multimeter to measure voltage at the module connector, especially during operation, to detect drops.
- Check the battery condition and alternator output, as weak power sources often cause voltage instability.
- Be cautious when adding aftermarket electronics, which can increase load and cause unexpected voltage drops.

Safety and High-Voltage Handling

Electrical voltage creates a potential danger when it comes to the possibility of electric shock or electrocution. Once the electrical pressure (voltage) reaches a point where it can overcome the natural resistance of the human body and a circuit is created with two points of contact in parallel to a power source, electric current will start to flow. The touch threshold (resistance) for dry human skin is often considered to be 50 volts; however, this value can be lower if the skin is wet, there are wounds present, or the electrodes penetrate the skin. Once current starts to flow, 80 milliamps (remember that a milliamp is jut 1000th of an amp) has the potential to cause injury or even death.

Communication Protocol & Voltage Regulation

Regarding the hazards of voltage and current (amps), voltage is often considered the dangerous element, which is why warning signs typically state 'Danger High Voltage'. If a voltage exceeds the touch threshold of dry human skin, it can cause an electric current to flow, and it's this current that can cause harm. Keeping the voltage potential low reduces the risk of electric shock or electrocution. However, even with low voltage, there's still a risk of a short circuit that can lead to arcing, fire, or explosion.
Make sure you are continually evaluating the risks of electricity when conducting any diagnosis or repair.

It is also important to consider the voltages being tested during a diagnostic procedure, in order to protect the operator, equipment and vehicle.

Application-specific diagnostics

Application-specific diagnostics involves focusing on particular systems within the vehicle and tailoring diagnostic techniques to meet the specific requirements of these components. For example, assessing the performance of hybrid and electric vehicles (EVs) requires specialised knowledge and tools to test critical components such as inverters, battery management systems, and motor controllers. The complexities of these systems necessitate a thorough understanding of the systems to identify potential issues accurately. Similarly, other systems require distinct diagnostic methods, each designed to detect and address specific problems.

Hybrid and EV system diagnostics

Working on hybrid and electric vehicles (EVs) presents unique challenges and hazards. You must exercise caution and adhere strictly to safety protocols when working on or around the high-voltage systems to prevent serious injury or death.

Work and diagnostic testing of high-voltage systems should only be conducted if you have received adequate training, using the correct Personal Protective Equipment (PPE), fully insulated tooling, and correctly rated and calibrated diagnostic electrical test equipment.

Any diagnostic descriptions in this book are designed to support knowledge and understanding, but do not act as a substitute for appropriate training. Never attempt any diagnosis or repairs unless you are suitably qualified and have the correct tools, equipment, and safety measures in place.

Communication Protocol & Voltage Regulation

Setup and testing of components

The successful diagnosis of hybrid and EV systems requires a thorough understanding of the components involved and the use of specialised diagnostic equipment. In-vehicle network systems may help with the control of high-voltage components in hybrid and electric vehicles (EVs), and although the communication circuits should be isolated from the high-voltage circuits, caution must be exercised when working close to these systems.

Due to the dangers involved with testing high voltage systems, test and diagnostic procedures in this book will be restricted to low-voltage network communication systems only. In order to diagnose high-voltage faults, you should undertake specific EV training and have access to certified equipment and Personal Protective Equipment. Further details can be found in the textbook *Principles of Electric Vehicle Technology*.

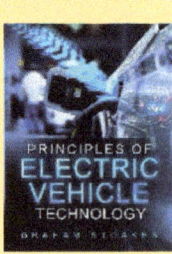

Isolation Techniques

In modern vehicles, high-voltage systems like hybrid or electric powertrains coexist with low-voltage communication networks such as CAN Bus. **Isolation** means physically and electrically separating these systems to prevent high-voltage currents or noise from damaging or interfering with sensitive low-voltage CAN circuits.

Why is isolation important?

- Protects low-voltage components: CAN controllers and ECUs operate at low voltages (typically 5V or 3.3V). Exposure to high voltage can cause permanent damage.
- Prevents electrical noise: High-voltage systems generate noise and voltage spikes that can corrupt CAN communication signals.
- Enhances safety: Isolation protects technicians and vehicle occupants by preventing dangerous voltage from traveling into low-voltage systems.
- Ensures reliable communication: Reduces errors and data loss caused by interference from the high-voltage environment.

Isolation uses special components and design techniques to block direct electrical connections while still allowing data signals or power to pass safely:

1. Optocouplers (Optical Isolation):
    - Use light to transfer signals across an electrical barrier.
    - Convert electrical signals into light on one side, then back into electrical signals on the other.
    - Completely separate electrical circuits while allowing communication.
2. Digital Isolators:
    - Use capacitive or magnetic coupling instead of light to transmit data across isolation barriers.
    - Provide fast, reliable data transfer with high noise immunity.
3. Isolated CAN Transceivers:
    - Specialised CAN **transceiver** chips with built-in isolation.
    - Separate the CAN controller (low voltage) from the CAN Bus lines (which may be exposed to higher voltages or noise).
4. Galvanic Isolation:
    - A general term for any method that prevents direct electrical connection, ensuring no current flows between isolated sections.

Communication Protocol & Voltage Regulation

Practical examples of isolation in vehicles

- Hybrid/Electric Vehicles: High-voltage battery systems are isolated from CAN networks controlling vehicle functions.
- Charging Systems: Isolation prevents voltage spikes from the charger affecting CAN communication.
- Body Control Modules: Often isolated to avoid interference from the car's 12V electrical systems and prevent ground loops.

Equipotential Bonding and shielding in EV cables to prevent EMI

In electric vehicles (EVs), powerful electrical systems run alongside sensitive communication networks like CAN Bus or Ethernet. EVs have high-voltage cables carrying strong currents for batteries, motors, and chargers. These high currents create electromagnetic fields, which can induce unwanted electrical noise in nearby low-voltage data cables. Noise or EMI can cause communication errors, leading to loss of data or malfunction of in-vehicle network systems like CAN Bus.

Two key methods used are:
- **Equipotential Bonding:** Connecting metal parts and cable shields together at the same electrical potential (voltage level) to avoid differences that cause noise currents.
- **Shielding:** Wrapping cables with conductive material to block external electromagnetic interference (EMI) from reaching the cables inside.

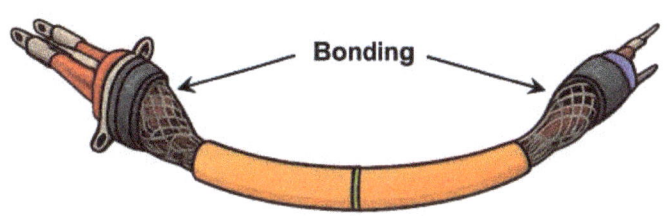

Figure 5.15 Equipotential bonding

How equipotential bonding works

- Equipotential bonding connects all metal parts and cable shields to a common ground or reference point.
- This creates a **uniform electrical potential**, so there's no voltage difference that would cause current to flow between parts.
- By preventing stray currents, it reduces the chance of interference leaking into communication cables.
- Bonding also helps protect technicians from electrical shocks by ensuring metal parts carry equal voltages in the event of a high-voltage circuit **insulation failure**.

How shielding works

- Shielding uses layers of metal foil or braided wire wrapped around cables.
- This conductive layer acts like a barrier, absorbing or reflecting electromagnetic noise before it can reach the sensitive wires inside.
- Shields are typically connected to ground through equipotential bonding, allowing any captured noise currents to safely dissipate.
- Shielding is especially important for CAN Bus, Ethernet, and sensor cables located near high-voltage wiring.

Equipotential Bonding	**Shielding**
Equalises voltage to stop stray currents.	Blocks external electromagnetic fields.
Connects metal parts and shields to ground.	Wraps cables with conductive materials.
Protects against voltage differences that cause noise.	Protects signal wires from picking up noise.
Enhances technician safety.	Improves signal quality and communication reliability.

Communication Protocol & Voltage Regulation

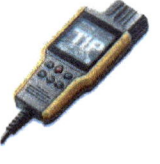

Working with EV Cables:

- Always ensure **shield continuity,** broken or loose shields can let EMI in.
- Check that equipotential bonding points are secure and free of corrosion.
- Avoid running low-voltage data cables too close and parallel to high-voltage cables without proper shielding and bonding.
- Use manufacturer-recommended cables and follow wiring guidelines to maintain proper shielding and bonding.

Working with Isolated CAN Networks:

- Always use the correct insulated diagnostic tools when working on high-voltage vehicles.
- Check isolation components if you encounter CAN communication faults near high-voltage sections.
- Avoid bridging or bypassing isolation barriers, they are critical for safety and proper function.
- Verify proper grounding and shielding to complement isolation and reduce noise further.

Isolation - keeping different electrical parts separate so that high voltages or electrical noise don't interfere with sensitive low-voltage components.

Transceiver - a device that both sends and receives data signals between electronic control units (ECUs) and the vehicle's communication network (like CAN Bus).

Equipotential Bonding (EPB) - connecting all metal parts and cable shields together so they share the same electrical voltage level.

Shielding - wrapping cables or components with a protective layer of metal to block unwanted electrical noise.

Uniform electrical potential - all connected metal parts or components have the same voltage level.

Insulation failure - the protective coating around wires or cables gets damaged, allowing electricity to leak or short-circuit.

Shield continuity - the metal shield around a cable is unbroken and properly connected from one end to the other.

Communication Protocol & Voltage Regulation

Protective Measures for Automotive Network Components

Vehicle communication networks like CAN Bus rely on sensitive electronic components, ECUs, transceivers and sensors that must operate safely and reliably. Electrical faults such as short circuits, voltage spikes, or overloads can damage these components or cause network failures. To prevent this, vehicles use protective devices including fuses, relays, and diodes.

Fuses: The first line of defence

- What they do: Fuses protect wiring and components by breaking the electrical circuit when current exceeds a safe level.
- How they work: Inside the fuse is a thin wire that melts if too much current flows, stopping electricity from reaching downstream parts.
- Why important: This prevents wires from overheating, components from burning out, and potential fires.
- Example: If a short circuit occurs in a CAN Bus module wiring, the fuse will blow to cut off power before damage happens.

Figure 5.16 Fuses

Relays: Controlled switching for safety

- What they do: Relays are electrically operated switches that control high current circuits using a low current signal.
- How they work: A small electric current activates an internal switch, allowing larger current to flow safely without running high power through control modules.
- Why important: Relays protect sensitive electronic control units by isolating them from heavy electrical loads and allowing safe power control.
- Example: A relay might switch power to a CAN Bus transceiver only when the vehicle ignition is on, protecting it from unwanted voltage surges.

Figure 5.17 Relays

Diodes: Preventing voltage damage and protecting directional flow

- What they do: Diodes allow current to flow in one direction only, blocking harmful reverse currents that could damage electronics.
- How they work: A diode acts like a one-way valve for electricity, ensuring current flows correctly and preventing voltage spikes from traveling backward through circuits.
- Why important: Diodes protect against voltage spikes from inductive loads (like motors or relays) and prevent damage to CAN network components.
- Example: A diode placed across a relay coil absorbs voltage spikes generated when the relay turns off, protecting nearby CAN electronics from sudden surges.

Figure 5.18 Diodes

How these protective devices work together

Device	Function	Protection Offered
Fuse	Breaks circuit during overcurrent.	Prevents overheating, fire, and damage.
Relay	Switches high current with low current signal.	Isolates control electronics from heavy loads.
Diode	Controls current direction and absorbs voltage spikes.	Protects against reverse currents and voltage surges.

Communication Protocol & Voltage Regulation

Inspecting Protective Measures
- Check fuses regularly for signs of blowing or damage; replace only with correct rating fuses.
- Test relays by listening for clicks or using a relay tester to ensure proper switching.
- Inspect diodes in relay circuits and protectors for damage or failure, especially if experiencing voltage spikes or erratic behaviour.
- Always follow manufacturer specifications when replacing or installing protective devices.

Protective measures like fuses, relays, and diodes are essential in safeguarding automotive communication networks. They prevent damage caused by electrical faults, control power safely, and ensure that sensitive CAN Bus components operate reliably.

Conclusion

This chapter has explored the critical aspects of communication protocols and voltage regulation that are vital to modern automotive systems, covering the origins of the CAN Bus and the importance of understanding frame structures, error detection, arbitration, and self-diagnosis for efficient data transmission between Electronic Control Units (ECUs). Additionally, it discussed the significance of a stable power supply and the methods for handling high voltage safely, including isolation techniques and protective measures. By mastering these foundational concepts, you are prepared to diagnose and maintain complex vehicle networks, ensuring safety, reliability, and efficiency in advanced automotive landscapes.

Diagnostics and Testing Principles

Chapter 6 Diagnostics and Testing Principles

In order to maintain and repair vehicle systems effectively, it is essential to understand how diagnostic and testing procedures are applied to CAN Bus and other in-vehicle networks. This chapter provides the key principles of network-based diagnostics, focusing on how faults are detected, interpreted, and addressed using onboard and external diagnostic tools. It covers how diagnostic trouble codes (DTCs) are retrieved and interpreted, and the analysis of networks using oscilloscopes. By developing a solid foundation in these testing principles, you will gain the skills needed to troubleshoot complex electrical systems with confidence and accuracy.

Contents

Diagnosing CAN Bus Systems	**124**
Symptoms of CAN Bus Faults	**124**
Network Topology Verification	**125**
OBDII & UDS	**129**
Using Diagnostic Tools	**135**
Oscilloscope Techniques	**138**
CAN Analysers	**155**
Advanced Diagnostics	**158**
8 Step Diagnostic Best Practice	**159**
Practical Training & Case Studies	**162**

When working on CAN Bus systems and vehicle networks, always remember that these circuits are part of the vehicle's critical control systems. Disconnecting, shorting, or applying the wrong voltage to CAN wiring can cause damage to electronic control units (ECUs), erase data, or even disable safety systems like airbags and ABS.
Before testing or repairing any CAN circuits:

- Always disconnect the battery if specified by the manufacturer's procedures.

- Use the correct diagnostic tools and avoid using standard test lights on CAN wires, as they can overload sensitive circuits.

- Never cut, splice, or tap into CAN wiring without proper guidance, as this can introduce faults and communication errors.

- Be aware that CAN systems operate even when the ignition is off; some ECUs stay awake for a short time after key-off.

Work methodically, follow the vehicle manufacturer's repair information, and always observe health and safety regulations. Taking care around CAN networks will help prevent costly damage and keep vehicle systems operating safely and reliably.

Diagnostics and Testing Principles

Diagnosing CAN Bus Systems

CAN Bus is essential for the proper operation of the vehicle's engine, brakes, airbags, infotainment, lighting, and more. When a fault occurs it can disrupt communication between ECUs, leading to a range of problems that may not be immediately obvious.
Even though CAN systems are designed to be robust and fault-tolerant, they are not immune to issues. Faults can occur due to wiring problems, electrical interference, damaged connectors, water ingress, or faulty ECUs. Diagnosing these problems is essential for ensuring the vehicle operates safely and reliably.

Symptoms of CAN Bus faults

Recognising the signs of a CAN Bus problem is the first step in diagnosing it correctly. Common symptoms include:

1. Intermittent Faults
- These are faults that appear and disappear unpredictably.
- An ECU might lose communication for a few seconds and then recover.
- Lights on the dashboard may flash briefly or warning messages might appear and then go away.
- Intermittent faults can be especially difficult to diagnose because they are not always present when you are testing the vehicle.

2. Network Failures
- A complete failure in the CAN Bus can cause entire systems to stop working.
- For example, if the ABS module loses communication with the powertrain control module (PCM), both systems may set diagnostic codes and disable certain functions.
- This can lead to multiple warning lights being displayed at once, such as ABS, traction control, and check engine.

3. Specific Component Issues
- Sometimes the fault affects only one ECU or sensor, even though the rest of the network is operating correctly.
- This could be due to a faulty control unit, poor grounding, or damaged wiring to that component.
- An example might be a door module that stops responding, resulting in power windows or central locking not working on that side.

When diagnosing faults related to the CAN Bus or other in-vehicle network systems, it's essential to approach the task methodically. Rushing into diagnosis without a clear plan often leads to guesswork, unnecessary part replacement, and wasted time. It can also cause frustration and obscure the real issue.
Instead, begin by carefully reviewing the symptoms.
- Take note of any warning lights, error codes, or unusual vehicle behaviour.
- Gather as much relevant information as possible, this might include customer complaints, scan tool data, and service history.

Doing so helps narrow the fault to a specific area, module, or communication pathway.
Even experienced technicians can fall into the trap of overconfidence, relying on memory or past cases rather than following a structured process. While experience is valuable, it should support, not replace an effective systematic diagnostic routine.

Best Practice: Before touching any tools or components, develop a clear diagnostic plan. Outline the steps you'll take, the tests you'll perform, and the data you'll need to confirm or eliminate possible causes. This disciplined approach improves accuracy, saves time, and builds confidence in your findings.

Diagnostics and Testing Principles

Because so many systems depend on reliable communication over the CAN Bus, diagnosing problems accurately is crucial. Replacing the wrong component can be costly and time-consuming. Using proper diagnostic tools, like scan tools that read live data and trouble codes, and understanding how to interpret CAN Bus waveforms with an oscilloscope, can help pinpoint the exact nature and location of a fault.
By learning to identify the signs of CAN-related issues and applying systematic testing methods, you can save time, reduce unnecessary parts replacement, and improve the quality of your repairs.

Network Topology Verification

In a CAN Bus system, **network topology** refers to the physical layout and wiring of the communication network connecting the ECUs. For the CAN Bus to function correctly, the wiring and electrical components, including **termination resistors**, must be properly installed and in good condition. When diagnosing network issues, verifying the integrity of this layout is a key step.

When investigating possible faults in the CAN Bus or other in-vehicle network systems, one of the most effective starting points is the use of a scan tool. This should be an integral part of your initial planning process.

Begin by retrieving any Diagnostic Trouble Codes (DTCs). These codes provide valuable clues about which systems or components may be affected.
However, modern scan tools offer more than just code reading, they can actively communicate with the vehicle's electronic control units (ECUs), also known as nodes. During the scan tool's initialisation phase, many advanced models will automatically poll each ECU on the network to check for a response. This process helps identify which modules are online and communicating, and which are not.

Visual Topology Mapping:
Some scan tools display this polling process as a simple visual map of the network, often referred to as a network topology diagram. This diagram shows each ECU as a node and highlights any that fail to respond. Non-responding nodes may indicate a fault in the module itself, a wiring issue, or a communication breakdown within the network.

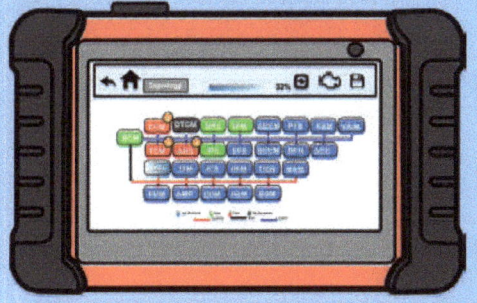

Termination resistors

At each end of the CAN Bus, there should be a 120-ohm termination resistor. These resistors are critical because they:

- Match the electrical impedance of the network.
- Absorb signal reflections.
- Stabilise voltage levels on the CAN lines.

Diagnostics and Testing Principles

It is often possible to conduct an initial diagnosis of network systems at the pins of the vehicle data link connector. Due to the standardised layout of the 16-pin connector the terminals can be identified from the image shown below. Pins 6 and 14 are used for CAN High and Can Low.

17. Manufacturer specific [sometimes used for network communication].
18. Bus positive SAE J1850 PWM and VPW.
19. Manufacturer specific [sometimes used for network communication].
20. Chassis ground.
21. Signal ground.
22. CAN High.
23. K-Line of ISO9141-2 and ISO14230-4.
24. Manufacturer specific [sometimes used for network communication].
25. Manufacturer specific [sometimes used for network communication].
26. Bus negative SAE J1850 PWM.
27. Manufacturer specific [sometimes used for network communication].
28. Manufacturer specific [sometimes used for network communication].
29. Manufacturer specific [sometimes used for network communication].
30. CAN Low.
31. L-Line of ISO9141-2 and ISO14230-4.
32. Battery voltage.

Note: Due to the introduction of security gateways, the DLC may need to be bypassed to access CAN data.

What to check:

- **Step 1**: Use a multimeter set to the ohms (Ω) setting.
- **Step 2**: Disconnect the battery and turn off all modules before testing. If necessary, connect breakouts or a breakout box to avoid damaging components or wiring.
- **Step 3**: Measure resistance across the CAN High and CAN Low pins at the diagnostic connector or at an ECU connector.

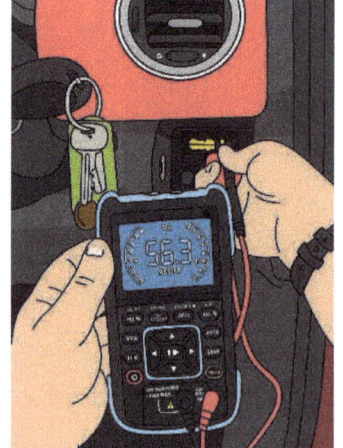

Diagnostics and Testing Principles

Always use non-invasive probing methods or a breakout box to avoid damaging terminals.
Verify termination resistors (\~60 ohms across pins 6 & 14) when the BUS is powered off. This can often be achieved with the ignition off and time given to allow the networks to go to sleep, however, it may sometimes be necessary to disconnect the battery to turn off all of the modules before testing.

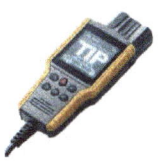

Termination resistances can give a good indication of correct circuit operation. If an ohmmeter is connected in parallel across CAN High and CAN Low (using pins 6 and 14 of the data link connector for example) with the circuit power switched off, then the total recorded resistance will be halved. With 120Ω termination resistors:

- If 60Ω is shown, CAN High and CAN Low should be OK.
- If O/L (infinity) is shown, an open circuit exists in both lines or to the DLC.
- If 0Ω is shown, a dead short exists.
- If 120Ω is shown, one CAN line may be at fault (confirm communication using an oscilloscope).

In most passenger vehicles, a standard CAN Bus uses two 120-ohm termination resistors, one at each end of the network. This setup works well for short to medium wiring lengths, such as those found in typical cars because it keeps the network electrically balanced and prevents signal reflections. However, in larger vehicles like trucks, buses, and commercial vehicles, the wiring length can be much longer, which sometimes requires different resistor values or network layouts to maintain reliable communication.

1. Lower Resistor Values for Short Buses
- In some systems with very short Bus lengths (less than 1 meter), like inside a small ECU cluster, the network may use only one 120-ohm resistor, or reduce resistance to prevent signal over-termination.
- These are usually internal sub-networks and are not as sensitive to reflections due to the short wire length.

2. Adjusted Termination for Long Buses
In very long CAN Bus wiring (over 40 meters), commonly found in articulated buses, trailers, or multi-section trucks, manufacturers may:
- Keep the standard two 120-ohm resistors but pay special attention to cable shielding and connector quality.
- In some custom or heavy-duty designs, use two 100-ohm resistors instead of 120-ohm to better match cable impedance and manage long-distance noise or resistance loss.
- In rare cases, install a third resistor at a midpoint to reduce reflections in unusually complex topologies, but this is manufacturer-specific and not typical of standard CAN designs.

Diagnostics and Testing Principles

Wiring integrity

The twisted pair of CAN wires must be intact and properly routed. Faulty wiring can cause signal degradation or complete communication failure.

What to check:

- Twisting and shielding: Visually inspect the wires to confirm they are twisted together and not running alongside high-voltage or noisy wiring that might cause interference.
- Wiring repairs: look for poor or incorrect wiring repairs, especially to one CAN line only; this can cause interference and communication errors.
- Continuity: Use a multimeter to check that the CAN High and CAN Low wires are continuous from one end of the Bus to the other. Any break will interrupt communication.
- Short circuits: Make sure that CAN High and CAN Low are not shorted together, or to power or ground. This may require the use of an oscilloscope.

Common issues found during topology checks:
- Corroded or damaged connectors (especially at exposed areas like under the bonnet or in door harnesses).
- Pinched, broken, or poorly repaired wires.
- Missing or incorrect termination resistors after ECU replacement or aftermarket installation.
- Water intrusion causing shorts between CAN wires or to ground.

Watch out for Aftermarket Electrical Equipment.
When diagnosing CAN Bus faults, one important thing to keep in mind is the effect of aftermarket electrical accessories. These can include things like:

- Alarm systems
- Remote start modules
- Dash cameras or GPS trackers
- Audio amplifiers and aftermarket infotainment systems
- LED lighting kits or underbody lights

Although these devices may seem unrelated to the vehicle's core systems, if they are installed incorrectly, they can cause serious problems on the CAN network.

Many aftermarket devices tap into the vehicle's wiring to get power, ground, or even connect to CAN wires for data. If this is done without proper knowledge or using improper methods, it can lead to:

- Electrical noise on the CAN lines
- Increased resistance or incorrect voltage levels
- Intermittent communication faults
- Complete CAN Bus failure

Diagnostics and Testing Principles

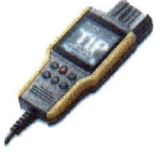

Some aftermarket modules splice directly into the CAN High and CAN Low wires, which can disturb the voltage balance or add extra resistance to the network. This interferes with the signal and may trigger false trouble codes, flashing warning lights, or cause some ECUs to stop responding entirely. When investigating CAN faults, especially intermittent or unusual ones, always ask the driver if any aftermarket devices have been installed. Then:

1. Visually inspect under the dash and near fuse boxes or wiring harnesses for non-OEM wiring, modules, or poorly wrapped splices.
2. Look for twisted pair CAN wires that have been cut or tapped into; this is a red flag.
3. Temporarily disconnect any aftermarket device you suspect may be interfering and recheck the CAN system.

If removing the aftermarket equipment resolves the issue, advise the customer on proper installation using manufacturer-recommended practices or refer them to a qualified installer.

OBD and UDS

Modern vehicles are equipped with an on-board diagnostic system, commonly known as OBD. This system continuously monitors the vehicle's performance, especially its emissions and powertrain, but also in-vehicle networks, and helps detect faults when something goes wrong. Technicians use this system to retrieve diagnostic trouble codes (DTCs) and other data during servicing or repair.

The two most common systems are:

- **OBDII (On-Board Diagnostics, Second Generation)**: used in North America.
- **EOBD (European On-Board Diagnostics)**: the European version, based on the same core standards.

Both systems serve the same purpose: to ensure that vehicles meet emissions standards and to assist in identifying faults through electronic monitoring.

In addition to this, vehicle manufactures have their own onboard diagnostic systems that operate in parallel with OBDII and EOBD.

While OBDII and EOBD provide standardised diagnostic information, mainly focused on emissions and powertrain systems, **OEM (Original Equipment Manufacturer)** diagnostic systems go much further. These manufacturer-specific systems can access detailed data across all vehicle systems, including electric drive, body controls, chassis, infotainment, advanced driver assistance systems (ADAS), and proprietary CAN Bus communications.

For example, an OEM system might show:
- Specific component test results (beyond standard **Mode 6**).
- Module programming options.
- System calibrations or re-learn procedures.
- Real-time data for non-emissions systems (e.g., climate control, air suspension).

However, this enhanced diagnostic information is often **proprietary,** which means:
- Standard scan tools may not be able to access it.
- Only OEM tools or licensed software can fully interact with the system.
- Access may be restricted or require a subscription from the manufacturer.

Diagnostics and Testing Principles

As a result, technicians working outside of a dealership may have limited visibility into some systems, especially for complex issues that require deep integration with OEM diagnostic routines.

Always check whether a fault can be diagnosed using standard OBDII/EOBD, or if OEM-level access is required for deeper troubleshooting.

OBDII (On-Board Diagnostics, Second Generation) - a standardised system in vehicles that monitors and reports on various engine and emissions-related functions.

EOBD (European On-Board Diagnostics) - the European equivalent of the OBDII system used in vehicles.

OEM (Original Equipment Manufacturer) - a company that produces parts, components, or complete vehicles that are supplied and branded by another company, typically the main automaker. OEM parts are made to the original specifications and standards as the parts used in the initial assembly of the vehicle, ensuring compatibility and quality.

Mode 6 - a diagnostic feature in vehicles that provides detailed, real-time testing and data about various sensors and systems.

Proprietary - technology, systems, or parts that are owned and controlled by a specific manufacturer. These are usually unique to that brand or model and may not be available for use or access by other companies or third parties without permission.

Why OBD systems matter

On-board diagnostics are required by law in many regions because they help reduce harmful emissions and make vehicle repair more accurate.

The system:
- Detects faults early, often before they become serious.
- Stores trouble codes for later retrieval.
- Activates warning lights, such as the check engine light (MIL – Malfunction Indicator Lamp).
- Provides real-time data for technicians using a scan tool.

Figure 6.1 A basic diagnostic scan tool

OBDII and EOBD

Table 6.1 describe some of the feature differences between OBDII and EOBD.

Table 6.1 Feature differences between OBDII and EOBD

Feature	OBDII (USA)	EOBD (Europe)
Introduced	1996 (petrol/gasoline), 2007 (diesel)	2001 (petrol/gasoline), 2004 (diesel)
Standard protocols	SAE J1850, CAN, ISO 9141-2	Primarily ISO 15765 (CAN)
Coverage	Emissions and powertrain systems	Emissions and powertrain systems
Connector type	16-pin standard DLC	16-pin standard DLC

Diagnostics and Testing Principles

Despite small differences in protocol or terminology, OBDII and EOBD are mostly interchangeable in terms of diagnostics. Most scan tools support both.

How on-board diagnosis works

The OBD monitors key systems in the vehicle using sensors and electronic control units (ECUs). When it detects a problem that could affect emissions or performance, it:
1. Logs a trouble code in memory (e.g., P0301 – Cylinder 1 misfire).
2. Turns on the MIL (Check Engine Light) if the issue is serious or repeated.
3. Stores freeze frame data (a snapshot of conditions when the fault occurred).
4. Allows access to live data from sensors for further investigation.

Types of Diagnostic Trouble Codes (DTCs)

OBDII and EOBD DTCs are standard across most makes and models, and follow a clear structure:

- **P**** – Powertrain (engine/transmission)
- **B** – Body (e.g., air conditioning, airbags)
- **C** – Chassis (e.g., ABS, steering)
- **U** – Network communication (e.g., CAN Bus faults)

In vehicle diagnostics, the letter 'U' is used at the beginning of a diagnostic trouble code (DTC) to indicate network communication faults. The 'U' stands for 'User Network', which refers to the communication system shared by multiple control modules in the vehicle, primarily the CAN Bus, but also other networks like LIN, FlexRay, or Ethernet.

A common format is:
P0420
- **P** = Powertrain
- **0** = Standard code (manufacturer-specific codes start with 1 or higher)
- **4** = Subsystem (emissions)
- **20** = Specific fault (catalyst efficiency below threshold)

Structure of a U-Code:

Like other DTCs, U-codes follow a standardised format:
- **U** = Network (communication fault)
- **0** = Generic (SAE standard), or **1** = Manufacturer-specific
- Next three digits = Specific system or module

Example:
- U0100 – Lost communication with ECM/PCM
- U0121 – Lost communication with anti-lock brake system (ABS) module

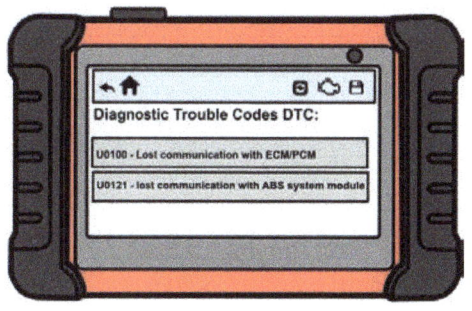

Figure 6.2 Diagnostic U-codes

Diagnostics and Testing Principles

When diagnosing a fault, always check:
- If the DTC is active or stored.
- The live data around the time of the fault.
- Whether the MIL is on or off.
- If the fault is intermittent or permanent.

Record all codes at the beginning of a diagnosis, regardless of whether you think they are relevant to the issue presented. Remember that due to in-vehicle network, faults on seemingly unrelated systems might be causing the problem.

Clear the code only after repairs are complete and you've confirmed the system is operating normally.

UDS

UDS stands for **Unified Diagnostic Services**. It is a **diagnostic communication protocol** used in automotive electronic control units (ECUs), defined in the **ISO 14229** standard.

Purpose: UDS is used to diagnose, test, and reprogram ECUs over in-vehicle networks like CAN, FlexRay, or Ethernet.

It allows technicians and tools to perform operations such as:
- Reading and clearing diagnostic trouble codes (DTCs).
- Reading sensor values and system status.
- Programming or updating ECU software (flashing).
- Performing system tests (e.g. turning components on/off).
- Security access to protected functions (e.g. immobiliser reset).

UDS vs OBD-II:
- OBD-II is a regulatory diagnostic protocol primarily for emissions-related systems.
- UDS is broader and more powerful, often used by manufacturers for deeper diagnostics and ECU development/testing.
- UDS is not limited to emissions and can be used throughout the vehicle, including chassis, body, and infotainment systems.

Common UDS services (Service Hex IDs):

Table 6.2 Common UDS services

Hex ID	Allocation	Mode
0x10	Diagnostic Session Control	Initiates and controls different diagnostic sessions such as default, programming, and extended.
0x11	ECU Reset	Resets the Electronic Control Unit (ECU).
0x14	Clear Diagnostic Information	Clears stored diagnostic trouble codes (DTCs).
0x19	Read DTC Information	Retrieves diagnostic trouble codes.
0x22	Read Data by Identifier	Reads specific data points from the vehicle systems.
0x27	Security Access	Controls access to security-related features.
0x28	Communication Control	Manages communication settings and parameters.
0x2E	Write Data by Identifier	Writes specific data points to the vehicle systems.
0x31	Routine Control	Initiates or controls certain routines for testing or reprogramming.
0x3E	Tester Present	Keeps the diagnostic communication active.
0x85	Control DTC Setting	Enables or disables the setting of diagnostic trouble codes.

Diagnostics and Testing Principles

 These services are used by diagnostic tools to communicate with a vehicle's control systems, perform diagnostics, and conduct various routines needed for maintenance or troubleshooting.

 **Unified Diagnostic Services (UDS)** - a standardised communication protocol used in automotive diagnostics. It facilitates communication between a diagnostic tool and a vehicle's electronic control units (ECUs).

Diagnostic communication protocol - rules that allows a diagnostic tool to communicate with a vehicle's electronic control units (ECUs).

ISO 14229 - an international standard that defines the UDS (Unified Diagnostic Services) protocol used for vehicle diagnostics.

Setting up and using a diagnostic scan tool for testing a CAN Bus network

By setting up and using a diagnostic scan tool effectively, you can efficiently troubleshoot and resolve issues within a CAN Bus network. Understanding how to interpret diagnostic trouble codes, analyse freezeframe data, and evaluate live data is essential in maintaining the health of a vehicle's communication systems and ensuring its smooth operation.

Setup and connection

Step 1
- Select the Appropriate Scan Tool: Begin by choosing a high-quality diagnostic scan tool compatible with the vehicle's make and model.

Step 2
- Connect the Scan Tool: Locate the vehicle's On-Board Diagnostics (OBD-II) port, typically found under the dashboard.
- Connect the scan tool to the OBD-II port using the appropriate cable or wireless/bluetooth VCI. Ensure the connection is secure to avoid any disconnections during diagnostics.

Step 3
- Power On the Scan Tool: Some scan tools may draw power directly from the vehicle's diagnostic socket, while others may require separate power sources.
- Once powered on, follow the on-screen instructions to select the make, model, and year of the vehicle being tested.

Step 4
- Automatic Node Topology Checks: High-quality scan tools will automatically perform checks to identify all nodes (control units) on the network. This feature helps in mapping the network and identifying any missing or malfunctioning nodes that could indicate deeper issues.

Diagnostics and Testing Principles

Code retrieval

Step 1
- Once the network is established, select the 'Read Diagnostic Codes' or similar menu.

Step 2
- Navigate through the scan tool menu to access the stored Diagnostic Trouble Codes (DTCs).
- Retrieve any active or pending codes that indicate specific problems within the CAN Bus or related systems.

Step 3
- After documenting the trouble codes, clear them to see if the issue persists. This can help confirm whether the problem is intermittent or has been resolved.

Review Freezeframe Data:
- Freezeframe data provides a snapshot of various sensor readings and system states at the moment a fault code was triggered.
- Analyse this data to understand the conditions under which the fault occurred, aiding in more accurate diagnostics.

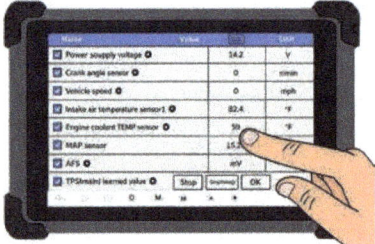

Checking live data

Step 1
- While the system is in operation, monitor 'live data.'

Step 2
- Access the live data stream from various sensors and control units on the CAN Bus.
- Monitor key parameters such as engine speed, temperature, and voltage levels in real-time. This information can help identify abnormalities or confirm the presence of an issue.

Step 3
- Cross-reference live data readings with manufacturer specifications to determine whether they fall within expected ranges.
- Any discrepancies can point to specific areas requiring further investigation.

Diagnostics and Testing Principles

Using Diagnostic Tools

Diagnostic tests on CAN Bus systems using a multimeter

Testing a CAN Bus system with a multimeter is a fundamental step in diagnosing communication issues within a vehicle. While a multimeter cannot read CAN messages, it helps check the physical layer, ensuring proper connections and voltages.

Equipment Needed:
- Digital multimeter.
- Vehicle wiring diagrams.
- Access to the CAN Bus lines (usually at the OBDII connector or near the CAN Bus junction blocks).

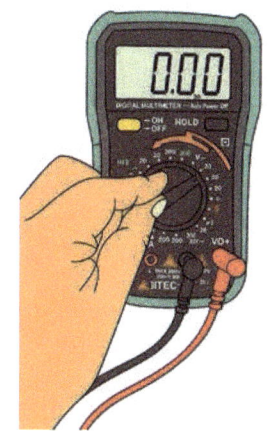

Set up your multimeter

Step 1
- Turn on your multimeter.

Step 2
- Set the multimeter to measure DC voltage. Usually, this is indicated by a 'V' with straight lines.

Step 3
- Select a voltage range higher than 12V (e.g., 20V) to cover typical vehicle voltages.

Step 4
- If your multimeter has a continuity test mode, it can be useful but is optional.

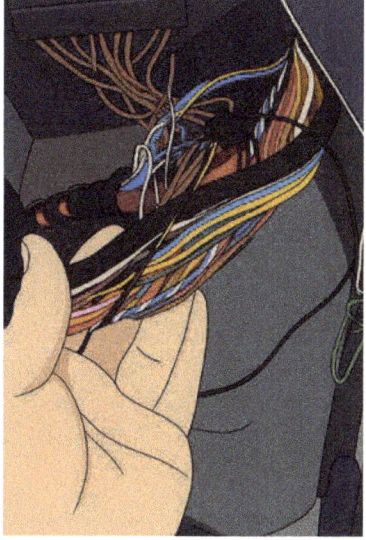

Locate the CAN Bus wires:

Find the CAN High (CAN H) wire and CAN Low (CAN L) wire.

These are usually color-coded:

- CAN H: typically, white/green, yellow
- CAN L: typically, white/blue, black

Use the vehicle wiring diagram to confirm the correct wires.

Figure 6.3 Locating the CAN Bus wiring

Diagnostics and Testing Principles

Measure the power supply to the CAN Bus

Step 1
- Connect the positive lead of the multimeter to the common CAN Bus power supply line to check system battery voltage. (This can be done at pin 16 of the diagnostic socket using a breakout).

Step 2
- Connect the negative lead to the vehicle chassis or battery negative terminal. (This can be done at pin 4 of the diagnostic socket using a breakout).

Step 3
- You should see approximately 12V to 14V with the engine running, or ready mode engaged with an EV.

Step 4
- If the voltage is low, close to 0 V or fluctuates wildly, there may be a power supply issue affecting the CAN system.

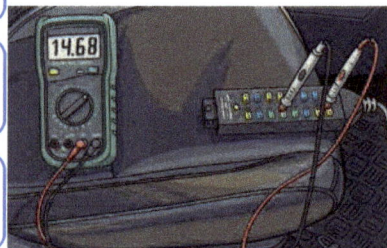

Check CAN High and CAN Low lines for voltage

Step 1
- Turn the vehicle's ignition to the ON position, with the engine off.

Step 2
- Place the multimeter positive lead on CAN H wire. (This can be done at pin 6 of the diagnostic socket).

Step 3
- Place the negative lead on ground; vehicle chassis or negative terminal. (This can also be done at pins 4 chassis ground or 5 signal ground, of the diagnostic socket).

Step 4
- Repeat the same for CAN L. (This can be done at pin 14 of the diagnostic socket).

Step 5
- For a healthy Bus, you should see:
- CAN H: approximately 2.5V to 3.5V - CAN L: approximately 1.5V to 2.5V.
- These voltages indicate the Bus is in a idle state, with the Bus lines idling and not actively communicating.

Step 6
- Check for voltage difference between CAN H and CAN L
- Keep the positive lead on CAN H and the negative lead on CAN L.

Step 7
- The voltage difference should be around 2V to 3V.
- This differential confirms the physical layer is functioning and the Bus is in idle mode.

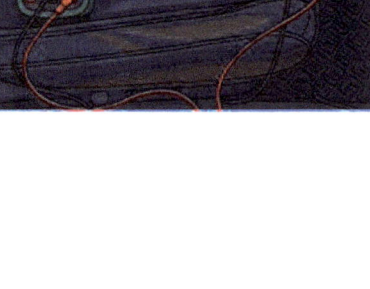

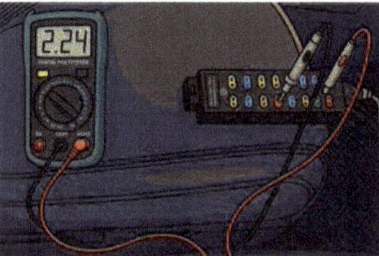

Diagnostics and Testing Principles

Testing for short to battery or ground

Step 1: Turn off the vehicle.

Step 2: Set multimeter to continuity test (if available).

Step 3:
- Check between CAN H/L and the battery positive terminal:
- Expected Result: No continuity. If there is continuity (beep), there may be a short to power.

Step 4:
- Check between CAN H/L and ground:
- Expected Result: No continuity. If continuity exists, the line may be shorted to ground.

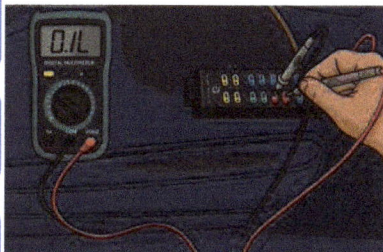

Testing for voltage at the vehicle data link connector (DLC)

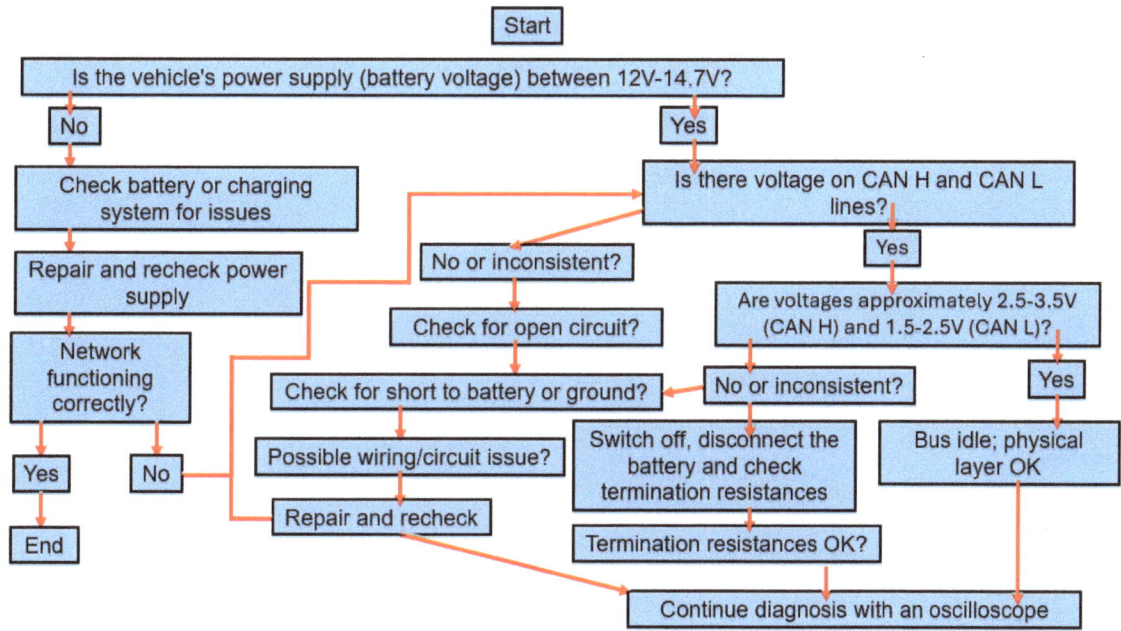

Figure 6.4 Voltage diagnosis

These tests do not guarantee the entire CAN system is functioning, but they help identify gross electrical issues such as wiring shorts, poor connections, or power supply problems. For more detailed diagnosis, specialised tools are recommended, but basic multimeter checks are a good starting point for troubleshooting.

Diagnostics and Testing Principles

Oscilloscope Techniques

As electrics and electronics continue to develop in modern vehicle design, technicians need to leverage the power of advanced diagnostic tools to remain current and effective in the field of automotive repairs.

The power of an oscilloscope to provide insights into the hidden world of electrical systems and components is unparalleled; it's like having X-ray vision. It is the oscilloscope (or scope) that can truly test the operation and health of a system component.

Equipment Needed:

- An oscilloscope with appropriate probes and breakout box.
- Vehicle wiring diagrams.
- Access to the CAN Bus lines (usually at the OBDII connector or near the CAN Bus junction blocks).

Analysing the shape, frequency, amplitude, pulse width and duty cycle of waveforms can help identify abnormalities and pinpoint faults.

More information on the setup and use of scopes can be found in the companion book: *Automotive Oscilloscopes Setup and Use*

Acquiring CAN Bus signals from the vehicle data link connector (DLC)

In order to capture CAN Bus signals from the vehicle data link connector you need to understand the pin layout of an EOBD (OBDII) configuration. Pin 6 is connected to CAN High and Pin 14 is connected to CAN Low; these pins carry differential CAN BUS data at 500 kbps (typical for high-speed CAN).

Using insulation piercing probes to measure CAN Bus signals is not recommended, because this can damage the integrity of the wiring and promote communication problems.

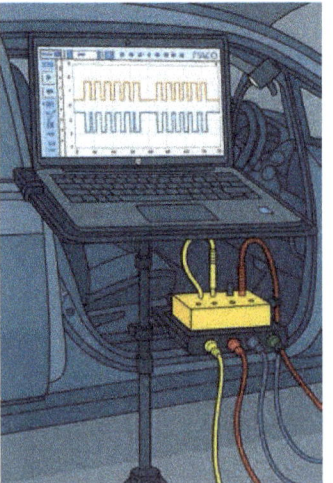

Figure 6.5 An oscilloscope connected to a CAN network with a breakout box

Diagnostics and Testing Principles

Setup and use

Step 1
- Connect the Scope:
- Channel A: Probe connected to pin 6 (CAN High).
- Channel B: Probe connected to pin 14 (CAN Low).
- Ground: Connect to pin 4 or pin 5 (chassis or signal ground).

Step 2
- Configure Oscilloscope Settings:
- Time base: Start at 20 µs/div to 50 µs/div.
- Voltage range: Channel A: 0 to 5V. Channel B: 0 to 5V (if preferred, invert Channel B for easier differential viewing).
- Trigger: Use edge triggering on Channel A (CAN H), set to trigger at \~3V.
- Coupling: DC. - Sample rate: At least 1 MS/s.

Step 3
- Capture the CAN Bus Waveform:
- Once configured, you'll see both:
- CAN High (CH A): idles at \~2.5V, rises to \~3.5V (recessive to dominant).
- CAN Low (CH B): idles at \~2.5V, drops to \~1.5V.

Step 4
- Analyse the Waveform:
- Look for: Normal CAN Communication.
- Clear, clean square-wave signals on both lines.
- Differential voltage of \~2V during dominant state.
- Symmetrical timing between High and Low.

Step 5
- Fault Indicators:
- Flat-line at 2.5V: no communication (Bus off or module asleep).
- Only one line changing: wiring or module fault.
- Over/under voltage: short to power or ground.
- Reflections, ringing: termination resistor issues.

Step 6
- Compare Against Known Good: If available, load a reference waveform for your specific vehicle make and model to identify any anomalies.

Step 7
- Save and Document Findings:
- Save the waveform capture.
- Annotate and timestamp observed issues or good performance.
- Note vehicle info, key-on status, and any connected modules.

Diagnostics and Testing Principles

Network diagnosis of in-vehicle network systems

If a critical network failure occurs, such as a short to positive or ground, the vehicle may suffer a complete communication loss. With a networked system, if communication is lost within a certain area, a number of items will not work, and numerous trouble codes may be generated.

Having connected a scan tool and retrieved the diagnostic trouble codes, you should look for the code that is the root cause. Communication failures are normally an effect of the original fault (i.e. 'unable to communicate' or 'communication lost'). You should ask yourself, 'Is this the cause or an effect created by the fault?'

CAN Bus systems report communication faults as live data. As a result, once you have identified the causal trouble code, you may be able to conduct a diagnosis by disconnecting (unplugging) and isolating components or sections of the network wiring loom until communication is re-established. With the oscilloscope connected and running watch the waveform communication as the network components are isolated.

Oscilloscope testing of CAN Bus

A CAN system can often be identified as a pair of twisted wires entering or leaving an ECU. An oscilloscope can be connected to these wires by 'back probing' at the ECU socket.

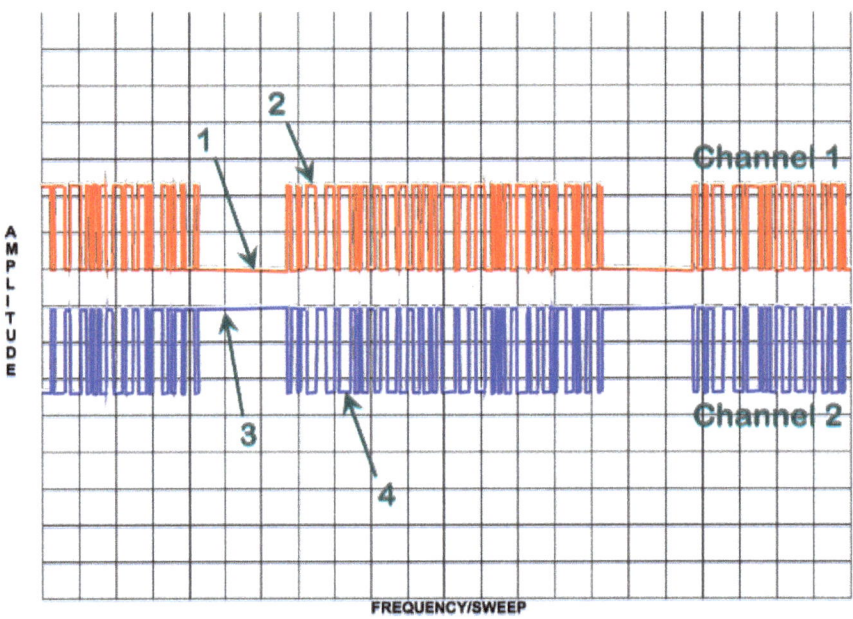

Figure 6.6 CAN Bus (CAN H and CAN L)

Table 6.3 Waveform analysis CAN High and CAN Low

Waveform component	Description
1	**Channel 1** is connected to CAN H (High) and switches positively. This means that the voltage is 0 or 2.5 volts in the off position depending on network speed.
2	**Channel 1**. When switched on, the voltage will jump to 3.5 or 4 volts depending on network speed.
3	**Channel 2** is connected to CAN L (Low) and switches negatively. This results in a voltage of 5 or 2.5 volts in the off position depending on network speed.
4	**Channel 2**. When switched on, the voltage will fall to 1 or 1.5 volts depending on network speed.

Diagnostics and Testing Principles

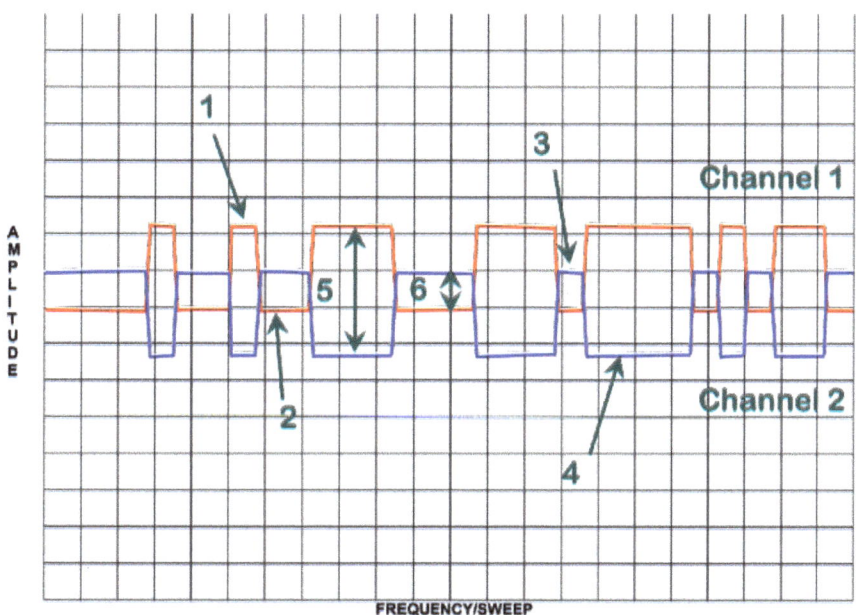

Figure 6.7 CAN Bus potential difference

Table 6.4 Waveform analysis CAN Bus potential difference

Waveform component	Description
1	**Channel 1** is connected to CAN H (High) and switches positively. This means that the voltage is 3.5 or 4 volts in the on position depending on network speed.
2	**Channel 1.** When switched off, the voltage will fall to 0 or 2.5 volts depending on network speed.
3	**Channel 2** is connected to CAN L (Low) and switches negatively. This results in a voltage of 5 or 2.5 volts in the off position depending on network speed.
4	**Channel 2.** When switched on, the voltage will fall to 1 or 1.5 volts depending on network speed.
5	This section of the waveform shows a dominant logic value of 0.
6	This section of the waveform shows a recessive logic value of 1.

By changing the frequency/sweep on the oscilloscope and aligning the voltage amplitudes between Channel 1 and Channel 2, it is possible to compare the two patterns and see the potential difference from CAN High and CAN Low. This can then be interpreted as a dominant or recessive logic value. *[see Figures 3.4 and 3.5].*
Recessive = Logic value of 1
Dominant = Logic value of 0
It is important to check that the patterns from CAN High and Low show equal and opposite with clean edges when examining the waveform. This indicates that the network wiring circuit is operating effectively, and that any non-responsive individual ECU is likely caused by the ECU itself.

Diagnostics and Testing Principles

Calculating network speed using an oscilloscope

It is sometimes necessary to know the speed of the network that you are diagnosing. This is especially useful when setting up a serial decoder.

Setup and Use

Step 1
- Connecting Probes: Attach the oscilloscope probes to the CAN High and CAN Low lines. These connections allow the oscilloscope to capture the differential signals transmitted across the network.

Step 2
- Start Communication: Switch on the vehicle/network and adjust time base and amplitude to acquire a stable capture. Pre-sets or guided tests can often help with this step and then be fine-tuned for accurate signal acquisition.

Step 3
- Analyse the waveform: Pause the capture and use the magnifier tool to zoom in on a section which shows a single data bit. This can often be identified as the narrowest dominent bit as illustrated in **Figure 6.8**.

Step 4
- Measure the data bit: Place rulers at the start and end of this single data bit and measure the time difference Δ (Delta). At this point, some oscilloscope software may calculate the network speed automatically.

Step 5
- To calculate the network speed manually use the following equation: One divided by the delta time, and then multiplied by one thousand to show the result in kilohertz.
- $1/\Delta \times 1000 = kHz$

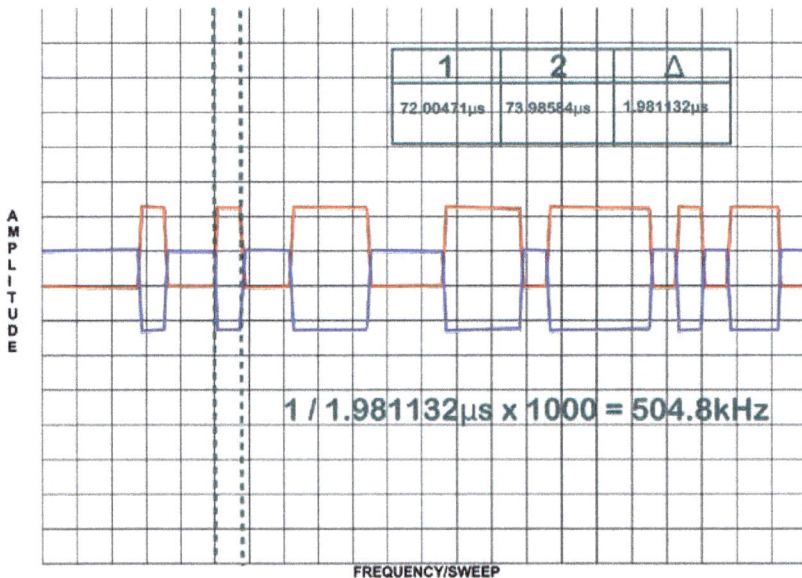

Figure 6.8 Using an oscilloscope to calculate network speed

Diagnostics and Testing Principles

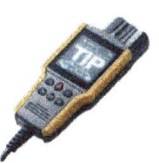

CAN Bus edge matching:

To prevent data corruption, CAN High and CAN Low must be synchronised and aligned. This can be evaluated using a method called edge matching.
Capture a CAN Bus trace from both High and Low channels.
Pause the waveform and use a ruler to verify the edge alignment.

To evaluate the amplitude of CAN High and Low, you can use the oscilloscope's invert function to flip one of the channels, displaying it upside down. By overlaying the waveforms, this technique allows for a quick and efficient comparison of the patterns, highlighting any discrepancies. This method simplifies the process of identifying potential issues that could cause communication failures, eliminating the need to interpret two separate waveforms simultaneously.

Table 6.5 shows examples of some CAN Bus issues. (In the image examples provided, the channels depicting CAN High and CAN Low have been separated to enhance visual clarity).

Table 6.5 CAN Bus faults and their effects on oscilloscope waveforms

Fault type	Waveform effect on oscilloscope	Diagnostic implications	Waveform example
CAN H to CAN L (direct short between Bus lines)	The differential signal collapses to zero volts, eliminating proper communication. The scope shows a flat-line or erratic signal.	Total network failure: modules lose communication.	
CAN H to CAN L (cross connection)	The signals are identical rather than being mirror images.	There is a fault, but it might not cause operational errors.	

Diagnostics and Testing Principles

Table 6.5 CAN Bus faults and their effects on oscilloscope waveforms

Fault type	Waveform effect on oscilloscope	Diagnostic implications	Waveform example
CAN H to ground	CAN H voltage drops, distorting the differential signal, causing erratic voltage swings or a weak signal.	Poor network performance, intermittent communication errors.	
CAN L to ground	CAN L voltage collapses, reducing the differential voltage and causing decoding errors.	Possible loss of lower-priority messages, erratic ECU behaviour.	
CAN H to power (+12V or battery)	Excess voltage pushes CAN H beyond acceptable levels, creating overvoltage trace.	Can damage transceivers, cause Bus shutdown.	
CAN L to power (+12V or battery)	CAN L voltage increases, creating an abnormally high differential voltage, leading to decoding errors.	Erratic data transmission, possible hardware damage.	

Diagnostics and Testing Principles

Table 6.5 CAN Bus faults and their effects on oscilloscope waveforms

Fault type	Waveform effect on oscilloscope	Diagnostic implications	Waveform example
Open circuit (CAN H or CAN L disconnected)	The affected signal flatlines, showing unstable or missing waveforms. If both lines open, the differential voltage may be near zero, causing Bus errors.	Communication loss or severely degraded signal integrity.	

 Please note that the examples provided in **Table 6.5** may not encompass all potential CAN Bus faults or issues. Given the multitude of possible errors and faults, any deviation from an established good example should be thoroughly investigated to determine the root cause of the issue.

Serial decoding

The data sent over CAN Bus is **digital**, structured as a series of bits (0s and 1s). These bits are grouped into messages containing information like sensor readings, switch positions, commands, or system status.
To properly diagnose and understand what's being sent on the CAN Bus, especially when using oscilloscopes with CAN decoders, you must understand how this binary data is represented in different number systems.

When viewing or decoding CAN Bus data, you'll most often see values displayed in one of these three formats:

1. **Decimal** (Base 10)
    - This is the standard number system humans use daily.
    - It uses ten digits: 0 through 9.
    - Example: 255 in decimal simply means 255 units.

Use in automotive: Sensor values, voltages, RPMs, temperatures, etc., are typically displayed in decimal on scan tools.

2. **Binary** (Base 2)
    - The language of computers and ECUs.
    - Uses only two digits: 0 and 1.
    - Each digit is called a bit.
    - Example: The binary number 11111111 is equal to 255 in decimal.

Use in automotive:
   - CAN messages are transmitted in binary at the electrical level.
   - Each pulse seen on the oscilloscope corresponds to a 0 or 1.
   - Used internally by CAN decoders before conversion to more readable formats.

Diagnostics and Testing Principles

3. **Hexadecimal** (Base 16)
    - A shorthand for binary data, often used in diagnostics and engineering tools.
    - Uses sixteen digits: 0–9 and A–F (where A=10, B=11, ..., F=15).
    - One hexadecimal digit represents four binary bits.
    - Example: FF in hex = 11111111 in binary = 255 in decimal.

Use in automotive:
    - CAN IDs and raw data bytes are commonly displayed in hex on oscilloscopes, scan tools, or data loggers.
    - Easier to read than long binary strings but still close to the actual transmitted data.

While oscilloscope CAN decoders often show raw hex values, always remember:

- The actual communication is in binary.
- Hex is just a compact, readable form of that binary.
- You may need to convert hex to decimal to understand what a data byte means (e.g., converting 0x1E to 30 km/h).

Quick conversion table		
Decimal	Binary	Hexadecimal
0	00000000	00
1	00000001	01
10	00001010	0A
15	00001111	0F
16	00010000	10
255	11111111	FF

Digital - data or signals represented as discrete values, typically 0s and 1s in binary form.

Binary - a numbering system that uses only two digits: 0 and 1.

Decimal - a number system based on powers of ten, commonly used in mathematics and everyday calculations.

Hexadecimal - a base-16 numeral system that uses 16 symbols: the digits 0–9 and the letters A–F to represent values 10–15.

Setting up serial decoding

To begin with serial decoding, the oscilloscope software must be capable of handling the specific protocol used in the vehicle's CAN Bus system.

- Always refer to the vehicle's service manual for specific safety procedures.
- Be careful not to short any pins in the CAN connector.
- Disconnect the battery if you're working with sensitive electronics to prevent damage.

Diagnostics and Testing Principles

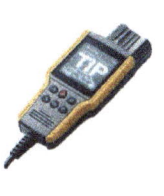

Diagnostic trouble codes (DTCs) can often indicate the general location of a network fault, helping you determine where to place the oscilloscope probes. Focus on codes that point to specific communication issues, as many other non-communication-related codes may be generated as a result of the fault and can be misleading. Whenever possible, connect to the CAN network close to the suspected fault area for more accurate diagnosis. If direct access isn't feasible, the DLC (Data Link Connector) pins 6 and 14 typically provide access to CAN High and CAN Low. Keep in mind, however, that some CAN communication may be blocked at the DLC due to a gateway, which could affect your diagnostic signals.

Setup and use

Step 1
- Connecting Probes: Attach the oscilloscope probes to the CAN High and CAN Low lines. These connections allow the oscilloscope to capture the differential signals transmitted across the network.

Step 2
- Start Communication: Switch on the vehicle/network and adjust time base and amplitude to acquire a stable capture. Pre-sets or guided tests can often help with this step and then be fine-tuned for accurate signal acquisition.

Step 3
- Protocol Selection: Navigate to the serial decoding menu and select the CAN protocol on the oscilloscope as illustrated in **Figure 6.9**.
- Create new serial decoder for both CAN High and CAN Low on two separate channels. Most oscilloscopes will have the parameters pre-set for the protocols used.

Step 4
- Ensure that the oscilloscope is configured to the correct bitrate and sample rate, aligned with the vehicle's CAN Bus specifications. Most oscilloscopes will have this information pre-populated but can be adjusted later if necessary.

Step 5
- Triggering: If possible, set triggering parameters to capture specific data frames or error conditions. This step ensures that the oscilloscope records relevant data without being overwhelmed by continuous traffic.

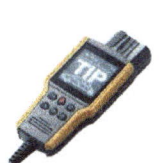

Because serial decoding on an oscilloscope depends on a clear and stable waveform, signal interference or noise can sometimes cause it to misinterpret data. When setting up the decoder for both CAN High and CAN Low, the decoded data should match; any discrepancies may indicate a corrupted signal. Since a CAN Bus network relies on the potential difference between High and Low signals rather than a simple on/off state, it is generally resistant to noise. In some cases, it can be helpful to decode the data using a maths channel, which can often cancel out network noise. This involves creating a maths channel that subtracts CAN Low from CAN High. For example, if CAN High is assigned to channel A and CAN Low to channel B, the equation should be A minus B. Once this new channel is set up, you can apply the serial decoder to it, providing a cleaner, more accurate view of the data being transmitted.

Diagnostics and Testing Principles

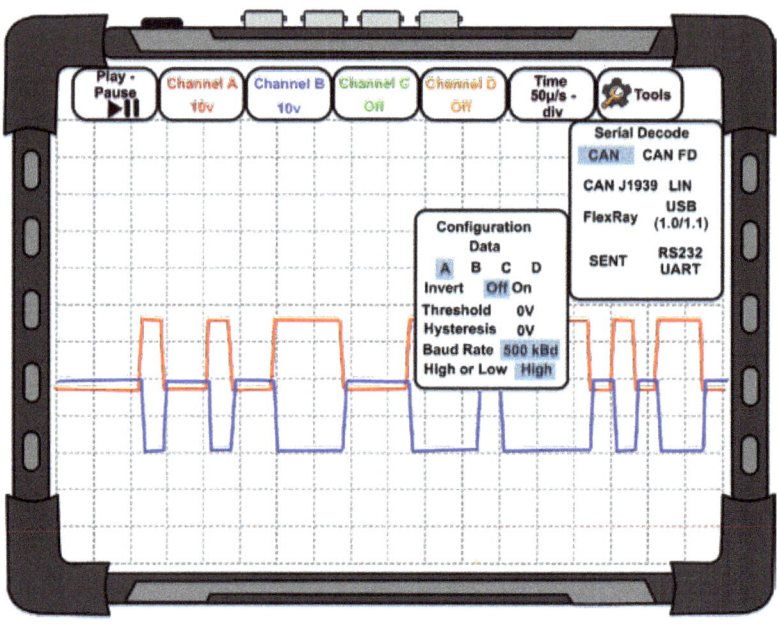

Figure 6.9 Serial decoding CAN Bus

Deciphering the data

Once the oscilloscope is set up, it begins to capture and decode the serial data from the CAN Bus. Deciphering this data involves understanding the structure of CAN messages:

- CAN Frames: Each CAN frame consists of several fields including the Identifier, Control Field, Data Field, CRC Field, ACK Field, and End of Frame. Recognising these fields is crucial for interpreting the message content. *[see Chapter 5]*.
- Identifiers: The Identifier field specifies the priority and purpose of the message. It can reveal which node transmitted the data and its intended recipient.
- Data Field: The Data Field contains the actual information being communicated, such as sensor readings or control commands.
- Error Detection: The CRC Field and ACK Field are used for error detection and acknowledgment, indicating whether the message was received correctly.

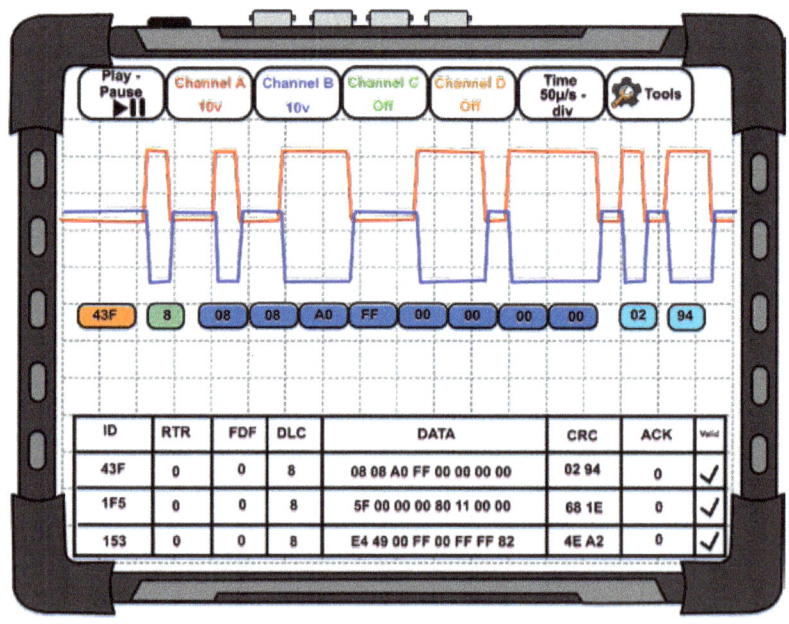

Figure 6.10 Decoded data example

Diagnostics and Testing Principles

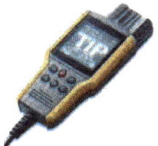

Using a Maths Channel to Calculate Potential Difference Between CAN H and CAN L
Oscilloscope Setup:
- Channel A → Connect to CAN High (CAN H)
- Channel B → Connect to CAN Low (CAN L)
  (Both measured with respect to chassis ground)

In a properly functioning CAN system:
CAN H and CAN L are differential signals — they mirror each other.
Typical values during transmission:
- CAN H rises to ~3.5V
- CAN L drops to ~1.5V
- Potential difference ≈ 2V

By calculating the instantaneous difference between CAN H and CAN L using a maths channel, you get a clean, direct representation of the true signal — noise common to both lines (common-mode noise) are naturally cancelled out.

Maths Channel Formula:
To calculate the potential difference:
A - B
Where:
- A = CAN H
- B = CAN L

This equation gives you the differential voltage, i.e., the signal the CAN transceiver actually sees.

Why This Is Useful for Diagnostics:
- Noise Immunity Check:
  Noise often appears on both CAN H and CAN L simultaneously (common-mode). By subtracting the two, the maths channel shows only differential changes, which are the actual data bits. Any common-mode spikes disappear, helping you dismiss harmless EMI.
- Quick Fault Confirmation:
  If your maths channel shows inconsistent or low-amplitude signals (far from the expected ~2V swing), you may have:
  > A wiring issue.
  > A termination resistor problem.
  > A faulty module pulling one line down.
- Visual Simplicity:
  Instead of visually comparing two complex waveforms, you get a single, stable waveform showing a truer representation of data transmission.

Because serial decoding using an oscilloscope works by analysing what it can see on the screen, if the data packet's frame is split (i.e., finishes on the next screen), it will see this as an error, recording this as a CRC fault. If you are receiving lots of CRC errors, try reducing the time base to see if it improves.

Diagnostics and Testing Principles

Decoding LIN Bus signals with an oscilloscope

Diagnosing LIN Bus issues requires understanding how to interpret the signals. An oscilloscope is a valuable tool for visualising and decoding these signals to identify communication faults.

Equipment Needed:
- An oscilloscope with appropriate probes and breakout leads.
- LIN Bus decoder software (may be built-in or an add-on for your oscilloscope).
- Vehicle wiring diagram indicating LIN Bus wire locations.

Setup and use

Step 1
- Locate the LIN Bus Wire: Refer to the vehicle's wiring diagram. LIN Bus wires are often labelled and may be a specific colour (check diagram).
- Common locations include: Communication networks between sensors and control units (e.g., climate control, door modules, seat modules) - Diagnostic connectors.

Step 2
- Connect the Oscilloscope Probe: Connect the oscilloscope probe to the LIN Bus wire using a back probe. Ensure the ground clip is securely connected to a known good ground point on the vehicle.

Step 3
- Set Up the Oscilloscope:
- Voltage Scale: Set the vertical scale to an appropriate voltage range (e.g., 0-20V), as LIN Bus operates at 12V. Time Scale: Start with a time scale of 1ms/div or 2ms/div and adjust as needed to see the data frames clearly. Trigger: Set the trigger to 'Normal' mode and adjust the trigger level to approximately half the LIN bus voltage (around 6V) to stabilise the waveform.

Step 4
- Activate the LIN Bus Decoder: Many oscilloscopes have built-in LIN decoding functionality or offer it as an add-on. Enable the LIN decoder through the oscilloscope's menu.
- Configure the decoder settings: - Baud Rate: LIN Bus typically operates at 19200 bps (bits per second). Set this correctly. Polarity: Ensure the polarity setting matches the LIN signal (usually positive). Data Format: Set the data format (e.g., 8 data bits, no parity).

Step 5
- Observe and Interpret the Waveform:
- Data Frames: A typical LIN data frame consists of - Break: A dominant (low) level signal to indicate the start of the frame. Sync Byte: Always the same value (0x55) to synchronise the receiver. Identifier (ID): Specifies the message type and destination. Data Bytes: The actual data being transmitted (0-8 bytes). Checksum: Used for error detection. Decoding: The LIN decoder will automatically interpret the waveform and display the data in a readable format, typically showing the ID, data bytes, and checksum.

Step 6
- Analysing the Decoded Data:
- Message IDs: Different IDs correspond to different functions or data. Refer to vehicle-specific LIN Bus documentation to understand what each ID represents. Data Values: The data bytes represent the actual values being transmitted. These could be sensor readings, control commands, or status information. Error Detection: Check for checksum errors, which indicate data corruption.

Step 7
- Troubleshooting:
- Missing signals: indicates no communication on the Bus.
- Malformed signals: corrupted communications or electrical issues.
- Incorrect data: indicates a faulty sensor or module may be sending incorrect data.

Diagnostics and Testing Principles

- Always refer to the vehicle's service manual for specific safety procedures.
- Be careful not to short any pins in the LIN connector.
- Disconnect the battery if you're working with sensitive electronics to prevent damage during repairs.

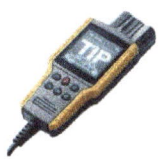

Example:

You might see a LIN message with ID 0x34, which (according to the vehicle's documentation) represents the driver's door module status. The data bytes might indicate the door lock status, window position, and mirror settings.

Important:
- Always consult the vehicle's service manual for specific LIN Bus information and troubleshooting procedures.
- Pay attention to the 'break' signal at the beginning of each frame. A missing or distorted break can indicate a master node problem.
- Ensure that the LIN Bus termination resistor (typically located in one of the modules) is present and functioning correctly.
- LIN Bus faults can be caused by wiring issues, faulty modules, or software problems. A systematic approach to diagnosis is essential.

Identifying IDs

Each message sent on the CAN Bus contains a unique identifier known as the CAN ID. Understanding these IDs is essential for effective diagnostics and troubleshooting, as they help you determine which device is sending or receiving specific messages. Knowing how to locate and interpret these IDs is a key step in diagnosing communication issues and ensuring the proper functioning of the CAN system.

IDs help with:
- Troubleshooting: Monitoring specific CAN IDs, can help you pinpoint the source of a problem.
- System Understanding: Knowing the IDs helps you understand which ECUs are talking to each other and what data they are exchanging.
- Module Verification: Confirm that modules are online by identifying the ID messages.

CAN ID identification

Equipment Needed:
- An automotive oscilloscope or CAN Bus analyser.
- A vehicle topology diagram.
- A computer-based spreadsheet.

Diagnostics and Testing Principles

Bus activity data

Step 1
- Connect and Capture Bus Activity: Use a CAN Bus analyser or automotive oscilloscope.
- Connect the oscilloscope to the vehicle's diagnostic port (typically OBDII or EOBD).
- Configure the scope to capture CAN Bus traffic. You'll see a waveform representing the Bus activity.

Step 2
- Determine Bus Speed (Baud Rate): The CAN Bus speed (baud rate) must be known to correctly decode the data. Common speeds are 250 kbps and 500 kbps.
- If Unknown: Use the oscilloscope to zoom in on the smallest bit of data and measure its length.
- Example: A bit length of 2 microseconds indicates a 500 kbps Bus speed (1/0.000002 seconds = 500,000 bits per second).

Step 3
- Decode the CAN Bus Data: Use your diagnostic tool's CAN decoding function.
- Configure the decoding settings: Select the appropriate CAN standard (CAN 2.0A or CAN 2.0B). Enter the correct baud rate. Set the voltage threshold. The tool will now display the decoded CAN messages, including the CAN IDs.

Analyse Bus data

Step 1
- Export and Organise the Data: Export the decoded CAN data into a spreadsheet; you will likely notice many repeated messages.

Step 2
- Eliminate Duplicate IDs: Focus on identifying unique IDs first.
- In your spreadsheet, select the ID column and use the 'remove duplicates' function, this will provide a list of unique CAN IDs.

Step 3
- Identify the Source of Each ID: To determine which ECU is transmitting a specific ID, systematically disconnect or remove power to one module at a time.
- Run the CAN Bus capture again and export the data.
- Compare the new list of CAN IDs to the original list. The missing IDs likely originate from the disconnected module.

Step 4
- Conditional Formatting for ID Comparison: After disconnecting a module and capturing the CAN data, copy the ID column into a new column next to all the modules' ID list.
- Highlight both columns, select Home > Conditional Formatting > Highlight Cells Rules > Duplicate Values. This will highlight the IDs that are present in both lists. The unique IDs (those only in the 'all modules' list) are associated with the module that was disconnected.

Create an ID definition file, listing your identified CAN IDs along with their descriptions in a simple table, then save it as a `.csv` or `.txt` file. You can load this file into your diagnostic tool to replace raw IDs with understandable descriptions, making analysis easier. Once IDs are named, you can filter and monitor specific IDs during tests, helping you identify issues like modules going offline during operation.

Diagnostics and Testing Principles

Important Considerations:
- Vehicle-Specific: CAN IDs vary widely between vehicle makes, models, and years.
- Standard vs. Extended IDs: CAN 2.0A uses 11-bit IDs, while CAN 2.0B uses 29-bit IDs. Ensure your tool is configured correctly.
- Data Interpretation: Identifying the ID is only the first step. Understanding the data contained within the message requires further analysis and vehicle-specific knowledge.

Decoding and analysing SENT messages

The acronym SENT, Single Edge Nibble Transmission (sometime known as Sensor Embedded Network Transmission) is a specific type of data encoding method used in some communication protocols, including certain automotive sensor signals. It involves transmitting data in small, discrete chunks called 'nibbles,' which are 4-bit segments (half a byte). SENT is designed to be simple, fast, and reliable for transmitting sensor information such as temperature, pressure, or position.

In SENT communication, the sensor sends out a series of pulses with varying widths. Each pulse width encodes part of the sensor's data. The longer the pulse, the higher the value it represents. These pulses are sent sequentially, forming a complete message that contains the sensor's measurement.

Decoding SENT

Step 1
- Understand the Pulse Pattern: Each SENT message begins with a synchronisation pulse, which helps the ECU recognise the start of a new message. After synchronisation, a series of pulses follow, each representing a specific data bit or piece of information. The pulse width correlates with the sensor reading. For example, a short pulse might indicate a low value, while a longer pulse indicates a high value.

Step 2
- Measuring Pulse Widths: To decode a SENT message, you need to measure the width of each pulse.
- Use an oscilloscope to capture and analyse digital signals: The pulses are measured in microseconds (µs).
- For example: 150 µs pulse = low or minimum sensor value - 250 µs pulse = maximum sensor value.

Step 3
- Converting Pulse Widths into Data: Each pulse width corresponds to a specific sensor measurement. By reading the entire sequence of pulses, you can reconstruct the sensor's data value. Some systems encode multiple bits in one pulse, so the sequence of pulse widths forms a binary number that represents the sensor reading.

Step 4
- Analysing the Data: Once you have the pulse widths, convert them into numerical values based on the sensor's calibration. Compare these values with expected ranges specified in the vehicle's manual. If the pulse widths or the resulting data are outside the normal range, it indicates a potential sensor fault or wiring issue.

Diagnostics and Testing Principles

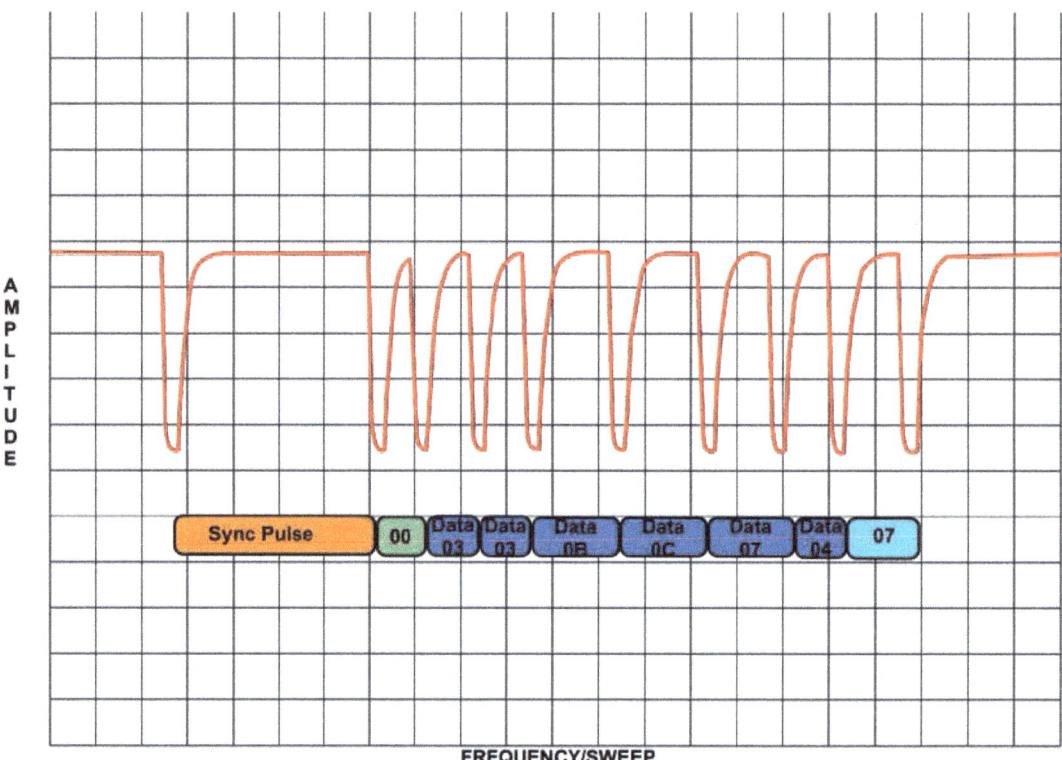

Figure 6.11 Decoded SENT

Suppose you are testing a vehicle's throttle position sensor that communicates via SENT. You connect your oscilloscope to the sensor wire and observe a series of pulses:
The first pulse is a synchronisation pulse, about 200 µs wide.
The following pulses are between 150 µs and 250 µs wide.
- A pulse measuring 180 µs might mean the throttle is slightly open.
- A pulse measuring 220 µs indicates the throttle is more open.

By analysing the pulse widths across multiple measurements, you can determine if the sensor is providing consistent and accurate data or if it's faulty.

Effective SENT Analysis:
- Use a suitable digital oscilloscope or decoding tool designed for automotive diagnostics.
- Always refer to the vehicle's service manual for the specific pulse width values and calibration details.
- Check the sensor wiring and connections if you notice unusual pulse patterns or inconsistent readings.
- Remember that environmental factors like electromagnetic interference can affect pulse accuracy; ensure your testing environment is clean.

Diagnostics and Testing Principles

CAN Analysers

A CAN analyser is a specialised tool used by vehicle technicians and mechanics to look into the digital communication between various control modules in a vehicle. The analyser helps us see what messages are being sent, receive real-time data, and detect communication problems.

CAN analysers are typically devices that connect to a vehicle's CAN network through an interface, usually via a USB cable to a computer or laptop. When connected, the computer essentially becomes one of the network's nodes. Special software then allows you to decode and display the live network traffic, often in a table format for easy analysis. Some advanced CAN analysers can also send messages onto the network, allowing you to influence system or component behaviour for diagnostic or testing purposes.

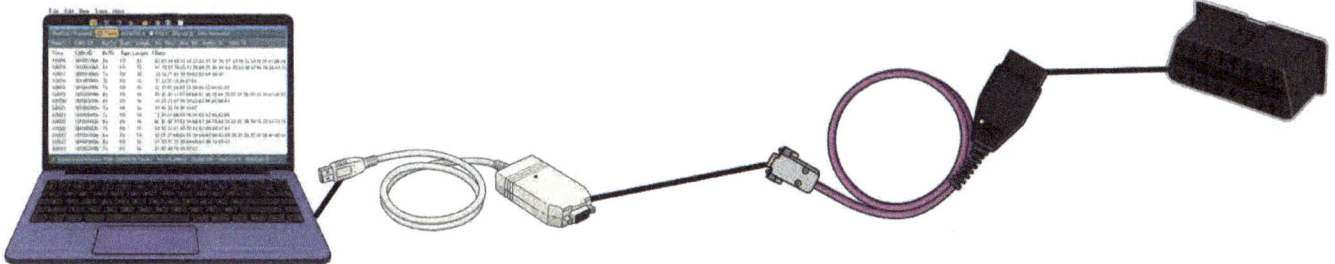

Figure 6.12 A CAN analyser

Features of a CAN analyser

- Real-Time Monitoring: The analyser displays live data and messages as they travel on the CAN network. This helps you see what signals are active at any given moment.
- Data Recording and Logging: Many analysers can record data over time. This is useful for analysing problems that happen intermittently, not just when the vehicle is stationary or easy to access. Often this data can be exported to other programs for deeper analysis.
- Filtering and Searching: They allow filtering specific message IDs or data to focus on particular systems, making troubleshooting faster and more efficient.
- Error Detection: Some analysers can identify faults, such as missing messages or corrupted data, which can point to wiring issues or malfunctioning sensors.
- Protocol Support: Besides standard CAN (Controller Area Network), advanced analysers may support other protocols like LIN, FlexRay, or CAN FD used in newer vehicles or specific systems.
- Display Options: Data can be shown in various formats, including raw hexadecimal data, interpreted text, or graphical charts, depending on user preference and task.

Capabilities of a CAN analyser

- Communication Testing: Verify if the control modules are communicating properly by checking their message exchanges.
- Troubleshooting Faults: Detect error codes, anomalies, or missing signals that can point to faults within the system.
- ECU Data Access: Access information from different Electronic Control Units (ECUs), such as engine, transmission, brakes, or airbag systems.
- Simulation and Testing: Some analysers can send custom messages or simulate signals to test system responses, aiding in pinpointing specific issues.

Diagnostics and Testing Principles

Connection methods

The way you connect a CAN analyser to the vehicle depends on the vehicle's network and the analyser's design. Common connection points include:

1. OBD Port: The most common connection point in most vehicles. Using an OBD cable or adapter, the analyser links directly to this port, providing access to the CAN network.

2. Direct Wiring: For certain vehicles or diagnostic situations, the analyser may connect directly to the CAN wiring harness or specific control modules. This requires knowledge of the vehicle's wiring diagram and careful handling to avoid damage.

3. Special Adapters: Some analysers come with adapters for different vehicle brands or protocols. These adaptors help connect to non-standard ports or different protocol networks.

Figure 6.13 CAN analyser connection

Practical applications of CAN analysers

A CAN Bus analyser is an essential tool for vehicle diagnostics. It facilitates the monitoring, deciphering, and troubleshooting of the Controller Area Network. Understanding how to set up and use a CAN Bus analyser is crucial for identifying faults and ensuring optimal vehicle performance.

Setting up a CAN Bus analyser

Step 1
- Understand the Vehicle's CAN Bus Architecture: Begin by reviewing the vehicle's wiring diagram to identify the CAN Bus network locations. This helps you locate the diagnostic connector or any other points where you can access the network directly.

Step 2
- Select the Right Analyser: Choose a CAN Bus analyser suited to your needs. While there are numerous types available with varying features, most serve the fundamental purpose of visualising and analysing CAN Bus traffic.

Step 3
- Physical Connection: Connect the analyser to the vehicle's diagnostic port using the appropriate adapter or cable. The On-Board Diagnostics (OBD) connector is a common access point in most vehicles.

Step 4
- Check Power Supply: Ensure your analyser is receiving power. Most analysers will be powered via the OBD port or a USB connection to a computer, but some may require an external power source, especially handheld or portable variants.

Diagnostics and Testing Principles

Using the CAN Bus analyser

Step 1
- Initialisation: Once connected, power on the analyser. Allow it to initialise and establish a communication link with the vehicle's CAN network. This usually involves configuring the analyser to the correct baud rate, which refers to the communication speed of the Bus (commonly 250 kb/s or 500 kb/s).

Step 2
- Select the Monitoring Mode: Set the analyser to the appropriate mode depending on your diagnostic needs. Options might include monitoring live data, recording data for analysis, or setting triggers to capture specific events.

Step 3
- Viewing Data: Monitor the CAN messages streaming through the network. The analyser will display these messages, often as hexadecimal identifiers and data bytes. Familiarise yourself with interpreting these codes to understand the communication between various electronic control units (ECUs).

Step 4
- Diagnosing Issues: Use the analyser to identify anomalies or error codes. This can include unexpected messages, dropped signals, or inconsistencies in the data stream, which may indicate faulty wiring/nodes, malfunctioning sensors, or software issues.

Step 5
- Data Logging: Enable logging if needed to record data over time for further analysis. This can be particularly useful for intermittent faults that aren't always present.

Monitoring traffic

Monitoring the CAN Bus traffic is the first step in diagnostics. A CAN Bus analyser allows you to capture real-time CAN messages flowing between ECUs. By viewing these messages, you can determine if the communication is normal or if there are signs of potential issues. Messages typically include an identifier, data bytes, and control information. Familiarising yourself with the common message formats used by the specific vehicle will aid in interpretation.

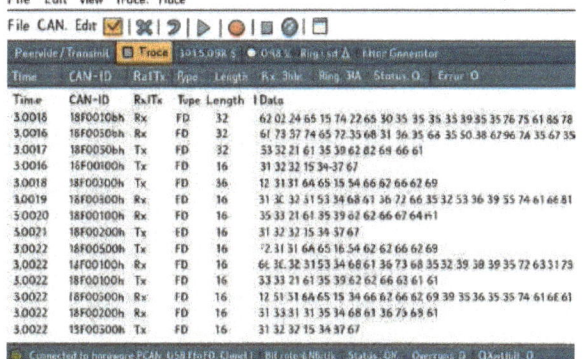

Figure 6.14 CAN Bus traffic

Filtering and triggers

The volume of messages on a CAN Bus can be overwhelming. To manage this, a CAN Bus analyser provides filtering and triggering features. Filtering allows you to specify conditions to display only relevant messages. For example, you can set filters for specific message IDs or data content. Triggers determine when the analyser starts or stops collecting data, ensuring you capture critical events without excess information.

Message injection

In some diagnostic procedures, you may need to simulate specific CAN messages to test system responses. CAN Bus analysers allow for message injection, where you can send crafted messages onto the Bus. This capability is useful for testing how ECUs react under certain conditions or verifying changes. Ensure that injected messages do not conflict with the vehicle's normal operation to avoid unintended consequences.

Diagnostics and Testing Principles

Error frame detection

Error frames are signals that indicate problems within the CAN network. These frames are automatically generated by the Bus when errors occur. A CAN Bus analyser can detect these frames, providing insight into issues like frame errors, bit timing problems, or faulty hardware. By analysing the frequency and cause of error frames, you can pinpoint and rectify underlying issues.

Advanced Diagnostics

In the realm of automotive networking, particularly with the CAN Bus, advanced diagnostics play a pivotal role in maintaining vehicle health and performance.

Bus load analysis

The Bus load refers to the amount of data being transferred across the CAN Bus at any given time. High Bus load can lead to delays or data collisions, affecting the vehicle's performance. By using diagnostic tools to analyse Bus load, you can determine if the network is operating within its capacity.

Imagine the CAN Bus as a busy main road filled with traffic. When the road is congested with cars, trucks, and motorcycles, new vehicles trying to join the flow have a hard time entering because the main road doesn't have enough space; they have to slow down or wait for a gap.
Similarly, on a busy CAN network, if many nodes (like vehicles on the road) are transmitting messages constantly, there's little room for new messages to get through. This high traffic load makes the network crowded, causing delays or missed signals, just like a congested road slows down traffic and prevents new cars from merging smoothly.

To analyse Bus load using an automotive oscilloscope, you can observe the traffic waveform on the screen. Under normal conditions, there should be clear gaps or spaces between messages, indicating the Bus has enough time to communicate efficiently. If the Bus is overloaded, these gaps become very small or vanish entirely, creating a crowded waveform with little to no space between signals. This crowded appearance suggests too much traffic on the network, which can lead to communication issues or delays. Monitoring the waveform in this way helps you determine if the CAN Bus is under strain and if there may be a need to diagnose or reduce network congestion.

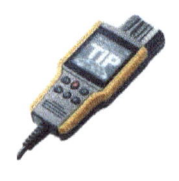

A common cause of high Bus load is when a node on the network keeps trying to send messages but never receives an acknowledgment. This causes the node to repeatedly resend the same message, which can flood the Bus and disrupt normal communication. To identify this issue, use your oscilloscope or diagnostic tool to look for repeated messages with identical timing and content.

Diagnostics and Testing Principles

By examining communication patterns, you can decipher the sequence and timing of messages between ECUs. This analysis helps in identifying nodes that may be silent (not transmitting), chatty (transmitting too much), or potentially malfunctioning. Recognising these patterns and identifying any deviations from the norm allows you to address issues before they manifest into more significant problems.

Gateway modules: Diagnosing faults in vehicles with segmented networks

In modern vehicles with complex systems, gateway modules act as communication bridges between different network segments. These gateways ensure seamless data flow across various proprietary and vendor-specific protocols. Diagnosing faults within gateway modules involves ensuring that they correctly route and translate messages between network segments.

If a gateway module fails, it can cause a loss of communication between different parts of the vehicle's system, which may lead to various display, sensor, or function issues. To verify whether the gateway is working properly, use your diagnostic tools to check for any error codes related to the gateway or communication issues. You can also examine the gateway's configuration and communication status by viewing live data streams on your scan tool. Additionally, inspecting the wiring and connections to the gateway ensures that signals are properly reaching the module. In some cases, performing a controlled reset or updates to the gateway module can help confirm if it's functioning correctly. By systematically checking the error codes, data communication, and connections, you can determine if the gateway module is at fault and take appropriate repair steps.

8 Step Diagnostic Best Practice

1 Check battery and charging circuit - unstable voltages will cause havoc on the vehicle's network system.

Begin by measuring the system's supply voltage, ideally at the battery, but also at the data link connector (DLC) and the network's power supply module. Don't assume the voltage is the same throughout the system—variations can cause communication issues. Additionally, check for any modifications or aftermarket equipment that might have been added. This may involve asking the owner or driver, but keep in mind they may not always have full or accurate information. Always verify any suspicions with your own investigation to ensure a thorough understanding of the vehicle's electrical state.

Figure 6.15 Verifying supply voltage

2 Decide how many things are malfunctioning – the number of failures can give clues to the potential issue.

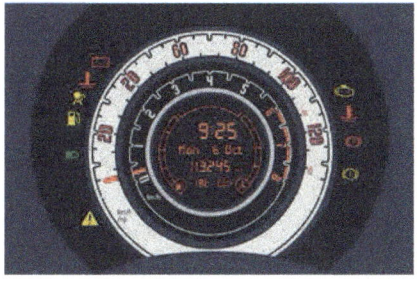

The number of malfunctions can help you identify the possible cause of a problem. If you find only one or two incorrectly operating vehicle systems units or devices, it is likely that the issue is with a specific component or module. However, if there are multiple or many issues, the problem may be related to the network itself or a failing node on the CAN Bus. Recognising this pattern allows you to focus your diagnostic efforts more effectively, starting with the suspected component if there are few errors, or investigating the network system if there are many. This approach helps you work more systematically and efficiently.

Figure 6.16 Multiple system errors

Diagnostics and Testing Principles

3 Scan vehicle – full/global scan, as a fault on an assumed unrelated system could be causing the issue.

Start by performing a full system diagnostic scan with a capable scan tool, rather than just a basic or system-specific scan. This allows the scanner to communicate with all ECUs on the network, helping it recognise which modules are responding and identifying any that may not be responding. Check the vehicle's software versions to see if any updates are needed, as outdated software can cause issues. Record all diagnostic codes for future reference and review the live data and freeze frame information, which can give clues about how the vehicle was operating when the errors occurred. After recording everything, clear the codes and operate the vehicle or system. Then, monitor the system carefully, especially paying attention to any codes that reappear, as these are often key to diagnosing the actual problem.

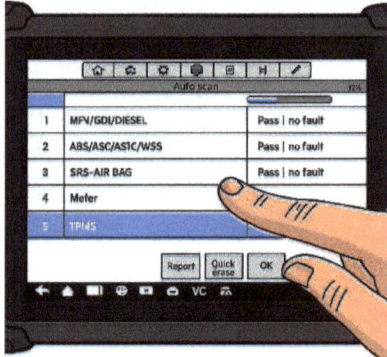

Figure 6.17 Scanning the vehicle

When performing an OBD scan for network errors, if there's no communication, first ensure the vehicle is awake and responsive, as some systems may be in sleep mode. Next, check the DLC (Data Link Connector) pins for physical damage or poor connections, especially pins 4, 5 and 16, which are power and ground lines. Also, verify the voltages on pins 6 and 14, which connect to CAN High and CAN Low lines. Proper voltages at these pins indicate the network's physical integrity, while abnormal readings may suggest wiring issues or faulty resistors that need attention.

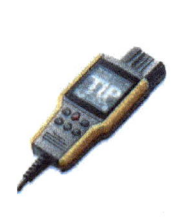

Remember that some network faults can generate many error codes, such as 'unable to communicate,' 'communication lost,' or 'communication stop.' These codes are a result of the underlying issue and can often be ignored during diagnosis. When reviewing a long list of network-related codes, focus on those that indicate a specific problem, such as voltage irregularities, short, or open circuits. Identifying these particular codes helps you pinpoint the real cause of the fault more effectively.
Always ask yourself the question cause or affect?

4 Conduct bi-directional testing (if available) - to rule out network or component

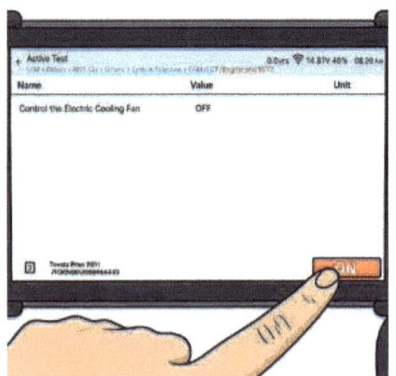

Using a diagnostic scan tool for bi-directional communication allows you to not only read trouble codes but also to directly interact with the vehicle's systems. This means you can activate or test specific components, such as switches, sensors, or actuators, to see if they respond correctly. By doing this, you can help determine whether the problem lies with the network or the component itself. If the component responds as expected when commanded, the network is likely functioning properly, and the issue may be with the part or its wiring. If it doesn't respond, it suggests a possible network or communication problem that needs further investigation. This approach helps you narrow down the cause more quickly and accurately.

Figure 6.18 Component activation

Diagnostics and Testing Principles

 Many modules need to be programmed or configured to work correctly with the vehicle's system. If this step is overlooked, the new part may not function properly, even if it is a good, functioning unit. Always check whether the component needs to be coded or programmed before condemning it as faulty.

5 Test the physical layer – voltages and terminating resistances

To test the physical layer of the CAN network, you can use a multimeter at the DLC (Data Link Connector). Check the voltages on the CAN High and CAN Low lines, typically, both should have a specific voltage range when the system is active. Also, perform short circuit tests to ensure there are no unintended connections between the CAN lines, to power or ground. Additionally, verify that the termination resistors are correctly installed at the ends of the network and functioning properly. Properly testing the physical layer helps confirm that the wiring and resistors are in good condition, which is essential for reliable communication on the CAN Bus. *[see Using Diagnostic Tools and terminating resistors]*.

Figure 6.19 Testing the physical layer

6 Scope CAN H and CAN L – at the DLC and different network connections if possible.

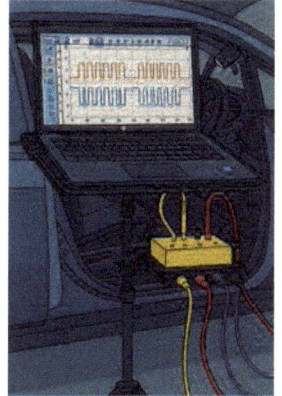 Using an oscilloscope to test the CAN network allows you to see the actual signals on the lines. Look for uniform and similar waveforms on both the CAN High and CAN Low lines, as they should mirror each other with consistent shape and timing. You can also add cursors or rulers on the screen to match the edges of the signals, helping you check for proper network resistance and signal quality. To further improve your analysis, you can use maths channels to subtract the signals, which helps cancel out any noise and gives a clearer view of the actual data. This method helps you identify issues like signal distortion or interference that could affect communication on the Bus.

Figure 6.20 Using an oscilloscope to test CAN Bus

7 Serial decode – to confirm the integrity of the waveforms/data packet.

After setting up your oscilloscope and capturing the waveforms from the CAN Bus, the next step is to use the serial decoding function. This feature helps interpret the raw signals and verify that the data packets are complete and correctly formatted. By decoding the waveform, you can confirm that the information being transmitted between modules is intact and accurate. If the decoded data shows errors or incomplete messages, it indicates a potential issue with the signal quality or wiring. *[see serial decoding]*.

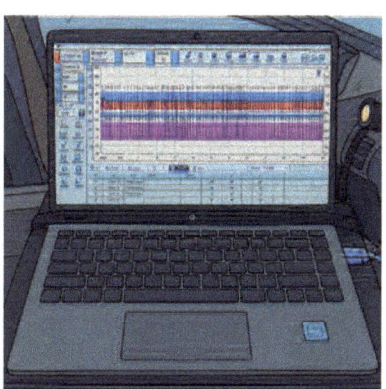

Figure 6.21 Serial decoding CAN Bus waveforms

Diagnostics and Testing Principles

8 If available use a CAN analyser – to check CAN id's and for any error count.

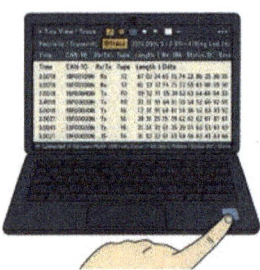

If you have access to a CAN analyser, it can be a very helpful tool for diagnosing network issues. The analyser allows you to see live data traffic on the CAN Bus, helping you understand what messages are being sent and received in real-time. It can also identify any errors or faulty messages that may indicate problems with the system. Additionally, many CAN analysers have a feature to inject messages into the network, which lets you test how the system responds to specific commands or signals. Using this tool helps you get a clear picture of the network's health and can quickly confirm whether the system is functioning correctly or if there are issues that need attention. *[see CAN analysers].*

Figure 6.22 CAN analyser

Performing an operation or road test on the vehicle can be helpful in identifying intermittent errors that don't appear during stationary diagnostics. When the vehicle is moving or under real driving conditions, some problems, like communication drops or sensor faults, may only happen at certain speeds or driving situations. During these tests, carefully monitor and record the CAN data and error codes.
Sometimes, understanding what these messages mean requires research or reverse engineering, especially if the vehicle uses unique or proprietary communication protocols.

Practical Training and Case Studies

To truly master CAN Bus diagnostics, hands-on experience is invaluable. This section focuses on practical training techniques and that can help you develop the skills needed to tackle complex vehicle network issues.

Real-world examples

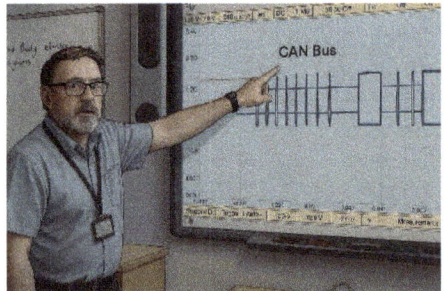

Learning from real-world examples offers invaluable insights. By studying cases where actual faults have been diagnosed and resolved, you gain a better understanding of common issues and effective troubleshooting methods. These scenarios provide a foundation for recognising patterns and symptoms in CAN Bus malfunctions, such as communication errors or ECU faults, allowing for faster and more accurate problem-solving.

Figure 6.23 Training and practice

Simulating faults

Simulating CAN Bus faults is an effective way to practice diagnostic skills without the risk of damaging actual vehicles. Training setups can introduce issues like incorrect messaging, node failures, or network noise. By creating these scenarios, you can hone your ability to diagnose and resolve problems under controlled conditions, building confidence for solving real faults.

Diagnostics and Testing Principles

Network reconstruction

Reconstructing small CAN Bus networks provides practical insights into their operation and design. By constructing a simple network with multiple nodes and ECUs, you can experiment with message flow, network configuration, and fault testing. This hands-on approach solidifies understanding of CAN Bus architecture and provides a platform for testing diagnostic strategies and tools.

Oscilloscope analysis

Practice using an oscilloscope to analyse CAN Bus signal waveforms; this is a critical diagnostic skill. An oscilloscope displays the electrical signals on the CAN lines, allowing you to assess signal integrity, timing, and synchronisation. By interpreting these waveforms, you can identify issues such as noise, signal distortion, or improper bit timing, which are often at the root of communication faults.

Voltage measurements

Proper voltage levels on the CAN High and CAN Low lines are essential for effective communication. You should use a multimeter or similar tool to measure and verify these levels. Typically, CAN High should be around 3.5 volts when dominant, and CAN Low should be around 1.5 volts.

Fault isolation

Fault isolation involves systematically identifying and addressing specific network issues.
Techniques include:

- Short Circuits: Checking for unintended connections between wires using continuity tests.
- Open Circuits: Verifying continuity in wiring to detect breaks or disconnections.
- Grounding Faults: Ensuring that all components are properly grounded to prevent communication errors.

By employing these fault isolation methods, you can accurately pinpoint and resolve specific issues that disrupt the CAN network's functionality.

Through practical training and real-world case studies, you can elevate your diagnostic capabilities, gaining the expertise required to maintain and repair sophisticated automotive networks.

Conclusion

In concluding this exploration of CAN Bus and in-vehicle network testing in automotive systems, it should be understood that covering every conceivable scenario, test method, and potential issue is beyond the scope of a single book. Nevertheless, this chapter has aimed to deliver an understanding of the essential principles and practical applications of CAN Bus testing. The objective has been to build your confidence in setting up and conducting comprehensive tests, while also igniting a sense of inquiry that encourages you to delve deeper into the intricacies of CAN Bus diagnostics.

Common Acronyms/Abbreviations

This section contains common acronyms and abbreviations: An acronym is a word that is formed from the first letters of a phrase or a series of words, usually to make it easier to say or remember. This list is not exhaustive, but provides some acronyms used in conjunction with the design and operation of vehicles and in-vehicle networks. Abbreviations may have different meanings or designations depending on context, and acronyms may be further adapted, reused, or reinterpreted as technology and engineering develops.

A - Amperes
A/F - Air Fuel Ratio
A/T - Automatic Transmission
AAT - Ambient Air Temperature
ABS - Antilock Brake System
AC - Alternating Current
AC - Air Conditioning
ACC - Automatic Climate Control
ACC - Air Conditioning Clutch
ACK - Acknowledge
ACR - Air Conditioning Relay
ABS - Antilock Braking System
ADAS - Advanced Driver Assistance Systems
ADU - Analogue-Digital Unit
AED - Automatic Electronic Defibrillators
AEV - All Electric Vehicle
AFR - Air Fuel Ratio
AGM - Absorbed Glass Matt
Ah - Amp Hours
AM - Amplitude Modulation
ATS - Air Temperature Sensor
AVD - Aqueous Vermiculite Dispersant
AVO - Amps Volts Ohms
AWG - American Wire Gage
BBW - Brake by Wire
BCM - Body Control Module
BCM - Battery Control Module
BEAN - Byteflight Enhanced Area Network
BEV - Battery Electric Vehicle
BHP - Brake Horsepower
BMS - Battery Management System
BMU - Battery Management Unit
BOB - Breakout Box
BPP - Brake Pedal Position Switch
Bps - Bits per second
BTS - Battery Temperature Sensor
Btu - British thermal unit
Bus N - Bus Negative
Bus P - Bus Positive
C - Celsius
CA - Cranking Amps
CAN - Controller Area Network

CAT - Category
CC - Catalytic Converter
CC - Climate Control
CC - Cruise Control
CC - Cubic Centimetres
CCA - Cold Cranking Amps
CCS - Combined Charging System
CCV - Closed Cricut Voltage
CFC - Chlorofluorocarbons
CL - Closed Loop
CLV - Calculated Load Value
CNG - Compressed Natural Gas
CO - Carbon Monoxide
CO2 - Carbon Dioxide
COSHH - Control of Substances Hazardous to Health
CP - Control Pilot
CPU - Central Processing Unit
CRC - Cyclic Redundancy Check
CTP - Closed Throttle Position
CTS - Coolant Temperature Sensor
CV - Constant Velocity
CVT - Continuously Variable Transmission
DBW - Drive by Wire
DC - Duty Cycle
DC - Direct Current
DMM - Digital Multimeter
DLC - Data Link Connector (OBD)
DLC - Data Length Control
DSO - Digital Storage Oscilloscope
DTC - Diagnostic Trouble Code
EBCM - Electronic Brake Control Module
EBD - Electronic Brake Force Distribution
ECC - Electronic Climate Control
ECM - Engine/Electronic Control Module
ECS - Emission Control System
ECT - Engine Coolant Temperature
ECU - Electronic Control Unit
EDL - Extended Data Length
EECS - Evaporative Emission Control System
EEGR - Electronic EGR (Solenoid)
EEPROM - Electronically Erasable Programmable Read Only Memory
EGO - Exhaust Gas Oxygen Sensor
EGR - Exhaust Gas Recirculation
EGRT - Exhaust Gas Recirculation Temperature
EMF - Electromotive Force (voltage)
EMI - Electromagnetic Interference
EML - Engine Management Light
EOBD - European Onboard Diagnostics
EOF - End of Frame
EPA - Environmental Protection Act
EPB - Electronic Parking Brake
EPB - Equipotential bonding

Common Acronyms/Abbreviations

EPROM - Erasable Programmable Read Only Memory
EPS - Electronic Power Assisted Steering
ESP - Electronic Stability Programme
ESS - Engine Start-Stop
EV - Electric Vehicle
EVAP - Evaporative Emissions System
EVAP CP - Evaporative Canister Purge
EVSE - Electric Vehicle Supply Equipment
EWS - Immobiliser (network acronym)
FDF - Flexible Data Frame
FM - Frequency Modulation
FOT - Fixed Orifice Tube
FSD - Full Scale Deflection
FWD - Front Wheel Drive
GND - Electrical Ground Connection
GPS - Global Positioning System
GWP - Global Warming Potential
HASAWA - Health and Safety at Work Act
H2O - Water
HC - Hydrocarbons
HCA - Hot Cranking Amps
HEGO - Heated Exhaust Gas Oxygen Sensor
HEV - Hybrid Electric Vehicle
HFC - Hydrogen Fuel Cell
HFC - Hydrofluorocarbon
HFO - Hydrofluoroolefin
HICE - Hydrogen Internal Combustion Engine
HO2S - Heated Oxygen Sensor
hp - Horsepower
HSE - Health and Safety Executive
HT - High Tension
HV - High Voltage
HVAC - Heating Ventilation and Air Conditioning
HVIL - High Voltage Interlock Loop
Hz - Hertz
I/O - Input / Output
IA - Intake Air
IAT - Intake Air Temperature
IC - Integrated Circuit
ICCB - In Cable Charging Box
ICE - In Car Entertainment
ICE - Internal Combustion Engine
ID - Identifier
IGBT - Insulated Gate Bipolar Transistor
IGN - Ignition
IHKA – Climate Control (network acronym)
ISO - International Standard of Organisation
KAM - Keep Alive Memory
Kg/cm2 - Kilograms/Cubic Centimetres
KHz - Kilohertz
Km - Kilometres
Kombi - Instrument Cluster (network acronym)

KPA - Kilopascal
KWP - Keyword Protocol
l - Litres
LA - Lead Acid
LAN - Local Area Network
LCD - Liquid Crystal Display
LED - Light Emitting Diode
LEV - Low Emission Vehicle
LFP - Lithium Iron Phosphate
LHD - Left Hand Drive
Li-ion - Lithium ion
LIN - Local Interconnect Network
LMO - Lithium Manganese Oxide
LOS - Limited Operating Strategy
LPG - Liquefied Petroleum Gas
LTO - Lithium Titanate
LWB - Long Wheelbase
LWR - Vertical Headlight Control (network acronym)
M/T - Manual Transmission
MAC - Mobile Air Conditioning
MCM - Motor Control Module
MEF - Methane Equivalency Factor
MF - Maintenance Free
MIL - Malfunction Indicator Lamp
MOST - Media Oriented Systems Transport
MPG - Miles per Gallon
MPH - Miles per Hour
MRE - Magnetic Resistive Element
MRS - Multiple Restraint System (network acronym)
mS or ms - Millisecond
MSD - Maintenance Service Disconnect/Manual Service Disconnect
mV or mv - Millivolt
N - Nitrogen
NCA - Nickel Cobalt Aluminium
NCAPS - Non-Contact Angular Position Sensor
NCM - Nickel Cobalt Manganese
NCRPS - Non-Contact Rotary Position Sensor
NGV - Natural Gas Vehicles
NIB - Neodymium Iron Boron
Ni-MH - Nickel Metal Hydride
Nm - Newton Meters
NOx - Oxides of Nitrogen
NPN - Negative Positive Negative
NTC - Negative Temperature Coefficient
O2 - Oxygen
OBC - Onboard Charger/Offboard Charger
OBD I - On Board Diagnostics Version I
OBD II - On Board Diagnostics Version II
OCV - Open Circuit Voltage
OE - Original Equipment
OEM - Original Equipment Manufacturer
OFN - Oxygen Free Nitrogen

Common Acronyms/Abbreviations

OL - Off Limits
OL - Open Loop
OS - Oxygen Sensor
OTA - Over the Air (Updates)
PAG - Polyalkylene Glycol
PATS - Passive Anti-Theft System
PCB - Printed Circuit Board
PCM - Powertrain Control Module
Pd - Potential Difference (volts)
PE - Protected Earth
PEF- Propane Equivalency Factor
PEM - Proton Exchange Membrane
PEV - Pure Electric Vehicles
PHEV - Plug-in Hybrid Electric Vehicle
PID - Parameter Identification Location
PID - Priority ID
PKE - Passive Keyless Entry
PLC - Powerline Communication
PNP - Positive Negative Positive
POE - Polyolester Oil
POF - Plastic Optical Fibre
POT - Potentiometer
PP - Proximity Pilot
PPE - Personal Protective Equipment
PPM - Parts Per Million
PPS - Accelerator Pedal Position Sensor
PROM - Programmable Read-Only Memory
PSI - Pounds per Square Inch
PTC - Positive Temperature Coefficient
PTM - Pulse Train Module
PUWER - Provision and Use of Work Equipment Regulations
PWM - Pulse Width Modulation
RAM - Random Access Memory
RBS - Regenerative Braking system
RCD - Residual Current Device
RCM - Reserve Capacity Minutes
RCM - Restraint Control Module
RDS - Radio Data System
RDW -Tyre Pressure Monitoring (network acronym)
RE EV - Range Extended Electric Vehicles
REF - Reference
RESS - Rechargeable Energy Storage System
RFI - Radio Frequency Interference
RHD - Right Hand Drive
RIDDOR - Reporting of Injuries Diseases and Dangerous Occurrence Regulations
RKE - Remote Keyless Entry
RMS - Recovery Management Station
ROM - Read Only Memory
RON - Research Octane Number
RTR - **Remote Transmission Request**
RWD - Rear Wheel Drive

SAE - Society of Automotive Engineers (Viscosity Grade)
SDT - Service Data Length Type
SEI - Solid Electrolyte Interphase/Interface
SENT - Single Edge Nibble Transmission
SIPS - Side Impact Protections System
SMR - System Main Relay
SoC - State of Charge
SOF - Start of Frame
SoH - State of Health
SRI - Service Reminder Indicator
SRS - Supplementary Restraint System (air bag)
SRT - System Readiness Test
STP - Shielded Twisted Pair
SWB - Short Wheelbase
SWL- Safe Working Load
SZM - Central Switch Module (network acronym)
TACH - Tachometer
TCM - Transmission Control Module
TCS - Traction Control System
TP - Throttle Position
TPM - Tyre Pressure Monitor
TPP - Throttle Position Potentiometer
TPS - Throttle Position Sensor
TSB - Technical Service Bulletin
TXV - Thermal Expansion Valve
UART - Universal Asynchronous Receiver-Transmitter
UDS - Unified Diagnostic Services
UJ - Universal Joint
ULEV - Ultra Low Emission Vehicle
USB - Universal Serial Bus
UTP - Unshielded Twisted Pair
UV - Ultraviolet
V - Volts
V2G - Vehicle to Grid
VAC - Vacuum
VAN - Vehicle Area Network
VCI - Virtual CAN interface
VCI - Vehicle Communication Interface
VDU - Visual Display Unit
VDE - Verband der Elektrotechnik
VIN - Vehicle Identification Number
VPE - Vehicle Protection Equipment
VPW - Vehicle Pulse Width
VR - Variable Reluctance
VSS - Vehicle Speed Sensor
WAN - Wide Area Network
W/B - Wheelbase
Wh - Watt Hours
WPT - Wireless Power Transfer
WSS - Wheel Speed Sensor
ZEV - Zero Emission Vehicle

Index

1

100BASE-T1 · 34, 111, 112

4

4G 5G · 30

8

8 Step Diagnostic Best Practice · 159

A

AC · 11, 14, 17, 64, 67, 86
Acronyms · 164
Actuators · 46
Advanced driver assistance systems (ADAS) · 112
Airbags · 46, 49
Alternators · 81, 85, 90
Amps · 11
Analogue · 22
AND Gate · 70
Anti-lock brakes · 49
Application-specific diagnostics · 117
Arbitration · 38, 39, 48, 49, 96, 97, 100, 103
Architecture · 41, 43, 51, 54, 108, 163
Asynchronous · 57, 112, 114, 115
Atom · 8
Atoms and molecules · 8

B

Bandwidth · 58
Base-10 · 65
Base-2 · 65
Battery Management Systems (BMS) · 86
Baud rate · 35, 77
BEAN (Byteflight Enhanced Automotive Network) · 57
Binary · 22, 52, 58, 61, 62, 63, 64, 65, 145, 146
Binary code · 22
Binary data · 58
Bipolar junction transistors (BJTs) · 68
Bit · 35, 39, 65
Bit rates · 48
Bit stuffing · 77, 78

Bit timing · 52, 76, 78
Boolean Logic · 69
Bootloading · 113, 115
Bosch · 26, 30, 34, 94
Broadcast · 37
Bus · 31
Bus cut relays · 43, 69
Bus load analysis · 158
Bus Network · 42, 43
Bus topology · 35
Bus-off · 36, 83, 102, 103

C

Calculating network speed using an oscilloscope · 142
CAN Analysers · 155
CAN Bus · 14
CAN Bus Frame Structure · 95
CAN FD · 30, 57, 75, 90, 91, 94, 96, 98, 155
CAN frame · 75, 95, 96, 97, 99, 148
CAN Message Structure · 74
CAN XL · 57, 98
Capacitance · 83, 84
Charge · 14, 84
Checksum · 96, 99, 100, 104, 107
Circuit · 10, 16
Climate control · 50, 105
Clock signal · 107
Clock speed · 41
Closed-circuit voltage (CCV) · 13
Coaxial · 72
Common-mode noise · 86, 88, 92
Communication Modules · 86
Components · 45
Computer · 28
Conductor · 10, 68
Continuity · 10, 16
Controller Area Network (CAN Bus) · 28, 30
Cooling Fans · 85
Cooling Systems · 86
Crash sensors · 45, 49
CRC · 75, 96, 97, 98, 99, 100, 104, 109, 111, 148, 149
Crosstalk · 81, 90
Current · 8, 14
Current divider · 16
Current flow · 85

Index

D

Daisy Chain · 41, 42
Data Link Connector · 36, 37, 73, 147, 160, 161
DC · 11, 17, 64, 67, 86, 91
Debugging · 113, 115
Decimal · 55, 61, 62, 63, 64, 65, 145, 146
Decoding and analysing SENT messages · 153
Decoding LIN Bus signals with an oscilloscope · 150
Deterministic communication · 39, 109, 110
Diagnosis · 11, 19, 74, 78, 102, 117, 118, 122, 124, 126, 131, 132, 137, 140, 147, 151, 160
Diagnostic communication protocol · 133
Diagnostic Tools · 135
Diagnostic Trouble Code · 37, 64, 102, 131, 132
Differential signal · 83
Differential signalling · 33, 34, 56, 58, 86, 87, 88, 90, 111, 113
Differential voltage · 60
Differential-mode noise · 87, 92
Digital · 22, 27, 51, 57, 118, 135, 146
Digital Signals · 51
Digital technology · 27
Diodes · 67, 121
Discharge · 92
DLC · 36, 73, 75, 126, 127, 130, 137, 138, 147, 159, 160, 161
Dominant · 34, 52, 54, 58, 60, 141
Dominant State and Recessive State · 34
Door locks · 50
Duty cycle · 22, 23, 24, 107, 138

E

Earth · 17, 92
ECU (Electronic Control Unit) · 14
Electric circuits · 15
Electrical noise · 18
Electrical Units & Terminology · 11
Electromagnetic interference (EMI) · 18, 58
Electromagnetism · 17, 79, 80
Electromotive Force (EMF) · 13
Electron · 10
Electronic and electrical safety procedures · 5
Electronic Control Units · 45
Electronic Control Units (ECUs) · 28
Electronics · 27
EMI (electromagnetic interference) · 18
EOBD · 36, 129, 130, 131, 138, 164
Equipotential Bonding · 119
Equipotential Bonding (EPB) · 120
Error Detection · 99
Error frame detection · 158
Error-checking · 99, 100

Ethernet · 30, 31, 34, 37, 38, 51, 56, 57, 89, 90, 91, 94, 98, 108, 110, 111, 112, 114, 115, 119, 131, 132
EV · 49, 81, 82, 86, 117, 118, 119, 120, 165, 166

F

Fast Charging Systems · 86
Fault isolation · 163
Fault-tolerant · 51
Ferrite beads · 83
Fibre optical · 72
Filtering and triggers · 157
Flexible communication · 109, 110
FlexRay · 34, 57, 110
FlexRay network protocol · 108
Floating · 92
Frame structure · 99
Freezeframe · 134
Frequency · 13
Fuel Cell · 86, 165
Fuel Injectors · 85
Fuel pumps · 81
Fuses · 121

G

Gateway · 37, 73, 108, 159
Gateways · 73
Ground · 17, 83, 165
Ground and earth · 17
Grounding · 18, 36, 80, 81, 85, 89, 90, 116, 120, 124

H

Hertz · 12
Hexadecimal · 61, 63, 64, 65, 146
High & Low Voltage · 19
High voltage · 51, 118, 122
High-bandwidth · 57, 115
High-resolution · 107
High-Speed · 49, 51, 60
High-Voltage Wiring · 86
HVAC · 86, 165
Hybrid · 26, 35, 86, 91, 98, 117, 119, 165, 166, 175
Hybrid topology · 35
Hydrogen · 8, 86

Index

I

Identifier · 38, 75, 96, 97, 99, 107, 132, 148
Identifying IDs · 151
Ignition systems · 81, 86
Impedance · 14, 35, 59
Induces · 81
Inductance · 83, 84
Information sources · 5
Infotainment · 85, 112
Insulation failure · 120
Insulator · 10, 68
Interference · 18, 81, 84, 85, 90, 102
Inverse · 58
Inversely proportional · 16
Inverters · 86
ISO 14229 · 132, 133
Isolation · 93, 118, 119, 120
Isolation Techniques · 118

J

Jargon · 38

K

Kilobits per second · 48, 49, 77
K-Line · 57

L

Light-emitting diode (LED) · 67
Lighting Systems · 85
LIN (Local Interconnect Network) · 57
LIN network protocol · 105
Local Area Network (LAN) · 30
Local Interconnect Network (LIN) · 33, 108
Logic Gates · 69
Low voltage · 19, 51, 52, 113, 117, 118
Low-latency · 107
Low-Speed · 49, 50, 51, 60

M

Magnetic field · 81
Magnetism · 81
Master/Slave · 32

Master-slave polling · 108
Media Oriented Systems Transport (MOST) · 33, 57, 115
Mediation · 78
Megabit per second · 49
Message injection · 157
Metal-oxide-semiconductor field-effect transistors (MOSFETs) · 68
Microchips · 28
Microcomputers · 27
Microprocessor · 28
Mobile phones · 81
Mode 6 · 129, 130
Molecule · 8
MOST network protocol · 114
Motors · 26, 57, 81, 85, 86, 90, 91, 105, 106, 107, 108, 119, 121
Multi-master · 94, 99
Multimedia · 57, 115
Multimeter · 54, 116, 128, 135, 137, 161, 163
Multiplexing · 29, 39, 41

N

NAND Gate (NOT + AND) · 71
Network · 14, 28, 30
Nibble · 33, 39, 57, 94, 103, 107, 153
Node · 32, 39
Noise · 36, 79, 86, 88, 90, 105, 119, 149
Nomenclature · 38
NOR Gate (NOT + OR) · 71
NOT Gate (Inverter) · 70
Nucleus · 8

O

OBD · 36, 57, 73, 129, 130, 131, 132, 156, 160, 164, 165, 174
OBDII · 36, 123, 129, 130, 131, 135, 138
OEM (Original Equipment Manufacturer) · 129, 130
Ohms · 12
Ohms law · 20
Onboard Chargers · 86
On-Board Diagnostics · 36, 73, 129, 130
Open circuit voltage (OCV) · 13
Optical fibre · 58, 114, 115
OR Gate · 70
Oscillate · 13
Oscillations · 85
Oscillator · 78
Oscilloscope · 12, 22, 54, 65, 102, 125, 127, 128, 138, 140, 141, 142, 143, 145, 146, 147, 148, 149, 150, 151, 154, 158, 161, 163

Index

Oscilloscope Techniques · 138
Over-the-air (OTA) updates · 112

P

Packets · 112
Parallel · 16, 31
Parallel circuit · 15
Parity bits · 108
Payload · 96, 98, 109, 110, 111
Peer-to-Peer · 32
Periodic table · 9
Personal Protective Equipment (PPE) · 6
Photodiode · 67
Physical layer · 71, 72, 135, 161
Point-to-point · 26, 28, 32, 57, 107
Potential Difference (Pd) · 13
Power · 13, 16
Power steering · 49, 108
Power Supply · 115
Practical Training and Case Studies · 162
Preamble · 109, 110, 111
Preparing for assessment · 4
Programs · 28
Proprietary · 57, 130
Protocol · 25, 38, 39, 47, 49, 95, 98, 155
Proton · 10
Pull-down · 23, 24
Pull-up · 23
Pulse Width Modulation (PWM) · 22, 107

R

Radio transmitters · 18, 81
Recessive · 34, 54, 58, 60, 141
Redundancy · 39, 75, 96, 97, 99, 100, 109, 110, 111
Reflections · 85
Regenerative Braking Systems · 86
Relay · 10, 67, 69, 71, 85, 121, 122
Resistance · 13, 14
Resistors · 66
RFI (radio frequency interference) · 18
Ring network · 42, 115
Ring topology · 35
Ringing · 85

S

Safety · 116
Scan tool · 37, 61, 64, 65, 73, 83, 102, 124, 125, 130, 133, 140,
Schottky diode · 67

Seat · 6, 50, 105
Self-Diagnosis · 102
Semiconductor · 10
Sensors · 46
SENT · 57
SENT network protocol · 103
Serial · 31
Serial communication · 29, 40
Serial decoding · 145
Series · 16
Series circuit · 15
Setup and testing of components · 118
Shield continuity · 120
Shielding · 5, 18, 36, 80, 81, 82, 83, 85, 87, 88, 89, 90, 91, 92, 119, 120, 127, 128
Shielding techniques · 82
Signal integrity · 85
Signal reflection · 59
Signals · 12, 13, 14, 18, 22, 26, 28, 29, 32, 33, 34, 35, 36, 37, 39, 40, 41, 45, 46, 48, 51, 52, 53, 54, 58, 59, 60, 61, 62, 65, 70, 72, 74, 78, 80, 81, 82, 83, 84, 85, 86, 88, 89, 91, 94, 96, 107, 115, 116, 118, 120, 138, 143, 146, 147, 149, 150, 153, 155, 158, 159, 161, 162, 163
Simulating faults · 162
Single Edge Nibble Transmission (SENT) · 33, 107
Single-Wire · 49, 50, 51
Solenoids · 85
Standard and extended CAN formats · 47
Star Network · 41
Star topology · 35
Starter Motors · 85
String Theory · 44
Suppression · 88
Symptoms · 123, 124
Synchronisation · 52, 76, 78, 114, 115

T

Termination · 59
Termination resistors · 35, 58, 73, 125
Terminology · 29
The discovery of electricity · 8
Time segments · 77, 78
Timeout · 102
Timing & Synchronisation · 52
Topology · 5, 35, 39, 55, 56, 57, 58, 125
Traction Motors · 86
Transceivers · 51, 118, 120
Transistors · 28, 68
Transmission · 33, 49, 57, 60, 74, 94, 96, 103, 107, 153
Tunnel diode · 67
Twisted copper · 72
Twisted pair · 33, 58

Index

U

UART network protocol · 112
Unidirectional · 105, 107
Unified Diagnostic Services · 132, 133
Uniform electrical potential · 120
Universal Asynchronous Receiver/Transmitter (UART) · 57, 115
Universal Serial Bus (USB) · 31
Unshielded twisted pair (UTP) · 115

V

Vacuum tubes · 28
VAN (Vehicle Area Network) · 57
Vehicle Protective Equipment (VPE) · 6
Virtual networks · 99
Volcano · 57
Voltage and wiring · 111, 113
Voltage Regulators · 85
Volts · 11

W

Watt's (power) law · 21
Watts · 12
What is a CAN Bus · 26
Wide Area Network (WAN) · 30
Wi-Fi · 30, 86
Windows · 33, 48, 50, 57, 124
Wireless Communication Modules · 86
Wiring Harness · 46
Wiring integrity · 128

X

Xenon · 85

Z

Zener diode · 67

Other Books

If you enjoyed this book, please check out other titles by the author:

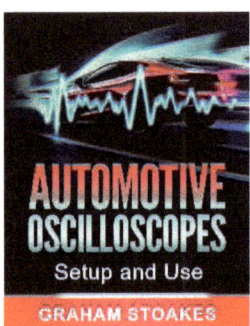

Paperback: 222 pages
Publisher: Graham Stoakes
(17 June 2025)
ISBN-10: 0992949297
ISBN-13: 78-0992949297

Automotive Oscilloscopes Setup and Use

Understanding how to interpret a waveform is essential but first, you need to capture it. A proper oscilloscope setup is where every great diagnostic story begins.
This companion to Automotive Oscilloscopes Waveform Analysis strips away the intimidation factor and shows you, step by step, how to get your oscilloscope out of the case, onto the car, and delivering results with confidence.
Too often, scopes are left to gather dust, not because they aren't useful, but because of the fear they're too complex or time-consuming. Designed for technicians who refuse to be limited by their comfort zone, this book breaks down the barriers of complexity.
With clear language, practical demonstrations, and real-world examples, it makes the process of setting up and using a scope both intuitive and repeatable. No rigid rules, just practical, adaptable techniques that fit real-world conditions.
Whether you're using a basic handheld unit or a high-end PC-based system, this book will help you master the essentials: grounding and connections, probe selection, voltage and time settings, trigger control, and signal stability. You'll learn how to create a ready-to-go diagnostic setup that integrates seamlessly into your workflow, so the oscilloscope becomes a tool you reach for instinctively.
Each chapter is built to demystify the process, delivering tips, shortcuts, and key principles that empower you to get accurate readings without second-guessing. By removing the barriers to setup, this book opens the door to the kind of diagnosis only an oscilloscope can deliver. Whether you're new to scopes or looking to refine your skills, the step-by-step guidance ensures you can confidently configure your equipment, connect to various vehicle systems, and capture high-quality waveforms.
With simplicity at its core, Automotive Oscilloscopes Setup and Use will help you turn your scope from a mysterious gadget into a trusted diagnostic partner.
Step beyond the scan tool, master the oscilloscope and take vehicle diagnostics to the next level.
Because the best diagnostic insights start with a signal worth analysing.

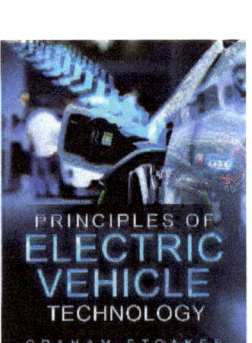

Paperback: 238 pages
Publisher: Graham Stoakes
(05 August 2024)
ISBN-10: 0992949270
ISBN-13: 978-0992949273

Principles of Electric Vehicle Technology

Electric vehicles (EVs) are a vital part of the world's infrastructure and are a fundamental component in the ongoing development that powers our future transportation needs.
Limited resources and environmental pollution mean that an alternative to traditional petrol- and diesel-powered internal combustion engines is necessary to maintain and propel a sustainable society that continues to thrive.
Regardless of fuel, it is electricity that has an elemental energy which produces no toxic pollutants at point of use.
Electricity can be generated from multiple sources, many of which can be considered environmentally friendly, making it a logical choice to charge our energy needs.
In our interconnected modern lives, electricity is indispensable, powering everything from our homes to our gadgets. Yet even though the first cars developed used electricity for their source of propulsion, internal combustion engines dominated the automotive landscape due to their seemingly inexhaustible and harmless hydrocarbon fuel.
As the world developed, it became increasingly clear that our reliance upon petrol and diesel was misguided.
We are perfectly happy with using electricity for nearly all of our daily energy needs, but many still struggle with the concept of using it for transportation due to the abundance of the internal combustion engine.
The inevitable rise in electrically powered vehicles means that we all need to learn about this new (yet old) technology if we are to integrate it into our everyday lives.
Often, the unknown poses the greatest barrier to a change in habits, leading to mental roadblocks that hinder progress.
We often know more than we give ourselves credit for, but it takes a spark of inspiration for this to be realised.
This book is designed to support knowledge relating to the technology employed in the operation and use of electric vehicles; helping technicians, engineers, first responders and vehicle operators understand how they work.

Other Books

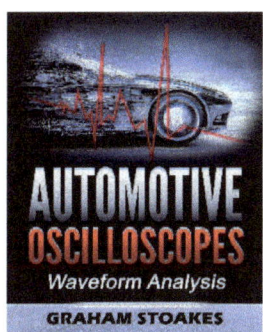

Paperback: 198 pages
Publisher: Graham Stoakes
(24 April 2017)
ISBN-10: 099294262
ISBN-13: 978-0992949266

Automotive Oscilloscopes Waveform Analysis

The rapid growth of technology used in cars has highlighted the need for a piece of diagnostic equipment that will give you X-ray vision and show you the heartbeat of a vehicles electrical and electronic system.
An OBD scan tool is vital for modern vehicle diagnostics; however, trouble codes will only take you so far. The problem can arise when the phrase 'fault code' is used in connection with diagnosis. A code will rarely point you directly to the root cause of a vehicle fault but can help you focus your diagnosis on a specific area and run functional tests.
It is the oscilloscope (or scope) that can truly test the operation and health of a system component. The important thing to remember about oscilloscopes, is that they should be easy to set up and use; otherwise, they will be passed over for a more familiar tool within your comfort zone.
Remember that nothing ever happens within your comfort zone.
There is a great deal of misconception about how difficult a scope can be to set up, and once you are used to your own equipment, if it is laid out and ready to use, it will soon become your diagnostic tool of choice.
This book has been written to help you get the most from your oscilloscope and has been designed to give straightforward and uncomplicated methods that can be used effectively for automotive diagnosis. It covers many of the most common automotive waveforms, assisting you in the analysis of the patterns produced, without restricting you to rigid equipment settings, or vehicle system design.
This will give you the 'scope' to develop your systematic diagnostic routines, with the flexibility to adapt to changing requirements.

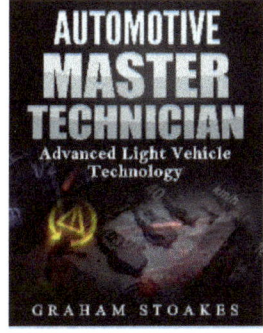

Paperback: 338 pages
Publisher: Graham Stoakes
(1 Feb. 2015)
ISBN-10: 099294922X
ISBN-13: 978-0992949228

Level 4 Automotive Master Technician - Advanced Light Vehicle Technology

'Technology needs technicians, and the ability to harness technical diagnosis calls for a Master Technician'.
The rapid growth in technology used in the production of cars has highlighted the need for a different approach to vehicle diagnosis and repair. The integration of complex electronic control with mechanical systems shows the brilliance in the engineering capabilities of designers and manufacturers.
While this technology has improved the comfort, safety, convenience and reliability of vehicles, it has also created an issue with established methods of maintenance and repair. As many of the control systems operate beyond our natural capabilities, diagnostic tooling is required to undertake most of the fault-finding duties traditionally conducted by vehicle technicians. Also, the sophisticated nature of advanced system faults will often lead to diagnostic requirements for which there is no prescribed method.
One of the fundamental roles of a Master Technician will be the diagnosis and repair of these complex and advanced system faults, for which diagnostic approaches need to be developed that can provide logical strategies to reduce overall diagnostic time. An effective diagnostic routine should always begin with a logical assessment of symptoms and then uses reasoning to reduce the possible number of options, before following a systematic approach to finding and fixing the root cause.

Other Books

Paperback: 154 pages
Publisher: Graham Stoakes
(6 July 2015)
ISBN-10: 0992949246
ISBN-13: 978-0992949242

Principles of Light Vehicle Air Conditioning

'As the number of vehicles on the world's roads rises, the demand for increased levels of comfort and convenience also grows'
While air conditioning and climate control may be seen as a luxury by some, the key benefits often outweigh the initial costs and resources required to implement these systems on newly produced vehicles; in fact most new cars come with some form of air conditioning as standard.
An environment which helps keep the driver and passengers comfortable and alert, maintaining the correct levels of ventilation and humidity, can increase concentration and the ability to devote more of their attention to the occupation of driving.
The downside of these systems is the environmental impact of the chemicals used to provide the refrigeration process.
Globally, anthropogenic, or 'man-made' emissions are believed to be the key factor in climate change and refrigerants have a larger influence than many others.
Small amounts of fluorinated gasses released to atmosphere may be causing irreparable damage to our planet, initiating ozone depletion and global warming.
Although many organisations are currently seeking alternatives to these harmful cocktails, at the present time we are restricted by the availability, cost and technology required to make viable replacements.
This means that for the time being, technicians and air conditioning professionals need to ensure that refrigerants are handled with due diligence and systems are maintained to the highest standards in order to contain and reduce emissions. Remember these chemicals only become dangerous when released to atmosphere.

Paperback: 196 pages
Publisher: Graham Stoakes
(1 July 2014)
ISBN-10: 0992949203
ISBN-13: 978-0992949204

Hybrid electric and alternative automotive propulsion

'A future without oil won't spell the end of the car but will simply drive engineering brilliance to find an alternative'.
As fuel demand and environmental pollution increases, it is important that substitutes are found for traditional methods of vehicle drive. An alternative propulsion vehicle is one that operates using something other than the established petrol or Diesel.
Whether you are a vehicle technician, automotive trainer, student or part of the emergency services, an awareness of current and emerging propulsion sources is vital to work on or around these vehicles safely.

www.grahamstoakes.com